Also by David Marshall Lang

The Armenians

A People in Exile

by
DAVID MARSHALL LANG
Professor of Caucasian Studies, University of London

London
GEORGE ALLEN & UNWIN
Boston   Sydney

GEORGE ALLEN & UNWIN LTD
40 Museum Street, London WC1A 1LU

© David Marshall Lang 1981

British Library Cataloguing in Publication Data

Lang, David Marshall
  The Armenians.
  1. Armenians
  I. Title
  909'.0491992   DS172

  ISBN 0-04-956010-7

Set in 11 on 13 point Baskerville
by Grove Graphics, Tring
and printed and bound in Great Britain by
William Clowes (Beccles) Limited, Beccles and London

Dedicated to the Dispossessed of
All Nations

Preface

This book is a companion volume to my earlier *Armenia : Cradle of Civilization,* now in its third edition. The original work was intended to give a picture of the ancient, semi-legendary region of Mount Ararat which served as a focus of early human life, from the Old Stone Age onwards. Coming to the classical and medieval periods, I attempted there to give some account of the contribution of the Armenian people to the political, social, artistic and literary life of the Near East.

From Roman times onwards, and throughout the periods of Iranian, Byzantine, Arab, Mongol and Ottoman supremacy, Armenia has been a prey to repeated invasions.

Armenians have been emigrating and settling abroad for nearly two thousand years. They have provided a leaven of originality and individual enterprise wherever they have made their home, have contributed greatly to economic prosperity in many adopted home-lands, have brought with them expertise in many aspects of the arts, including painting and music (not forgetting cooking), and have shared these attainments with the peoples of the lands where they have settled.

Their fierce individuality, a certain secretiveness, and marked acquisitive tendencies have combined to render them unpopular among some of their neighbours. Since I received the special award of 'Friend of the Armenians' from the Primate of the Armenian Apostolic Church of America in 1978, I have sometimes been accused of being starry-eyed about the Armenians. This is by no means the case. During recent years, I have had dealings with hundreds of Armenians – the vast majority being hard-working, sincere and intelligent men and women. However, where flowers bloom, noxious weeds are often to be found. Among such Armenian weeds with whom I have had contact I may include one burglarious, poker-playing patriarch, one adulterous archbishop, two pornographers, one phoney musicologist, one crooked solicitor and several rich misers. Our libel laws prevent me from naming them here, but they will figure in my posthumous memoirs.

A French philosopher once remarked that to understand everything is to forgive everything. This is why I have begun this book with what I hope is a reasonably accurate and objective account of the genocide practised against the Armenians by successive Ottoman rulers, between the years 1894 and 1918, and continued with variations under the regime of Kemal Atatürk. This holocaust left mental and emotional scars on the survivors, which affect their attitudes to community issues and international problems. These scars show little signs of healing. As time passes, the feeling of frustration and deprivation turns into a veritable obsession.

This obsession can cloud judgement and give rise to grave dangers to the community at large. I refer to the wave of murderous attacks perpetrated by 'Armenian freedom fighters' on Turkish diplomats and their families. These attacks are justified in some sections of the militant Armenian press, as allegedly tending to attract world opinion to the wrongs suffered by the Armenian nation, and as contributing to the eventual return to Armenian suzerainty of the large territories of historical Armenia now submerged in eastern Turkey.

No genuine friend of Armenia can view these terrorist attacks with anything but disapproval and alarm. At a time when the Soviets are trampling over Afghanistan, and the Persians are defying all known norms of international law, the idea of the NATO powers handing over eastern Turkey to a handful of Soviet-backed Armenians is too ludicrous to entertain seriously. Even worse, terrorist violence seriously jeopardizes the position of the surviving Armenian community left within Turkey – estimated at between 80,000 and 100,000 – and headed by the respected Istanbul Patriarch Shnork Kaloustian. This Turkish Armenian community constitutes a large band of hostages to fortune. The young, impulsive Armenian element would surely be well advised to lay off violence, and concentrate on peaceful, civilized ways of projecting a good image of Armenia and its people throughout the world at large.

Let it not be thought that I am unsympathetic to the Armenians' desire for recognition of their just claims to redress. After the Turkish invasion of Cyprus in 1974, I addressed a letter to *The Times,* which got me into serious trouble with the Turkish Embassy in London and with my own college authorities. Mr Christopher J. Walker and I compiled jointly and published in December 1976 a Minority Rights Group report on the Armenians, which has gone into four editions and been translated into French and Armenian.

The present work is to a great extent a labour of love. It embodies memories and impressions deriving from visits made over the past thirty-five years to centres of Armenian emigration, situated geographically as far apart as Los Angeles and Teheran. I have been amazed by the way in which so many Armenians, driven relentlessly from their homeland in Turkish Anatolia, have made a success of life in new and alien surroundings.

It is my hope that this book, which is partly autobiographical, and to some extent impressionistic, will show the world what human courage and endeavour can achieve in the face of apparently insuperable odds. It has not been put together according to any set chronological plan, and I have avoided as far as possible repeating any of the material which has gone into my earlier publications. Here and there I have 'let my hair down', and included some ideas and impressions which purists would not expect to find in the writings of a purely 'academic' author.

Let me thank my publishers, Messrs George Allen & Unwin, for patience and encouragement over twenty-five years. I am particularly grateful to my witty and helpful editor, Mr Peter Leek. Among organizations and individuals who have materially supported my research on this book, I would express appreciation to Messrs Gregory and Victor Aftandilian of Massachusetts; the Armenian Ladies' Association, Teheran; the Calouste Gulbenkian Foundation, Lisbon; Mr Vachik Khachatourian; Mr K. K. Mazloumian and Dr Toros Toranian, of Aleppo; Mr Christopher J. Walker, of London; the Very Reverend Dr Mesrob K. Krikorian, of Vienna; Mr James H. Tashjian, of Boston.

School of Oriental and African Studies
University of London

DAVID M. LANG

Contents

Maps

List of Illustrations

I

The Armenian Holocaust

THE OTTOMAN genocide perpetrated in 1915 against the Armenian citizens of Turkey was the first systematic attempt in modern times to bring about the complete, deliberate extermination of a nation.[1] The genocide ('murder of an entire people') was ingeniously planned and brilliantly and effectively carried out, making the fullest use of terrain, climate and the auxiliary aid of local populations who were jealous of and hostile to the victims.

The campaign of mass murder was, to a large extent, the practical result of the adoption of an overtly racialist ideology by the Young Turk junta ruling in Turkey during the First World War. The members of this junta, and their racist policy, were much admired by Adolf Hitler, in spite of their final humiliating overthrow. The Führer's own work in the field of mass extermination, though on a larger scale, was slow and cumbrous when compared with the deadly speed with which the Young Turks pounced on their largely unsuspecting and predominantly loyal Armenian prey.

The execution of the genocide of the Armenians in 1915 was preceded two decades earlier by widespread massacres perpetrated by Sultan 'Abdul Hamid between 1894 and 1896. These massacres, which aroused the horror of Europe, may be regarded as an overture or perhaps as a dress rehearsal for the 'final solution' of 1915.

[1] Some people might qualify this statement by citing American policy towards the North American Indians.

The Armenian massacres of the late Ottoman period were the result of complicated historical processes. They were precipitated by the events surrounding the collapse of Ottoman power in the Balkans and eastern Mediterranean. Universally derided as the 'sick man of Europe', the Ottoman regime and its ruling class were forced in upon themselves, and obliged to abandon the old multinational system for a narrow and overtly racialist form of state organization. The Armenians and the Greeks, in addition to the Bulgarians and the Arabs, presented themselves as convenient scapegoats – 'fifth column-ists' – on whom could be blamed inevitable disorders and upheavals which were really the result of centuries of Turkish misrule, tyranny, inefficiency and sheer intolerance.

By the accession of Sultan 'Abdul Hamid II in 1876, the Armenians and Turks had lived side by side for over eight centuries – if not in harmony, at least with a modicum of mutual forbearance. Although the Armenian, in the eyes of the Turkish Muslim religious and political hierarchy, was a *giaour* or infidel, and hence a second-class citizen, he occupied a recognized and relatively secure place in Ottoman society. Ottoman Armenians, as members of the Armenian *millet*, or national community, came under the jurisdiction of the Armenian Patriarch of Constantinople. The Patriarch in turn exercised wide powers delegated to him by the Sultan and the Grand Vizier. The Armenians were often referred to by the Ottoman authorities as 'the loyal Millet'.

This delicate balance of interests was shattered by the intrusion of the European powers, who regarded Ottoman Turkey as an overripe fruit which might fall into their laps at any moment. The decline of Ottoman power in the Balkans and the Black Sea region had gathered pace in the eighteenth century. Tsar Peter the Great (1682–1725) had been fully aware of the simmering discontent among Balkan Slav, Greek, Georgian and Armenian Christians, and did his best to turn this discontent to Russia's advantage – a policy ably continued later in the century by Empress Catherine the Great. This disaffection was well known to the Ottoman government, whose response was mass repression accompanied by the erection of such gruesome monuments as the Tower of Skulls, at Nish in Yugoslavia, which I visited in 1968.

During the 1820s, two important events contrived to damage community relations within the Ottoman Empire – firstly, the libera-tion of Greece through the War of Independence; and, secondly, far to the east, the capture of Erevan and Eastern or Persian Armenia by the Russian general Count Paskevich-Erivansky in 1827. Paskevich then advanced into Turkish Armenia and captured Erzerum. Thousands of Armenian families migrated from Turkish Armenia into Russian Armenia, now reconstituted as a province of the Tsarist empire.

Tsar Nicolas I (1825–55) repeatedly asserted his status as supreme protector of Christians within the Ottoman Empire. All this naturally made both the Tsar and his Christian protégés suspect to successive Sultans, and also led directly to the outbreak of the Crimean War in 1853.

During the nineteenth century, the Armenians built up two main cultural centres, which also became focuses of national revival in the political sense. These centres were Tbilisi (Tiflis), capital of the Russian viceroyalty of the Caucasus, and the Ottoman capital of Constantinople.[1] An Armenian named Hagop founded the first regular Turkish-language theatre in Constantinople (1870), and the Armenians had their own opera there. Erevan, present-day capital of Soviet Armenia, was an obscure provincial town, and remained so until after the 1917 Russian Revolution.

In the Ottoman capital, the Armenians came into increasingly close touch with British, French and other European commercial interests, who employed them as clerks, managers and local agents, thus arousing the envy of the largely illiterate Turkish populace. Western missionaries, including the American Protestants, selected the Armenians as prime targets for their proselytizing activities. After studying in American-supported schools, Armenians began to travel abroad and study in European universities, returning home to suffer acute frustration as second-class citizens in a backward Muslim society.

During the 1860s, two events sowed the seeds of trouble to come. The first of these was the conclusion of the prolonged negotiations for a new constitution of the Armenian Millet (national community), which the Armenians imagined would result in democratic participation in the affairs of this community, hitherto dominated by the venal Constantinople Patriarchate and an oligarchy of *amiras* or Armenian magnates. The Imperial 'Regulation of the Armenian National Com-

---

[1] James Etmekjian, *The French influence on the Western Armenian Renaissance, 1843–1915* (New York, 1964).

munity', signed by Sultan 'Abdul Aziz in 1863, was seen by Turkish officialdom as an attempt to set up a state within a state. It was in fact suspended by Sultan 'Abdul Hamid II between 1898 and 1906.

The second event leading to friction was the insurrection of the sorely tried Armenian mountaineers of Zeitoun, in the *sanjak* or province of Marash, in 1862. Suppressed with the utmost vigour by Ottoman troops, this rebellion focused the attention of the European powers on the sufferings of Armenian villagers in remote parts of Anatolia and Cilicia.[1]

A milestone in the development of the 'Armenian Question' was the Russo-Turkish War of 1877–8. This conflict was sparked off by Turkish massacres perpetrated in Bulgaria in 1876 and vigorously denounced by Gladstone and other Western statesmen. Russian armies advancing through the Balkans and also on the Caucasian front soon brought Ottoman Turkey to its knees, and Russian statesmen dictated to the Sultan's government a humiliating treaty signed at San Stefano, close to Constantinople, on 3 March 1878.

Armenian interests were fully safeguarded in the San Stefano treaty, which ceded to Russia the areas of Kars, Ardahan and Bayazid. It was stipulated that administrative autonomy should be guaranteed to the provinces of eastern Turkey which were inhabited by Armenians. The implementation of necessary reforms was to be a prior condition for withdrawal of the Russian troops which had occupied a substantial part of eastern Anatolia during the 1877–8 war.

The treaty of San Stefano was rendered abortive and inoperative, largely through pressure applied by the British Conservative Prime Minister, Benjamin Disraeli, Earl of Beaconsfield. On the initiative of European powers hostile to Russian dominance of the Balkans and over the Ottoman Empire, a conference was summoned at Berlin, where a definitive treaty was signed on 13 July 1878.[2]

The clause of the San Stefano treaty involving Armenian autonomy was drastically modified. The corresponding clause of the Berlin treaty, Article 61, embodied an innocuous and vague undertaking by the Sublime Porte to effect certain reforms in Turkish Armenia after (and not prior to) the withdrawal of Russian troops, and to inform the interested Powers from time to time of the progress of these measures. As a reward for his services to Ottoman interests, which

---

[1] Louise Nalbandian, *The Armenian Revolutionary Movement* (University of California Press, Berkeley and Los Angeles, 1963).

[2] W. N. Medlicott, *The Congress of Berlin and After* (2nd edn, London, 1963).

included the realignment of the Russian-Turkish frontier line in Armenia, Disraeli was able to annex Cyprus to the British Crown.

An Armenian delegation from Constantinople visited Berlin and attempted to secure certain guarantees and basic civil rights for the Armenian community inside Turkey. They returned home bitterly disappointed. Indeed, the Armenians had prematurely thrown in their lot with Turkey's foreign enemies, and thereby compromised themselves fatally with the new Sultan, 'Abdul Hamid II. The Sultan quite understandably regarded the Armenians' relations with foreign powers at San Stefano and at Berlin as treasonable. Many Armenians rather credulously regarded Article 61 of the Berlin treaty as a talisman, assuring automatic protection against Ottoman misrule. All this gave rise to endless misunderstanding and rancour. As the years went by, the Western powers became even less inclined to intervene effectively on behalf of the Armenians, inspiring the Duke of Argyll to remark: 'What is everybody's business is nobody's business!'

Documents now available to us indicate that even before 1878 the Ottoman General Staff had already been making contingency plans for the defence of the inner Turkish dominions in Anatolia. The loss of most of the Balkan lands and of areas of eastern Anatolia in 1877–8 meant that Turkey's armies had to regroup and prepare to defend the central Anatolian heartland. To quote Turkish military reports of the time, the Balkan and Arab lands could be regarded as the limbs of the Ottoman Empire, and might perhaps be amputated without fatal effect. Asia Minor and Anatolia, on the other hand, were the heart and lungs of the body politic, and if they were cut into, the entire organism must perish.[1] Since the Armenians were closely intermingled with the Turkish population of Asia Minor and Anatolia, the prospect of voluntary agreement on regional autonomy for the Armenians was increasingly dim.

During the 1880s, the Armenian community in Turkey nevertheless took a rosy view of their prospects, as 'guaranteed' by Article 61 of the 1878 Berlin treaty. The Constantinople intellectuals made grandiose plans for the future of the 'nation', as satirized in Baronian's mordant short novel, *Honourable Beggars*.[2] Had Sultan 'Abdul Hamid II (1876–1909) made some statesmanlike move towards resolving the

---

[1] See M. Krikorian, *Armenians in the service of the Ottoman Empire, 1860–1908* (London, 1978), p. 7. Erzerum was singled out as hub of the military defence of eastern Turkey, to be held at all costs.

[2] Trans. M. Kudian (London, 1978).

Armenian question, he would have enjoyed the overwhelming support of the Ottoman Armenian community at large.

Sultan 'Abdul Hamid II was a master of diplomacy, intrigue and repression. He suspended the 1876 Constitution after only two years' trial, and built up a formidable secret police. Although his mother is supposed to have been an Armenian lady, the Sultan himself detested Armenians. He encouraged Kurdish tribesmen from the south to move into traditional Armenian rural areas of the six Armenian *vilayets* or provinces of eastern Turkey. These Kurds billeted themselves on Armenian families and committed all kinds of vandalism and outrage, aggravating the state of anarchy and oppression long endemic in eastern Anatolia. Armenians began to quit their native villages. They moved into Russian Armenia, also into the supposed security of Turkish towns and cities, as well as migrating abroad.

Largely in self-defence, the Turkish Armenians set up several political groups and secret societies, notably the Armenakans (1885), the social-democratic Hunchaks (1887), and the more militant Dashnaks (1890) – the latter having their original headquarters outside Turkey, in Tbilisi, capital of Georgia and centre of the Russian Causasian viceroyalty. (Some Armenian political extremists regarded Tsarist Russia as an obstacle to national advancement.)

Sultan 'Abdul Hamid's response was to organize the Kurdish tribesmen into the so-called Hamidiye cavalry regiments, which terrorized the civil population of eastern Turkey in the same way as the Cossacks did in Russia immediately before the 1917 Revolution. Such was the audacity of these Kurdish irregular units that they even assaulted British consular officers who were supposed to supervise the implementation of the Berlin treaty as it affected Armenia.[1]

During this period, a distinctive Armenian community life evolved and flourished for a time in the *vilayet* or province of Mamuret ul-Aziz (Elazig) and in the adjoining *sanjak* of Marash, both situated directly between Cilicia and historical Great Armenia. Among the main centres of Armenian settlement were the cities of Kharput, Mezré, Malatya, Arapkir and Hozat, and also Marash itself. Foreign missionaries spread education and encouraged Armenian self-confidence. Even under Sultan 'Abdul Hamid, Armenians played a significant part in local administration, medicine, finance and engineering.

---

[1] Sir Robert Windham Graves, *Storm Centres of the Near East* (London, 1933), pp. 113–14.

Armenians and Turks lived side by side, though usually in separate quarters of the towns. Conditions were better than in the Kurdish-dominated villages of eastern Anatolia, but friction was never far beneath the surface. For instance, the local courts openly discriminated against Armenians and other Christians, in favour of Muslim Turks. Thus, Turkish bullies would attack individual Armenians or provoke them to a fight, and then fake simulated injuries, so that their Armenian victim would be sent to prison.

The novelist Vahan Totovents (1889–1937), in his autobiographical *Scenes from an Armenian Childhood*,[1] provides vivid glimpses of his youthful days in Mezré. On one occasion, the town-crier and public executioner murdered his wife and her young Turkish lover, and then accused the Armenians of the crime; many Armenians were arrested and beaten up, and only released weeks after the incident had been cleared up. The Armenians themselves were not all angels. The young Vahan Totovents's father kept a mistress in Constantinople, and Vahan himself enjoyed the embraces of the youngest wife of the local mullah. Once, the headmaster of the Armenian school was found stabbed to death; after a great outcry against 'Turkish murderers', it was found that the criminal was a young Armenian who harboured a personal grudge against the headmaster. At one unsettled period, an Armenian barber cut the throat of a Turk he was shaving, thinking that revolution had broken out. Such incidents, obviously, did nothing to help inter-community relations.

One of the mainstays of the Armenian cause had earlier been implicit faith in the power and benevolence of the Russian tsar in St Petersburg. After the 1877–8 war, a number of circumstances undermined this Russian good will towards the Turkish Armenians.

The assassination of Tsar Alexander II in 1881 was followed by the dismissal of his liberal chief minister, Loris-Melikov, himself an Armenian. The Tsars Alexander III and Nicolas II, at grips with Georgian and Armenian nationalists in the Caucasus, had absolutely no sympathy for Armenian revolutionaries in Turkey, and 'Abdul Hamid was well aware of this. In fact, Russian opposition towards the idea of an autonomous Armenia was almost as marked as 'Abdul Hamid's own. Later on, in 1903, Nicolas II even attempted to confiscate the property of the Armenian National Church, as well as

[1] Trans. M. Kudian (Oxford University Press, 1962).

closing down Armenian schools and other institutions through Russian Transcaucasia.

Fortified by Russian sympathy, and by the burgeoning friendship of the German Kaiser Wilhelm II in Berlin, 'Abdul Hamid resolved to hazard a 'show-down' with the Armenian nationalists. Provocative acts by Armenian extremists had indeed become a regular feature of the Turkish scene, particularly between 1890 and 1894. Their aims and activities are described as follows by a British consul serving at Erzerum at that time :

They proposed to create, not a genuine rebellion, but at least a semblance of revolt, by organizing armed attacks on isolated gendarmerie stations and postal escorts by small bands of 'Comitadjis',[1] directed by the local agents of the secret societies; by the cutting of telegraph wires, and the occasional bombing of government buildings when this could be done without much danger. They counted upon the proneness to panic of the Sultan, and the stupidity, misplaced zeal or deliberate malevolence of the local authorities to order and carry out unnecessarily severe punitive measures, which would degenerate into massacre as soon as the fanaticism and blood-lust of the ignorant Turk and Kurd populations had been sufficiently aroused. Then would come the moment for an appeal to the signatory Powers of the Treaty of Berlin to intervene and impose upon the Sultan such administrative reforms as would make life at least endurable for his Armenian subjects. They were quite cynical when remonstrated with on the wickedness of deliberately provoking the massacre of their unfortunate fellow-countrymen, with all its attendant horrors, without any assurance that the lot of the survivors would be any happier, saying calmly that the sacrifice was a necessary one and the victims would be 'Martyrs to the National Cause . . .[2]

The signal for armed confrontation between the Armenians and the Ottoman government was given in 1894, when a Hunchak agitator named Murat persuaded the Armenian mountaineers of the Sassoun district to refuse payment of the customary *hafir*, or protection tribute, to local Kurdish chieftains. This *hafir* was a thinly dis-

---

[1] Balkan-style outlaws and bands of guerilla fighters.
[2] Windham Graves, *Storm Centres of the Near East*, p. 139.

guised form of extortion, as the Kurdish chiefs and their followers were merely glorified brigand gangs. However, the Ottoman government treated the Armenian activities in Sassoun as a rebellion against the state and sent troops to quell it, which they did with great brutality.

An international commission of inquiry was set up to investigate the Sassoun incident. On 11 May 1895, Great Britain, France and Russia sent a memorandum to Sultan 'Abdul Hamid, urging reforms in the six Turkish Armenian provinces. The Armenians organized a demonstration in the Turkish capital (18 September 1895).

The Sultan responded by instituting a reign of terror which affected all the Armenian provinces, and also many important Turkish cities which had Armenian communities, including Constantinople itself. In some instances, Armenian civilians were herded into their own churches, which were then set on fire by Turkish troops, and the victims burnt alive. At ports along the Black Sea coast, thousands of Armenians were dumped into the harbours and left to drown.

In June 1896, the Armenians began to fight back, notably in the city of Van. Members of various patriotic organizations rose in defence of their homes and families. They engaged invading Turkish military units in action, saving the inhabitants of Van from the wholesale massacre which had been planned on the Sultan's orders.

On 24 August 1896, twenty-six Dashnak revolutionaries, led by a seventeen-year-old-youth named Babken Siuni, seized the Ottoman Bank building in Constantinople. Their aim was not to rob the bank of its valuables, but to force the Western powers who controlled the institution to intervene in the chaotic affairs of Turkey and support Armenian demands for reform and a 'new deal'.

The Armenian revolutionaries issued an ultimatum, embodying twelve demands for reform, and redress of the Armenian community's grievances. Failing satisfaction within forty-eight hours, the Dashnaks threatened to blow up the bank, killing themselves and the bank staff, and destroying the valuables deposited inside the premises.

The chief director of the Ottoman Bank, Sir Edgar Vincent (later Lord d'Abernon), opened negotiations with the Dashnaks, through the intermediary of Maximov, dragoman of the Russian Embassy. The Western embassies undertook to support the Armenian revolutionaries' demands.

Four of the Dashnaks had already perished in the fracas. The survivors eventually agreed to evacuate the bank, under guarantee of safe conduct. They were escorted through angry mobs on to Sir Edgar Vincent's private yacht; seventeen of them were soon afterwards shipped to Marseilles.

Furious at this challenge to his authority, the Sultan immediately gave orders for a wholesale massacre of Armenians resident in Constantinople. Indeed, advance orders had already been given for this bloodbath, since the Ottoman secret police had got wind of an impending Armenian raid on the Ottoman Bank, and were glad of a chance to vent their anger on the Armenian civil population. Under the very eyes of the Western ambassadors and European residents, mobs of ruffians launched a frenzied assault on every Armenian they could find. Government soldiers, *softas* (bands of theological students from the mosques), and uniformed police officers led on and incited bands of Turks in their murderous fury.

Women and children were ruthlessly cut down in the streets. Many houses and shops were broken into. The reign of terror lasted for several days, resulting in terrible carnage and destruction. Impartial estimates by the various diplomatic eyewitnesses put the number of Armenian dead on the streets of the Ottoman capital at between six and eight thousand. A collective note, sent by the ambassadors of the great powers on 27 August 1896, demanded cessation of the atrocities: a number of Armenians connected with or employed by the various embassies and foreign business concerns had been murdered or seriously wounded.

The question of 'Abdul Hamid's deposition was actively debated in government circles in the capitals of Europe. The Russian Ambassador, Nelidov, was convinced that the British and French would take advantage of the situation to seize Constantinople and the Dardanelles. In the autumn of 1896, contingency plans were laid in St Petersburg for mobilization of the Russian Black Sea fleet, to be combined, if necessary, with a commando-type landing at the Turkish capital.[1]

The Armenian atrocities aroused intense indignation in Great Britain and also in America. The total death toll over the years from 1894 to 1896 was not less than 200,000 – some estimates put it as high as a quarter of a million.

The veteran statesman Gladstone toured leading British cities, preaching a crusade against the unspeakable Turk. 'To serve Armenia

[1] H. Pasdermadjian, *Histoire de l'Arménie* (2nd edn, Paris, 164), p. 355.

is to serve civilization,' he declared. The Archbishop of Canterbury, Dr Edward Benson, on the other hand, refused to intervene publicly, and received a number of indignant letters reproaching him for failing in his Christian duty.[1]

The unenviable task of representing British interests in this crisis fell to the 3rd Marquis of Salisbury (1830–1903), who defeated Gladstone's Liberal administration in 1895. In Liberal eyes, Lord Salisbury's reputation had been compromised by his association with Disraeli during the Eastern Crisis of 1877–8.

Lord Salisbury, a reasonable and humane statesman, made no attempt to turn the Armenian problem to his political advantage, as his former chief, Disraeli, had done. But Salisbury's freedom of action was far more circumscribed than had been the case when Disraeli was in power twenty years previously. After studying the documents, I have come to the conclusion that Lord Salisbury's biographer, Lady Gwendolen Cecil, sums up the position fairly when she writes:[2]

Since he was last in office the German emperor had quarrelled with England over Far East politics, and never afterwards paid more than lip service to the old friendship. The breach with France was not yet healed, and, though Lord Salisbury's personal authority remained and the influence of his initiative, England was isolated in European sympathy throughout this period.

He found diplomacy once more absorbed in the Near East problem as the result of a peculiarly atrocious outbreak of Turkish cruelty and misgovernment in Armenia. After failing in a private proposal to Germany to join in some drastic enterprise – its details are not known – for the dismemberment or subjugation of Turkey, he appealed in 1896 to the Christian Powers as a whole to take combined action for enforcing reform on the Porte. They agreed and accepted his initiative. . . .

But as regarded the lot of the unhappy Armenians it proved a sore disappointment to its author – Russia, who, in the strange whirligig of time, had become the champion of Turkish independence, vetoing, with German support, any form of coercion at Constantinople.

---

1 Lambeth Palace papers.
2 *Encyclopaedia Britannica* (14th edn, vol. 19, p. 885).

The only European sovereign now to cultivate 'Abdul Hamid's friendship immediately after the Armenian massacres was Kaiser Wilhelm II, who had already paid one state visit to Turkey, in 1889. This time, in 1898, the Kaiser arrived in Constantinople, anxious to finalize one of his favourite projects, the Berlin–Baghdad railway. After presenting the city of Constantinople with a hideous fountain of his own design, to be erected on the site of the ancient Hippodrome, Wilhelm set off for the Holy Land.

The German monarch entered Jerusalem dressed in shining armour, in imitation of the Crusader knights. The Kaiser proclaimed himself a friend of Muslim, Jew and Christian alike – 'the knight of peace and labour, interested not in riches but in the healing of souls'. The true value of this statement was revealed to all in 1915 and the following years, when over a million Christian Armenians were murdered by Germany's Turkish allies, without the Kaiser uttering a word in their defence.

2

False Hopes

THE FINAL decade of 'Abdul Hamid's long reign was a time of political unrest and economic difficulties. In 1898, the Sultan was compelled to hand over the island of Crete to international control. What remained of Turkish dominions in the Balkans was seething with unrest. In the back streets of Salonika, young Turkish officers, Freemasons, and political exiles were concocting a new revolutionary ideology, that of the Young Turk movement. In 1905, an Armenian revolutionary committee organized an unsuccessful attempt on 'Abdul Hamid's life. They planted a carriage filled with dynamite in the square outside the Hamidieh Mosque while the Sultan was at prayers. The carriage exploded and several bystanders were killed. For a time, the secret Society of Union and Progress joined forces with the Dashnaks in plotting Sultan 'Abdul Hamid's overthrow.

The revolt broke out in July 1908, when the Turkish Commander-in-Chief in Northern Macedonia was assassinated by mutineers at Monastir. From all over the southern Balkans came news of Turkish garrisons and Christian insurgents throwing in their lot with the mutineers. On 23 July 1908, an ultimatum signed by the Central Committee of Union and Progress in Monastir informed the Sultan that unless the Ottoman Constitution of 1876, suspended in 1878, was restored within twenty-four hours, the Second and Third Army Corps would march on Constantinople.

The decree proclaiming the restoration of the Ottoman Constitution was published on 24 July 1908. Constantinople gave itself up to a delirium of rejoicing. In Damascus and Baghdad, in Van and

Trebizond, the restoration of the 1876 Constitution was hailed as the dawn of a new era.

Contemporary eyewitnesses describe the astonishing scenes which took place on Galata Bridge and in the square of Aya Sofia, where Kurds and Armenians, Greeks and Bulgars embraced one another as brothers. Young Turk officers harangued the crowds, proclaiming that Muslims, Christians and Jews were no longer divided, but would work together for the glory of the Ottoman nation. Even mullahs were seen wearing the red and white cockade of liberty.

In April 1909, partisans of 'Abdul Hamid's absolutist regime launched a counter-revolutionary coup. A great number of young officers and other adherents of the constitutional movement were massacred, parliament was raided and several deputies murdered. Leading members of the Committee of Union and Progress went into hiding. Talaat, the future Minister of the Interior, formerly a telegraph clerk, was sheltered by Agnuni, leader of the Constantinople Dashnaks. (Agnuni was rewarded for his hospitality in 1915, when he was one of the first Armenian notables whose death warrant was signed by Talaat Pasha.)[1]

Almost simultaneously, a massacre of Armenians was unleashed at Adana, in Cilicia. It is not clear which faction was responsible for the outbreak – the Young Turks or partisans of 'Abdul Hamid. It is possible that it was simply a spontaneous outbreak of mob violence and Muslim fanaticism. About 30,000 Armenians perished.

The victims would have been more numerous still had it not been for the bravery of Major Doughty-Wylie, British Vice-Consul at Konia. Doughty-Wylie put on his military uniform, gathered up a small group of Turkish troops and rode through the centre of the trouble in the towns of Adana and Mersin, in pursuit of the rioters. A bullet smashed his right arm, but a few days later he was on patrol again when the killing resumed. According to press reports, his action saved thousands of lives; he was awarded the CMG and the Turkish order of Mejidieh for his bravery.[2]

Because of his complicity in the unsuccessful counter-revolution,

---

[1] Stephen G. Svajian, *A Trip through Historic Armenia* (New York, 1977), p. 401.

[2] H. V. F. Winstone, *Gertrude Bell* (London, 1978), pp. 119—20. C. H. M. Doughty-Wylie was a close friend of Gertrude Bell; he died a hero's death at Gallipoli in 1915, and Gertrude Bell never recovered from this loss, which haunted her until she took her own life in 1926.

Sultan 'Abdul Hamid was deposed in 1909, and succeeded by his brother, who reigned as Sultan Muhammad (Mehemet) V.

Nothing better illustrates the state of Turkey in those times than the life and career of this pathetic old gentleman, who was not only nominal ruler of Turkey, but also Caliph or Supreme Head of the Muslim religion everywhere. The new Sultan had spent the last thirty years in gilded captivity in a palace, surrounded by spies, and with only the ladies of his harem for company. 'So long as he remained quiescent, the heir apparent was comfortable and fairly secure, but he knew that the first sign of revolt, or even a too curious interest in what was going on, would be the signal for his death.'[1]

He was simply 'a quiet, easy-going gentlemanly old man'. The Committee of Union and Progress proceeded to rule him, as they ruled all the rest of Turkey – by intimidation. On one occasion, the new Sultan's own son-in-law was condemned to death by the Young Turk junta. Sultan Mehemet V went down on his knees before Talaat Pasha, but his son-in-law was hanged just the same, in full view of the palace. Nobody doubted any longer who was master in the 'reformed' Ottoman Empire.[2]

The Young Turks had begun in idealistic fashion, inaugurating parliamentary government and a whole series of liberal reforms. Members of the Christian communities, including the Armenians, were for the first time given the right and the duty to serve in the Ottoman army and navy.

But internal dissensions and foreign wars, combined with the adoption of a chauvinist pan-Turk ideology, helped to turn the Young Turk regime into a military dictatorship. Foreign pressure added to the new government's difficulties. In 1911, the Italians suddenly started a war against Turkey which ended in their annexing Libya and the Dodecanese islands. In 1912–13, a Balkan alliance wrested from the Ottoman Empire most of its remaining possessions on the European continent.

A crucial event in the development of the Young Turk movement was the *coup d'état* of 26 January 1913. On that day, Colonel Enver together with Talaat and two hundred of their partisans invaded the Sublime Porte, seat of the central administration, murdered the liberal War Minister Nazim Pasha, and turned out the veteran Grand

[1] Henry Morgenthau, *Ambassador Morgenthau's Story* (New York, 1919), p. 17.
[2] *Ambassador Morgenthau's Story*, p. 18.

Vizier Kiamil Pasha. Enver consolidated his position by recapturing Adrianople (Edirné) from the Bulgarians (July 1913). Within a few months, Enver Pasha (known as 'Napoleonlik' – the little Napoleon) was War Minister. Enver's backer and hatchet man Talaat was Minister of the Interior. With their associate Ahmed Djemal Pasha, the Navy Minister, they formed a ruthless and determined triumvirate. When US Ambassador Henry Morgenthau arrived at Constantinople in 1913, he assessed the situation as follows :

The Young Turks had disappeared as a positive regenerating force, but they still existed as a political machine. Their leaders, Talaat, Enver, and Djemal, had long since abandoned any expectation of reforming their state, but they had developed an insatiable lust for personal power. Instead of a nation of nearly 20,000,000, developing happily along democratic lines, enjoying suffrage, building up their industry and agriculture, laying the foundations for universal education, sanitation, and general progress, I saw that Turkey consisted of merely so many inarticulate, ignorant, and poverty-ridden slaves, with a small, wicked oligarchy at the top, which was prepared to use them in the way that would best promote its private interests.[1]

Ambassador Morgenthau goes on to comment on the Young Turks' fall from 'the highest idealism to the crassest materialism'. The Committee of Union and Progress, he says, functioned like a corrupt American party machine in control of some US provincial city – a gang which filled every public office with its own henchmen. 'No man could hold office, high or low, who was not endorsed by this committee.'

This view of the moral principles of the Young Turk regime was not confined to those associated with the cause of the Western allies. Morgenthau's opinion of the regime coincided rather closely with that of a wartime German Imperial ambassador to Turkey, Count von Wolff-Metternich. Writing to the German Chancellor Bethmann-Hollweg in June 1916, the Count noted that no one in Turkey could withstand the ruling Committee of Union and Progress – 'a many-

---

[1] *Ambassador Morgenthau's Story*, p. 13.

headed Hydra, the personification of chauvinism and fanaticism'. The German Ambassador further noted that the Committee dominated not only the Ottoman capital, but also the most outlying provinces of the empire. Each provincial governor or village headman had a Committee member at his side, to control his every action. The 'hungry wolves' of the Committee were activated by both fanaticism and greed. The programme of 'Turkification' meant in practice the expulsion or murder of all non-Turkish elements – and the seizure of other people's property. 'Herein, and in the parroting of slogans about liberty culled from the French Revolution, consists for the time being the celebrated rebirth of Turkey.'[1] These scathing phrases are notable, since they emanate from the pen of the personal representative of Turkey's friend and ally, Kaiser Wilhelm II.

The policies of the Young Turk junta were given a veneer of respectability by the adoption of a new ideology known as pan-Turkism or pan-Turanianism. The best-known exponent of this doctrine was Zia Gökalp (1876–1924). Gökalp was a devotee of the French sociologist Émile Durkheim (1858–1917) and his published works are notable for their reasonable tone and persuasive style. However, as a close friend of the Interior Minister Talaat Pasha, and a member of the Central Council of the Committee of Union and Progress, Gökalp carries a heavy burden of responsibility for the Armenian genocide of 1915.

Gökalp's philosophy was coloured by the Turkish military disasters of the late nineteenth and early twentieth centuries. The Turks had been set upon by Russian, British and Italian imperialists and driven from their ancient dominions in the Balkans, the Mediterranean and North Africa. Therefore the Turks must take refuge in their ancient national traditions, and be proud, instead of being ashamed, of their Turkic ancestry.

It was now the duty of the Turks to 'know themselves', to rediscover the soul of the people, which could be done by research into the history and culture of the ancient Turks, and by examining those aspects of Turkish popular culture which faithfully retained their authentic character.

Gökalp's essays glorified the warlike Turks of old, and described their political and cultural achievements, their extensive pre-Islamic

---

[1] German original printed by J. Lepsius, *Deutschland und Armenien, 1914–1918* (Potsdam, 1919), p. 277.

Turkish kingdoms, and the feats of Attila, Jenghiz Khan, Timur, Babur and the early Ottoman sultans. For Gökalp, the ancient Turks were distinguished by many excellent qualities: hospitality, modesty, courage, and so on. They did not oppress other nations, their god was one of peace, and they eschewed imperialistic ambitions. The great Turkish conquerors sought only to unite the scattered Turkic tribes. The Turks, both in ancient and in modern times, had a worthy mission, namely to realize the highest moral values and to prove that sacrifices and heroic deeds were not beyond human strength.[1]

This fine-sounding programme looks very well on paper. But, in the hands of the Young Turks, who had seized power by terror and assassination, Gökalp's theories were political dynamite. They could be and were exploited as the basis for a typical 'master-race' ideology, jointly glorifying both ethnic 'Turkism' and the Islamic faith, and consigning non-Turkish non-Muslims like the Greeks and Armenians to exile or extermination.

The irony of all this is that the leaders of the Young Turk party were themselves of the most diverse ethnic origins: Talaat Pasha was a Muslim Bulgarian 'pomak', while Enver Pasha's mother was Albanian, and he had a Circassian grandmother. The original centre of the movement was Salonika, a city of Greek Macedonia.

It is also worth noting that the Anatolian Turks generally differ greatly from their distant kinsmen in Turkestan and other Turkic areas of Asia and eastern Europe. Ethnologically, the Anatolian Turk represents the most varied conglomerate imaginable. He is a mixture of descendants of the invading Seljuq Turks, combined with Greeks, Slavs, Kurds, Persians, Armenians, Georgians, Circassians and Arabs; many Turks may be described as barbarized Byzantines and Cappadocians. The pure 'Turanian' type has become so effaced that traces of it are rarely seen among the settled population.

Authentic Turkish and Turkmen tribes in Anatolia and Asia Minor tended until recently to live a separate, nomadic existence. The most numerous were the Yürüks, who lived in small groups from Izmir (Smyrna) to the eastern Taurus. Their language retained a number of old Turkish words, and they used tents of the circular Central-Asian type. Turkmen tribes form another Turkic group in Anatolia. More distinctively Asiatic even than the Yürüks, they cluster in the level plains around the salt lake (Tüz Gölü) in the centre of the

---

[1] C. W. Hostler, *Turkism and the Soviets* (London, 1957), p. 106.

country, and also live in the eastern Taurus region.[1] They have never had any interest in or indeed knowledge of theoretical pan-Turkism as a doctrine.

Following their *coup* of 26 January 1913, the triumvirate of Enver, Talaat and Djemal were unchallenged dictators of Turkey. Enver had been Ottoman Military Attaché in Berlin between 1909 and 1911 and was an undisguised admirer of Prussian militarism. He adorned his handsome features with a Kaiser Wilhelm moustache, sharply turned up at the ends.

The onset of a world war was already on the horizon. Turkey's future alignment became clear with the arrival in December 1913 of a special German military mission under General Liman von Sanders (1855–1929), an honourable but unbending Prussian, who enjoyed the personal confidence of Kaiser Wilhelm.

Thus, by January, 1914, seven months before the Great War began, Germany held this position in the Turkish army : a German general was Chief of Staff; another was Inspector General; scores of German officers held commands of the first importance, and the Turkish politician who was even then an outspoken champion of Germany, Enver Pasha, was Minister of War.[2]

The open dominance of Germany over the Ottoman armed forces aroused resentment among rival foreign governments. It was partly to counter this feeling that the Young Turks ostensibly agreed to a new scheme for reform in the eastern, Armenian provinces. A Dutchman named Westenenk and a Norwegian named Hoff were nominated to supervise the long-awaited reforms in that area. Hoff actually arrived in Van and began his work in July 1914, on the eve of the First World War.

The members of the Young Turk inner circle were laughing up their sleeves. At secret meetings of the Committee of Union and Progress, the fate of the Armenians had been discussed and decided in principle months, if not years, before the outbreak of war. The prime war aim of the Young Turks was the reunification of Ottoman Turkey with Turkish Caucasia and Central Asia. Right in the middle

---

[1] Hostler, *Turkism and the Soviets,* pp. 15–16.

[2] *Ambassador Morgenthau's Story,* p. 42.

of the projected pan-Turk empire lay a monstrous blot on the horizon – the Armenian table land, inhabited by well over two million Christian non-Turks. They were in the way – and were duly scheduled for elimination.

The fact that the Armenian genocide was planned by the Young Turk junta well before the outbreak of the First World War is shown by the skilfully laid plans for the scheme and its lightning execution when the signal was given in the late spring of 1915. From 1913 onwards, in all towns and villages inhabited by Armenians, governors and police chiefs had been appointed who were known for their devotion to the aims and dictates of the Young Turk regime. Specially briefed in Constantinople, they were supplied with secret orders giving detailed instructions for the extermination operation. In cases known to me from personal inquiry, friendly Turkish officials got wind of these projected measures, and gave timely warning to Armenian friends some weeks before the genocide began.

The essence of the plan was secrecy. Since many telegraph operators, cipher clerks and local government officials were themselves Armenians, care was taken to avoid putting detailed instructions on paper. In many cases, the extermination scheme was to be put into operation on receipt of the simple message: 'Take care of the Armenians.'[1] The carrying out of this meticulously planned annihilation programme forms the subject of the following chapter – and it does not make pleasant reading.

[1] This detail kindly supplied by Right Reverend Bishop Nerses Bosabalian, London, 1980.

1   Noah with his family in the Ark, sailing towards Mount Ararat. From a
14th-century manuscript of Rashid al-Din's *Universal History*, copied in Iran.
(Royal Asiatic Society)

2   Bronze head of the goddess
Anahit/Aphrodite, Hellenistic
period. Found at Satala, eastern
Turkey. *(Trustees of the British
Museum)*

3 Ruins of Anavarza or Anazarbus castle, Cilician Armenia. Crusader period. *(Gertrude Bell collection, University of Newcastle)*

3

Abomination of Desolation

ON 28 JUNE 1914, the murder of the Austrian Archduke Franz
Ferdinand and his wife at Sarajevo sparked off a fuse which
within a brief span of time exploded the European magazine
in a series of detonations. By noon on 1 August a state of war existed
between Russia and Germany, and on the next day German troops
entered French territory.

Responsible Turkish public opinion stood for strict neutrality in
the world conflict. Senior Ottoman diplomats and officials were aware
of the dangers and potential disasters which involvement in the world
conflagration would bring to the Empire.

The Young Turk triumvirate had no such misgivings. It was only
eighteen months since they had staked their own lives on the success
of the *coup* of 26 January 1913. They saw the outbreak of the First
World War as an unrepeatable chance to secure their objective of
'Turkey for the Turks', combined with domination of Turkic Central
Asia and perhaps of Egypt and the Balkans also.[1]

On the day when Germany was invading France, 2 August 1914,
Enver Pasha signed a protocol with the German Ambassador, von
Wangenheim, the terms of which were known only to the inner
circles of the Young Turk movement. A few days later, two German
dreadnoughts, the *Goeben* and the *Breslau*, arrived at Constantinople

[1] cf. *Ambassador Morgenthau's Story,* p. 51.

from the Mediterranean, where the British navy had failed to intercept them. The vessels were promptly 'purchased' by the Turkish navy, while remaining under effective German control. Their commander, the German Admiral Souchon, skilfully steered Turkey into the war by sending Turkish torpedo boats to bombard Odessa (29 October 1914). Far away to the south, Ottoman bedouin troops crossed the Egyptian border and had a minor clash with British soldiers. War was declared forthwith, and four moderate members of the Ottoman Cabinet – one an Armenian, Özkan – resigned.

The Turkish alliance was of immense military and political value to the Central Powers. The Turkish armies, still firmly entrenched in Syria, Mesopotamia and Palestine, were able to offer an immediate and serious threat to the Suez Canal and to the British position in Egypt. By their dogged and successful defence of the Dardanelles, they prevented effective co-operation between Russia and the Western powers. Their Balkan position assured the supremacy of the Central Powers in that important area. The Turks were still the greatest independent Muslim power, and Ottoman prestige among Muslims elsewhere (exercised through the decrepit Caliph, Sultan Mehemet V) created a series of problems in the British and French empires.

In spite of Turkish assertions to the contrary, the Turkish Armenians, in the vast majority of cases, behaved as loyal Ottoman citizens. At its eighth party conference held at Erzerum in August 1914, the Dashnak Party had called on its members to carry out their patriotic duties as Turkish subjects, in the event of war breaking out between Turkey and Russia. Nearly a quarter of a million Armenians were conscripted into the Ottoman armed forces, and they performed sterling service during the first battles of the war.[1]

During December 1914 and January 1915, Enver Pasha himself took part in the fighting at Sarikamish, on the Russian Caucasian border. His army was almost annihilated, and the Young Turk War Minister would himself have been captured or killed but for the help of some devoted Armenian troops. There is no evidence that the Armenians in eastern Turkey had any plans for insurrection. In April 1915, the German commandant at Erzerum in eastern Anatolia, General Posseldt, testified to the German Embassy in Constantinople that 'the Armenians would have stayed perfectly quiet, if they had not been harassed and provoked by the Turks'. According to General

---

[1] Sir Winston Churchill, *The World Crisis* (London, 1929), vol. 5, p. 404.

Posseldt, the local Armenians' conduct had been exemplary (*tadellos*) throughout.[1]

During February 1915, panic reigned in the Turkish capital, as news reached Constantinople of allied naval operations in the Aegean, which were then followed by landings on the Gallipoli peninsula late in April. This is not the place to go into the reasons for the ultimate failure of the Dardanelles operation – a failure caused in part by infantile wranglings between Churchill, Kitchener and Lord Fisher, in part by the incompetence of British naval and field commanders on the spot, but most of all by the grit and heroism of the Turkish and German defenders. Among the main leaders of the defence of the Dardanelles was the future reformer of Turkey, Mustafa Kemal.

For the time being, the majority of the Young Turk junta was convinced that defeat was near. The Russian army of the Caucasus was advancing slowly but surely into eastern Anatolia. It seemed that the British and French fleets might arrive at any moment in the Bosphorus, in which event it was quite likely that revolution would break out in the Ottoman capital.

The Turkish Committee of Union and Progress had already realised that war could provide them with ideal conditions in which to carry out the extermination of the Armenians which they had long meditated – without the awkward complications which had plagued poor, bungling Sultan 'Abdul Hamid, who was now langushing in enforced retirement. A member of the Committee's Central Council, Mevlanzadé Rifat, has left a record of a Council meeting held early in 1915, in which the practical details of the operation were worked out. The Executive Secretary, Dr Nazim, remarked:

'We are now at war; there is no more auspicious occasion than this; the intervention of the Great Powers and the protests of the newspapers will not even be considered; and even if they are, the matter will have become an accomplished fact, and thus closed for ever.'

Another participant, Hassan Fehmin, observed:

'I am thinking of an easy method of extermination: We are at war. We can send those young Armenians who can bear arms to the front lines. There, coupled between fire by Russians facing them and by special forces in their rear dispatched by us for that purpose, we can trap and annihilate them. In the meantime, we can order our

---

[1] J. Lepsius, *Deutschland und Armenien*, p. 51, document no. 31, report dated 26 April 1915.

faithful adherents to plunder and to liquidate the old and infirm, women and children, who remain behind in their homes... This seems a suitable method.'[1]

It was resolved that this 'suitable method' of extermination should be administered by a three-man committee consisting of Dr Nazim, Dr Behaettin Shakir, and the Minister of Education, Shoukrie, under the personal supervision of Talaat Pasha.

The Russian advance in the east, and the Gallipoli operations, caused the Turkish dictators to speed up their extermination plans. During early spring of 1915, Turkish police and gendarmes all over Anatolia stepped up their systematic harassment of the Armenian civil population. This was a 'softening up', preparatory to the final solution which had been decided on in the central councils of the Young Turk movement.

A favourite device was to raid Armenian towns and villages, ostensibly in search of hidden arms. Individuals were taken in for questioning, and subjected to tortures. Priests in particular were victimized: their nails were torn out with pincers, their teeth knocked out one by one, their beards burnt off, and their eyes gouged out. Victims were beaten on the soles of their feet until the whole foot swelled up and the tendons burst, and the foot sometimes had to be amputated. American missionaries reported cases in which women accused of concealing weapons were stripped naked and whipped with branches freshly cut from trees, and such beatings were even inflicted on those who were pregnant.

Djevdet Bey, the Vali of Van and brother-in-law of War Minister Enver Pasha, specialized in nailing horseshoes to the feet of his Armenian victims. He then forced them to execute a kind of grotesque tap dance, until they fell senseless and were bayoneted or clubbed to death. A senior Turkish official boasted to the American Ambassador Henry Morgenthau that the Union and Progress Committee had unearthed a book about the tortures of the Spanish Inquisition, and had successfully adapted for current use most of the refined torture methods described there.[2]

The date of 24 April 1915, when the leaders of the Constantinople Armenian community were rounded up and sent away to their deaths, is still commemorated annually by Armenians everywhere as marking

---

[1] E. K. Sarkisian and R. G. Sahakian, *Vital Issues in Modern Armenian History* (Watertown, 1965), pp. 33–4.

[2] *Ambassador Morgenthau's Story*, pp. 304—7.

the crucial event which sealed the doom of the Turkish Armenian population, then numbering around two and a half millions. The indiscriminate nature of this 'purge' is shown by the fact that among the first victims was the great Armenian composer Komitas, a harmless clergyman, intent only on his research on Armenian church music and folklore. When eventually rescued from a Turkish concentration camp, the poor man had been driven mad by his experiences, and never composed another note of music. He died twenty years later. A great Armenian poet, Siamanto (nom-de-plume of Atom Yarjanian) was among those members of the Armenian intelligentsia who were slaughtered.

Early in 1915 also, the Armenian military units, who had rendered loyal service to the Ottoman government, were disarmed and turned into labour detachments. They were then systematically starved, beaten and overworked. Compared with their miserable fate, that of an American chain-gang convict was enviable. The US Ambassador Henry Morgenthau reported :

Army supplies of all kinds were loaded on their backs, and, stumbling under the burdens and driven by the whips and bayonets of the Turks, they were forced to drag their weary bodies into the mountains of the Caucasus. Sometimes they would have to plough their way, burdened in this fashion, almost waist high through snow. They had to spend practically all their time in the open, sleeping on the bare ground ... They were given only scraps of food; if they fell sick they were left where they had dropped, their Turkish oppressors perhaps stopping long enough to rob them of all their possessions – even of their clothes. If any stragglers succeeded in reaching their destinations, they were not infrequently massacred.[1]

As time went on, the Armenian military labour units were simply shot down in cold blood. Squads of fifty or a hundred Armenians would be bound together in groups of four, and then marched out to a secluded spot, and there shot. Sometimes the victims were forced to dig their own graves before being killed. According to an American consular report, two thousand Armenian military workmen were

[1] *Ambassador Morgenthau's Story,* p. 302.

sent out from Kharput in July 1915, ostensibly to build roads; practically all of them were slaughtered, and their bodies piled into a deserted cave. The same fate befell two thousand disarmed Armenian soldiers ordered to march towards Diarbekir: Turkish government agents mobilized local Kurdish tribesmen, and the Armenians were massacred to the last man. Most of the victims' corpses were later discovered stark naked, the Turks and Kurds having stolen all their clothes.

The senseless slaughter of useful workmen provoked impotent rage and frustration among Turkey's German allies. In June 1916, the Turks liquidated large numbers of Armenians working on vital sectors of the Berlin–Constantinople–Baghdad railway, then nearing completion. (It was the important Amanus sector, bordering on Cilicia, which was affected.) The German Ambassador in Constantinople, Count von Wolff-Metternich, stormed to the Sublime Porte and directly accused Talaat Pasha and Halil Pasha, the Foreign Minister, of deliberate sabotage of the joint war effort. 'These measures', the German envoy declared to them, 'create the impression that the Turkish government itself is intent on losing the war.[1]

The Ottoman ministers simply shrugged their shoulders; for them the 'final solution' of the Armenian question was more important than any military engineering operations. The Turks and Germans later replaced the murdered Armenians with British and Indian war prisoners captured at the surrender of Kut, near Baghdad. These British prisoners, contrary to all civilized rules of war, were forced to work until they dropped from exhaustion, and then were brutally flogged.

When they had the opportunity, Armenian soldiers and volunteer irregulars fought bravely in defence of their homes and families. In Van, for instance, they barricaded themselves in the old city, and held out with great valour until relieved by Russian and Armenian units from the Caucasus (May 1915). Equally successful was the epic defence of Musa Dagh near Antioch, in the Gulf of Alexandretta. Four thousand Armenians entrenched themselves on the hillside and held out against overwhelming Ottoman forces. After more than forty days, they were relieved by a French naval contingent, one of whose leaders was a French naval officer of Armenian extraction, Charles

---

[1] Lepsius, *Deutschland und Armenien*, p. 227, report no. 282, 30 June 1916. That the persecution of Armenians was harmful to the Turkish war effort is stressed by Allen and Muratoff, *Caucasian Battlefields* (Cambridge, 1953), p. 332.

Diran Tekeian. The story is told in Franz Werfel's epic novel, *The Forty Days of Musa Dagh.* Other Armenian attempts at collective self-defence ended in tragedy and disaster, as at Urfa (Edessa).

With the young Armenians of military age out of the way, the Turkish Ministry of the Interior next eliminated Armenian fathers of families and other males over the age of forty-five. These men were ordered to report to the local prisons, were locked up without being charged with any offence, and later on were taken out, often by night, and shot, bludgeoned to death, or hanged. Ample documentary evidence of these proceedings exists – including group photographs of the victims taken by Turkish police for their records.[1] Nearly all the provincial Armenian bishops and clergy were slaughtered. Those that survived followed their flock into exile and ministered to them until they themselves fell victim to disease or starvation or both.

The fate of the Armenian men was, perhaps, enviable compared with what was in store for the women and children. The Interior Minister Talaat Pasha, telegraphed the Governor of Aleppo on 15 September 1915 :

You have already been informed that the Government has decided to exterminate entirely all the Armenians living in Turkey. No-one opposed to this order can any longer hold an administrative position. Without pity for women, children and invalids, however tragic the methods of extermination may be, without heeding any scruples of conscience, their existence must be terminated.[2]

To save money and ammunition, the Young Turk ruling junta decided on a programme of mass deportation, through which they could also give the operation a semblance of legality. This semblance of legality, of course, is farcical when we consider that the mass movement was decreed for the summer months of 1915, at a time of maximum heat and drought, and that the victims were to be systematically denied access to food and water en route.

Their destination was the desolate and poverty-stricken Syrian

[1] For instance, the group photograph of fifty prominent Armenian citizens of Kayseri, whose pictures were taken in front of the Kapu Alti prison. They were all hanged, or else deported and killed en route. See Stephen G. Svajian, *A Trip through Historic Armenia* (New York, 1977), plate facing p. 359.

[2] The *Daily Telegraph*, London, 29 May 1922; French version in Pasdermadjian, *Histoire de l'Arménie,* 2nd edn, (Paris, 1964), p. 410.

wilderness of Deir al-Zor, which in most cases could be reached only by a trek of two or three hundred miles over precipitous mountains infested by Turkish ruffians and Kurdish bandits. Since many of the deportees were old women in their seventies and eighties, or little babies and children of two or three years of age, it is clear that the deportation orders were death sentences and were intended as such. The vast majority of the Armenian families had no more chance of reaching their destination alive than they had of walking barefoot across the Sahara desert.

Even in the midst of this ghastly business, the Young Turk officials, police and army officers, managed to feather their own nests. Kaiser Wilhelm's representative at Constantinople, Count von Wolff-Metternich, noted with contempt how the members of the Committee of Union and Progress forced condemned Armenian families to sell their houses and property to them for a small fraction of their real value.[1]

Not that this mattered much to the hapless Armenians, because their escorts systematically robbed them of their cash and valuables in the course of the ensuing death march. The Ottoman Bank President showed bank-notes soaked with blood and stuck through with dagger holes. Some torn ones had evidently been ripped from the clothing of murdered people – and these had been placed on ordinary deposit in Bank current accounts by Turkish army officers.[2] Dr J. Lepsius estimated in 1919 that the profits accruing to the Young Turk oligarchy and its 'hangers-on' from the expropriation of the Armenians amounted to not less than a thousand million German marks – about three hundred million dollars in modern money.[3]

For political and strategic reasons, the pattern of events varied from region to region. The deportations were not generally enforced in the cities of Constantinople, Izmir (Smyrna) and Aleppo, partly because of the presence there of numerous European residents – diplomats, journalists, businessmen and missionaries. In some provincial cities of Asia Minor, such as Kayseri, the deportations and murders were selective, and certain doctors and government officials were exempted.

In Angora, the modern Ankara, the Vali or governor was a humane and enlightened man, and refused to carry out orders from

[1] Lepsius, *Deutschland und Armenien*, p. 277.

[2] Viscount Bryce, *The Treatment of Armenians in the Ottoman Empire, 1915–16*, 2nd edn (Beirut, 1972), pp. 385–6.

[3] Lepsius, *Deutschland und Armenien*, p. lxvi.

the central government to deport and kill Armenians. He was supported in this by the local police chief and the military commander of the province. They knew that the Angora Armenians, mostly Roman Catholics, were loyal to the Ottoman government. They were some 20,000 strong, and leaders in commerce and industry. The Armenians' houses and shops were searched in July 1915, and neither weapons nor incriminating documents were found.

However, the Vali of Angora and his colleagues were soon dismissed, and replaced by reliable Party men from Constantinople. These quickly exterminated the Angora Armenians. Most of the Armenian men were carried out in the night to a spot called Asi Yozgad, where Muslim Turkish tanners and butchers had been specially assembled carrying the knives and choppers of their trade. These tanners and butchers made short work of the unarmed Armenians. The bodies were thrown into a river from a bridge nearby. So horrible was the sight from the bridge that traffic was suspended during the hours of daylight. Travellers passing over the bridge by night complained of being nearly suffocated by the stench of decaying flesh.[1]

As one moves further eastward, the picture becomes if possible still more horrible. Knowing that Russian troops including Armenian contingents were advancing on Van and Erzerum, the Vali Djevdet Bey destroyed entire Armenian villages, sparing neither men, women nor children. At Siirt, south of Bitlis, a general massacre of Armenian, Nestorian and Jacobite Christians took place on 17 June 1915. The scene was inspected immediately afterwards by Rafael de Nogales, a Venezuelan soldier of fortune serving with the Turkish armed forces. Nogales found a hill 'crowned by thousands of half-nude and still bleeding corpses, lying in heaps, or interlaced in death's final embrace'. The same eyewitness goes on to say :

Fathers, brothers, sons, and grandsons lay there as they had fallen beneath the bullets and yataghans of the assassins. From more than one slashed throat the life gushed forth in mouthfuls of warm blood. Flocks of vultures were perched upon the mound, pecking at the eyes of dead and dying, whose rigid gaze seemed still to mirror the horrors of unspeakable agony; while the scavenger dogs struck sharp teeth into the entrails of beings still palpitating with the breath of life.[2]

[1] Bryce, *The Treatment of Armenians*, pp. 382–5.
[2] Rafael de Nogales, *Four Years beneath the Crescent* (London, 1926) p. 124.

Soon afterwards, Nogales came upon a caravan of several hundred deported Christian women and children, resting in a village market-place :

Their sunken cheeks and cavernous eyes bore the stamp of death. Among the women, almost all of whom were young, were some mothers with children, or, rather, childish skeletons, in their arms. One of them was mad. She knelt beside the half-putrefied cadaver of a new-born babe. Another woman had fallen to the ground, rigid and lifeless. Her two little girls, believing her asleep, sobbed convulsively as they tried in vain to awaken her. By her side, dying in a scarlet pool, was yet another, beautiful and very young, the victim of a soldier of the escort. The velvety eyes of the dying girl, who bore every evidence of refinement, mirrored an immense and indescribable agony . . .

When the hour struck for departure, one after another of those filthy, ragged skeletons struggled to its feet and, taking its place in that mass of misery that shrieked silently to heaven, tottered off, guarded by a group of bearded gendarmes. Behind them pressed a mob of Kurds and ruffians, whom the escort tried to frighten off with a volley of stones. However, it was in vain. Those tough scoundrels did not consider turning back for a slight thing like that, but kept fluttering about their future victims like carrion buzzards, hurling curses and brandishing weapons in the faces of the unhappy creatures.

The governmental Secretary . . . told me confidentially that a number of similar caravans had marched past towards Sinan during the week, but that none had reached their destination. When I inquired why not, he answered with a resigned air, 'Because Allah is great and All-powerful.'[1]

Some modern Turkish apologists dismiss Armenian accounts of these atrocities as mere propaganda. That is why I have been careful to include authentic testimonies from German, British, American, Turkish and even Venezuelan sources. Let us now add a denunciation of these horrors from the mouth of the Italian Consul-General at Trebizond, Signor G. Gorrini, published in the journal *Il Messaggero* of Rome on 25 August 1915. The Consul-General stated that out of 14,000 law-abiding Armenians living in Trebizond up to 1915 –

[1] *Four Years beneath the Crescent,* pp. 130-1.

Gregorians, Catholics and Protestants – not one hundred remained alive when he left the city on 23 July of that year :

From the 24th June, the date of the publication of the infamous decree, until the 23rd July, the date of my own departure from Trebizond, I no longer slept or ate; I was given over to nerves and nausea, so terrible was the torment of having to look on at the wholesale execution of these defenceless, innocent creatures.

The passing of the gangs of Armenian exiles beneath the windows and before the door of the Consulate; their prayers for help, when neither I nor any other could do anything to answer them; the city in a state of siege, guarded at every point by 15,000 troops in complete war equipment, by thousands of police agents, by bands of volunteers and by the members of the Committee of Union and Progress; the lamentations, the tears, the abandonments, the imprecations, the many suicides, the instantaneous deaths from sheer terror, the sudden unhingeing of men's reason, the conflagrations, the shooting of victims in the city, the ruthless searches through the houses and in the countryside; the hundreds of corpses found every day along the exile road; the young women converted by force to Islam or exiled like the rest; the children torn away from their families or from the Christian schools, and handed over by force to Moslem families, or else placed by hundreds on board ship in nothing but their shirts, and then capsized and drowned in the Black Sea and the River Deyirmen Dere – these are my last ineffaceable memories of Trebizond, memories which still, at a month's distance, torment my soul and almost drive me frantic.[1]

We now pass on to contemplate the fate of those Armenians who somehow survived the death march over the Taurus mountains into Syria, to be sent on to the dreaded desert concentration camps at Deir al-Zor. The death toll on the marches was frightful. Out of one convoy of 18,000 from Sivas and Kharput, only 150 survivors reached Aleppo. Their tongues had turned as black as charcoal with thirst. Ambassador Morgenthau reported that many of the women had been stripped stark naked by their guards and by brigands in league with them. The poor creatures could hardly walk for shame; they staggered into the city bent double.

---

[1] Bryce, *The Treatment of Armenians,* pp. 291–2.

This tale is again described by the Venezuelan mercenary Nogales, who saw the survivors tottering to what was literally to be their journey's end.

> After crawling for a long time like wounded animals, shrieking to their families, they finally fell at the roadside, to die and become carrion. Among them I saw many a very old man, many an aged woman, carrying a great-grandchild in withered arms, perhaps the last survivor of a once numerous family. I saw children covered with hideous sores, with suppurating eyes black with flies, bearing a little brother, dead or new-born, whose mother had died along the way.[1]

The transit camps rapidly became centres of infection and epidemic diseases, including typhus and smallpox. Camps and roads in Syria became clogged with stinking bodies, which attracted hyenas from the desert. The epidemics attacked the local population, and thousands of Arab civilians and Turkish soldiers died. In Aleppo alone, 35,000 persons dies of typhus between August 1916 and August 1917. Even military transport was impeded and dislocated by the passage along narrow highways of these straggling processions of walking corpses. I have searched anxiously in the enormous mass of records extant for any redeeming features, any honourable exceptions among the general run of brutish Turkish officials or rapacious Turkish and Kurdish villagers through whose domains the sorry processions passed. I regret to state that instances of human kindness are very few indeed. It was not until the caravans emerged, sadly depleted, into Arab lands that any compassion was shown to the wretched survivors. The only class of refugee whom the Turks showed interest in saving were attractive girls, who were forced to adopt Islam and married off to Turks or Kurds; or else they were bought for a few piastres and exploited as prostitutes until they died of exhaustion and venereal disease.

Some of the little boys were salvaged from the human wreckage and sent to special orphanages, to be brought up as Muslim Turks, under the general tutelage of that Turkish feminist virago, Halidé Edib Adivar.[2]

---

[1] *Four Years beneath the Crescent*, p. 171.

[2] Born 1883, died 1964. A woman of enormous originality and strength of character; author of 2-volume autobiography, published in English, full of self-pity and attempted justification of Young Turk atrocities.

German, Austrian, Swiss and American missionaries in Syria did their best to relieve the appalling distress, against a background of obstruction and harassment on the part of the Ottoman authorities. In 1916, German relief agents based at Aleppo reported that they had seen thousands of deported Armenians cringing under tents in the open desert, struggling along in convoys on the march, descending the Euphrates in open boats, and all in the most miserable condition. Only in a few places did the Turkish government issue any rations, and these were quite insufficient.

The relief agents found the deportees eating grass, herbs and locusts, as well as dead animals and human bodies. The death rate from sickness and starvation was very high, and was increased by the brutality of the guards, whose attitude to the exiles as they were driven back and forth over the desert was that of common slave-drivers. The hopelessness of the situation was such that many Armenians resorted to suicide.[1]

But still the Armenians did not die fast enough to satisfy the Young Turk junta headed by Enver, Talaat, and Ahmed Djemal. A Turkish soldier captured by British forces in Mesopotamia reported that in February 1916 his battalion had passed through a place called Ras ul-Ain, where 12,000 Armenian refugees were concentrated under the guard of some hundreds of Kurds, drawn from the 'urban riff-raff' of Mosul, Bitlis and Diarbekir.

These Kurds were called gendarmes, but were in reality mere butchers; bands of them were publicly ordered to take parties of Armenians, of both sexes, to various destinations, but had secret instructions to destroy the males, children and old women . . . One of these gendarmes confessed to killing 100 Armenian men himself . . . They were dying of typhus and dysentery, and the roads were littered with decomposing bodies. The empty desert cisterns and caves were also filled with corpses.[2]

Particular zeal in the work of extermination was shown by the governor of the Deir al-Zor district, a certain Zekki. This man would ride on horseback past Armenian refugee families, sweep up a small child from the ground, twirl the helpless form around in the air, and

[1] Bryce, *The Treatment of Armenians*, p. 684.
[2] H. V. F. Winstone, *Gertrude Bell*, pp. 183–4.

then hurl it down on a heap of stones, to a shattering death. On one occasion, he imprisoned five hundred young Armenians in a stockade in the blazing sun for a week, without food or water. Almost every one of them went raving mad; they turned on their companions, strangled or beat them to death, and then drank their blood or devoured their flesh. During Zekki's term of office at the Deir al-Zor deportation area, he was responsible for the death of well over 20,000 Armenians.

The Ottoman and German censorships prohibited all mention of these horrors in newspapers under their control, and reports of the massacres had to be smuggled abroad secretly. In private conversation, however, such Young Turk leaders as Talaat Pasha made no secret of their joy at the success of their plans. Talaat himself became Grand Vizier, and boasted to the American envoy Mr Morgenthau that he had done more in three months to solve the Armenian question than poor old 'Abdul Hamid had achieved in thirty years. When Morgenthau remonstrated and protested about the massacres, Talaat retorted: 'The massacres! What of them! They merely amuse me!'[1]

Talaat also tried to induce Mr Morgenthau to furnish him with a register of life insurance policies taken out with American companies by wealthy Armenians now dead, so that the Ottoman government (i.e. the Young Turk junta and their friends) could sequester (i.e. steal) the proceeds from the policies. Ambassador Morgenthau indignantly refused to co-operate.[2]

The question of German complicity in the Armenian massacres from 1915 onwards has often been discussed. It is undeniable that the Germans had reorganized the Turkish army, and manoeuvred the Ottoman Porte into the First World War, thus providing Enver, Talaat and their associates with ideal conditions within which to carry out their plans.

But members of the German Embassy in Constantinople, apart from Ambassador Wangenheim himself, had no idea of the planned extermination of the Armenians. (Wangenheim was a mortally sick man, and died before the end of 1915.) When the news of the Armenian massacres filtered through from the provinces in the summer of 1915, the German Embassy lodged vigorous protests with the Sublime Porte. These protests, as we know from the documents later published by Dr Lepsius, lay unanswered for six months and

---

[1] Cited by Nogales, *Four Years beneath the Crescent*, p. 137.
[2] *Ambassador Morgenthau's Story*, p. 339.

were eventually rejected by the Ottoman Foreign Office with the utmost insolence and rudeness.[1]

Many German and Austrian diplomats, honourable men, were horrified at the monster which their masters had helped to conjure up. But, once the First World War had broken out, Kaiser Wilhelm could not risk losing this valuable ally – any more than Great Britain could have dispensed with the military might of Soviet Russia after 1941, however much British Conservatives disliked Stalin and all that he stood for. Nogales states:

> The Ottoman Empire was without question the most important ally that Germany had during the World War. This is an incontestable fact which the Germans themselves are the first to recognize. While the Austrians openly pleaded for peace, and the Bulgarians kept up a continual complaint because of the constant decrease in rations, the Turkish soldier kept on bleeding and dying of starvation among the snows of the Caucasus and the sands of the desert without ever letting a complaint or a whisper of dismay cross his livid, fever-paled lips.[2]

Locked in mortal combat on the battlefield of France, and in Poland to the east, the German General Staff had vital need of the invaluable support of Ottoman Turkey. The Young Turk ruling junta were well aware of their overwhelmingly strong bargaining position.

Thus it was that the Germans in Turkey had to acquiesce in the murder of Armenian employees of their own consulates and business concerns, and of Armenian pupils from their own German mission schools. In 1916, the German Ambassador, Count von Wolff-Metternich, finally made himself so obnoxious to the Ottoman government through his humanitarian efforts that Enver and Talaat had him recalled to Berlin under a cloud of disfavour.

Thus it was also that the German socialist leader Karl Liebknecht, who courageously raised the Armenian issue in the German Reichstag, had to be fobbed off with the following declaration by the Political Department of the German Foreign Ministry (11 January 1916):

> It is known to the Imperial Chancellor that revolutionary demonstrations, organized by our enemies, have taken place in Armenia, and that they have caused the Turkish Government to expel the

---

[1] Lepsius, *Deutschland und Armenien,* pp. 210–11, document 218.
[2] Nogales, *Four Years beneath the Crescent,* p. 12.

Armenian population of certain districts and to allot them new dwelling places. An exchange of views about the reaction of these measures upon the population is now taking place. Further information cannot be given.[1]

The only really effective and successful German action on behalf of the Armenians was a vigorous intervention by General Liman von Sanders towards the end of 1916, in favour of the Smyrna Armenian population. Liman von Sanders was then General Officer commanding Turkish and German forces in the Smyrna (Izmir) district, and his objections were based as much on military as on humanitarian grounds. The Smyrna Armenians were finally wiped out by the forces of Mustafa Kemal in 1922.[2]

It is worth noting that the conflict of interest between Germany and Turkey became quite acute at the end of the war, following the 1917 Bolshevik Revolution in Russia and the disintegration of the Russian Caucasian front. The Turks were anxious to overrun and annex the whole of Transcaucasia, including Georgia. However, the astute Georgians declared their independence (26 May 1918) and placed themselves under German protection.[3]

The Armenians also had independence forced upon them, in the most tragic circumstances. Turkish troops occupied Kars and other strategic cities, and any surviving Armenian civilian refugees were massacred. The Ottoman army bypassed independent Armenia and occupied Baku briefly in the autumn of 1918. Fifteen thousand Armenians were butchered by the local Tatars.

It is impossible to count the number of those who died in the terrible famine which affected Armenia from 1918 to 1920. The British High Commissioner in Transcaucasia saw dozens of emaciated victims collapsing and dying on the streets of Erevan. It is estimated that there were half a million homeless refugees from Turkish Armenia in and around Erevan in 1918. It is doubtful if more than half of them survived the famine, epidemics and freezing cold.[4]

---

[1] Bryce, *The Treatment of Armenians*, p. xxvii. Liebknecht was murdered by German officers while in custody in January 1919, together with Rosa Luxemburg.

[2] Marjorie Housepian, *Smyrna 1922: The Destruction of a City* (London, 1972).

[3] Firuz Kazemzadeh, *The Struggle for Transcaucasia (1917–1921)* (New York and Oxford, 1951).

[4] Richard G. Hovannisian, *The Republic of Armenia* (University of California Press, 1971) vol. 1. I have included further notes on independent Armenia in Chapter 9, below.

4   Illuminated title page of St Luke's Gospel. Decorated by Sargis Pidsak for King Levon IV at Sis, Cilician Armenia, in 1329. *(Chester Beatty Library, Dublin)*

5 Geghart monastery, So-
viet Armenia. 13th century.
(*Czechoslovak. Academy of
Sciences*)

6 17th-century Armenian
cathedral at New Julfa, near
Isfahan. Embroidered pic-
ture, in a woven rug. (*Arax
Printing*)

Further heavy loss of Armenian lives occurred during the early years of the Kemalist regime in Turkey. In 1919, the victorious British and French occupied Cilicia and adjoining regions of southern Turkey, where there had been a large Armenian population dating from the period of the Crusades. The ignominious rout of the French from the Marash region early in 1920 entailed a heavy death toll among those Armenians who had been bold enough to return from exile in Syria.[1]

Kemalist reprisals against Armenian civilians reached a climax at the Turkish recapture of Smyrna from the Greeks in September 1922. On this occasion, more than 100,000 Greek, Armenian and other refugees perished in a terrible holocaust, when the Turks burnt down the Armenian, Greek and European quarters, and machine-gunned families attempting to reach allied warships anchored close to the harbour.

And so the abomination of desolation had come to pass. A peaceful population of well over two million men, women and children, the most skilled, industrious and educated element in Anatolia and Cilicia, had been murdered or dispersed. About a million and a half persons of both sexes perished by violence or hardships over the seven years from 1915 to 1922,[2] and more than half a million were refugees in a score of foreign lands. Only about a hundred thousand Armenians remained, concentrated mostly in Istanbul and a few other urban centres.

Talaat Pasha and his gendarmes did not keep regular count of their dead victims. But, according to the American relief worker Stanley Kerr, out of 86,000 Armenians living in the district of Marash (eastern Cilicia) in 1914, only 12,000 survived in exile, in 1922. Before the First World War, the ancient city of Sivas numbered 80,000 inhabitants, including 30,000 Armenians; only 1,500 Sivas Armenians survived the war and today, in 1980, there are not more than eighty Armenian families left in the city, under constant pressure to become assimilated or get out.[3] Rafael de Nogales informs us that 15,000 Armenians perished at Bitlis and in the surrounding district on a single day in 1915. According to the official Turkish census of 1960, the

---

[1] Stanley E. Kerr, *The Lions of Marash* (State University of New York Press, Albany, 1973).

[2] This figure of 1½ million dead is also given by Bernard Lewis in his book, *The Emergence of Modern Turkey*.

[3] Kerop Bedoukian, *The Urchin* (London, 1978).

once great city of Van, former metropolis of Turkish Armenia, now numbered only two Armenian speakers.

The principal Young Turk leaders made their escape when Turkey surrendered to the Allies in October 1918. Other members of the Committee of Union and Progress were briefly interned by the British in Malta. A Turkish military tribunal condemned to death, *in absentia*, the former rulers of the defeated Ottoman Empire, notably Enver, Talaat, Ahmed Djemal, and Nazim; among the charges was complicity in the mass murder of Armenians.

The Turkish war criminals had escaped from the tribunal's jurisdiction. It was left to Armenian patriots to put the sentences into effect. Talaat was assassinated in Berlin by an Armenian student on 15 March 1921. (The assassin was acquitted by a German court, partly on the grounds that his sufferings and the loss of his family had deprived him of his reason.) Ahmed Djemal was dispatched by an Armenian in Tbilisi, capital of Soviet Georgia, on 21 July 1922. Rather bizarre and yet strangely appropriate was the end of Enver Pasha, the 'Little Napoleon' and military exponent of Pan-Turanianism. Taking refuge in Central Asia among Turkic tribes of the Bukhara region, Enver headed there an unsuccessful revolt against Soviet power, and was killed near Bukhara on 4 August 1922.

4

Land and People:

Historical Introduction

HISTORICAL ARMENIA in Classical and Byzantine times covered a large area to the east of Asia Minor and to the south of the Caucasus range. To the south-east was the land of the Medes and Persians. The Black Sea lies north-west of Armenia, and the Caspian to the north-east. However, the Armenians have never enjoyed continuous access to these important seas.

The best known landmark of Armenia is Mount Ararat, on which according to the Book of Genesis Noah's Ark alighted after its long voyage from Mesopotamia. Mount Ararat – which the Armenians call 'Masis' – is situated today a few miles inside the Turkish frontier, but is fully visible from many parts of Soviet Armenia. This fact helps to keep alive the feelings both of frustration and of national pride which are characteristic of Armenians everywhere.

The geographical name 'Ararat' is closely linked with that of Urartu, which is the name given by the Assyrians to the ancient kingdom which once existed on the territory of historical Armenia. This kingdom, originally a confederation of local tribes, flourished as a unified state from the ninth to the early sixth century BC; it constituted a formidable rival to Assyria for supremacy in the Near East.

The Urartian capital was the ancient city of Van, today in modern Turkey. Van is situated on the eastern shore of the large lake of that name. The plain of Van is very fertile, and this fertility was enhanced by magnificent aqueducts built by the ancient Urartians – some of the water channels remaining in use right up to modern times. Another

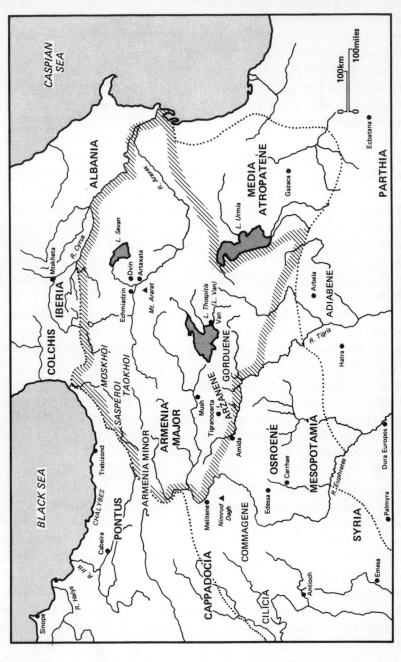

ARMENIA AT THE TIME OF THE ROMAN EMPIRE

Armenian granary is the broad Araxes valley, particularly in the vicinity of Erevan and near the ancient capital of Artashat. Some authors have even maintained that this region of Armenia was the original Garden of Eden.

Soon after 600 BC, Urartu was invaded by various warlike hordes,[1] including the Scythians, the Medes (ancestors of the modern Kurds), and also a tribe known as the people of Hayasa. These Hayasa people came from central Anatolia, close to the old Hittite state. The Armenians call themselves 'Hai-k', and their country, Hayastan, and many modern scholars consider that this Hayasa element forms an important constituent in the makeup of the modern Armenian nation.

Less than a century after these invasions, we find the ethnic names 'Armina' and 'Armenians' or 'Armenioi' mentioned in Persian inscriptions and in Greek sources. Thus, the people of Armina were known to Great King Darius I Hystaspes of Iran (521–485 BC), who mentions them in an important royal inscription, and Herodotus, Father of History, was familiar with the Armenians.

The Armenian language is an independent, one-language subgroup within the Indo-European language family. However, the identification of ethnic origins with linguistic affinity is deceptive. It seems clear that the Armenians themselves, in the majority of cases, belong to an ancient population stratum of eastern Anatolia, akin to the ancient Hurrians and Urartians. We have only to look at ancient Hittite, Assyrian and Achaemenid sculptures to pick out the prototypes of the modern Armenians, praying, toiling, and bringing tribute to the Great Kings of the ancient world.

I have dwelt on this geographical and linguistic background at some length, because the Armenians are themselves very conscious of their ancient origins, and are fond of referring to their roots among the peoples of antiquity. Even if he has lived all his life close to sea level – perhaps at Beirut in the Lebanon, or in Belgium and Holland – an Armenian yearns for the twin peaks of Ararat and for the Anatolian highlands. Patriotic Armenians see this sentimental attachment to the original homeland in Anatolia and Transcaucasia as a kind of spiritual sheet-anchor, preventing them from being absorbed into the alien communities among whom their destiny has led them to settle.

[1] B. B. Piotrovskii, *Urartu: The Kingdom of Van and its Art,* trans. Peter S. Gelling (London, 1967).

Indeed, up to the great dispersal between 1895 and 1915, Armenian life was generally marked by ethnic continuity and social conservatism. Considering the pressures which the Armenians have undergone over the centuries to become assimilated in various foreign environments, they have contrived to maintain a remarkable ethnic and cultural individuality, especially where they have been able to set up an offshoot of their ancient Apostolic Church. Some Armenian communities are in fact rather inbred, and many Armenians are still reluctant to tolerate intermarriage with non-Armenians, who are referred to rather contemptuously as 'odars' – an equivalent of the term 'gentile'. Like the British in India under the Raj, Armenians have sometimes tended to create various taboos and erect invisible barriers to maintain their community ethos intact. This group solidarity has in turn helped to preserve over the centuries certain readily identifiable physical traits.

The 'Armenoid' physical type is well known to anthropologists, and forms one of the three brunette subgroups of the broad-headed complex of white races. This Armenoid type is quite conspicuous – it has the skull abruptly flattened behind, while the head is characterized by a lofty vault, with what physical anthropologists call 'outward-drooping orbits'.[1] The hair is usually brown or black. The eyes are large, mostly hazel, brown or black in colour, often framed by bushy eyebrows. Occasionally one meets Armenians with lustrous blue eyes, which are very striking.

The Armenian physique is renowned for toughness and endurance. This befits the rugged terrain of most of the Armenian homeland. Although the Araxes valley and the Van region can be described as a land of milk and honey, more than half of historical Armenia consists of barren upland with a harsh climate. The landscape is cut up by enormous mountains, and prevailing weather conditions are more like those of the Scottish Highlands or the Rocky Mountains than those of most of the Fertile Crescent lands.

Nowadays, the Armenian mountaineers are athletic and relatively tall. However, the general type found in the older generations both in Soviet Armenia and the diaspora communities is rather short and compact. The nose is often prominent and bulbous or else aquiline and high-bridged. The facial complexion is rather swarthy, and features are strongly marked. There is a tendency to chunky solidity

---

[1] *Encyclopaedia Britannica*, 14th edition, vol. 2, p. 384.

in middle age. A bristling moustache, turned up at the ends, is often seen in the older generation of men.

In the Near and Middle East, an Armenian 'Levantine' type is in evidence, especially where there has been intermarriage with Greeks, Syrians or Iranians.

Armenian girls are often very lovely in their sultry splendour. On my visits to Erevan in 1977 and 1978, I met Armenian students and young married women as ravishing as any one could see on the boulevards of Paris.

In modern times, Armenians have adapted well to their surroundings. In the United States, Armenian teenagers brought up on a healthy diet with plenty of milk and cereals, and playing baseball and other sports, grow several inches taller than their parents, and become slim and athletic.

Marked differences in temperament and character between members of various Armenian communities owe much to environmental influences. The Armenian peasant and mountaineer in his native habitat, say Zeitoun, Sassoun or the Karabagh, is closer in his ways to the mountaineer of Georgia or Daghestan than he is to a prosperous Armenian merchant in London or Cairo. Those Armenian highlanders were, and still are, renowned for their energy, patriotism and patriarchal attitude to the family; they are both brave and hospitable.

Most Europeans are more familiar with Armenian businessmen, and with Armenian artists and musicians. Armenian businessmen have a reputation for shrewdness and financial ruthlessness. No doubt this is partly due to the Armenians' long association with cities and bazaars of the East, where it is a case of 'eat or be eaten'. Immigrants, of course, have to be very clever to succeed in such Western centres of Armenian enterprise as Marseilles, Amsterdam, Detroit or New York.

It is interesting to see how the traditionally demure and submissive Armenian wife and mother can blossom forth in the 'open society' of the United States. The liberated Armenian lady driving round in her Chevrolet and organizing all kinds of community, Church, and local government activities is now an accepted feature of the American social scene. As she grows older, she happily develops the middle-class American matron's conventional 'blue rinse' attitudes to the economic and social problems of modern life.

One wonders how stern Armenian grandfathers responded to a recent photograph in the *National Geographic Magazine* showing a blonde Armenian College girl wearing a blazing red T-shirt emblazoned with the slogan: 'Kiss me, I am Armenian!' Many older Armenians, surely, must be proud of this emancipation, a sign of the acceptance of their young people on equal terms in contemporary Western society.

Wherever fate may have led them, one is impressed by the Armenians' intelligence and quick-wittedness. 'Nothing escapes them,' remarks that seasoned traveller, Sir Fitzroy Maclean. 'They have read one's thoughts almost before they have had time to take shape.'[1] Even in pagan times, two thousand years ago, Armenians were renowned as poets and musicians, as builders and sculptors, as orators and philosophers, as generals and as hotel keepers.

In modern times, Armenians consistently display a high intelligence and are successful in a wide range of professional activities. They are renowned as scientists, mathematicians, doctors and dentists. They excel in the arts and in literature. Armenians are numbered among film directors, book illustrators, and among orchestral conductors and soloists. They are excellent cooks and famed for their hospitality. In spite of their tragic history, Armenians are noted for their sense of humour. They have also produced many outstanding administrators and military leaders. I shall be expanding on these themes in succeeding chapters of this book.

We have no need to linger over the early history of the Armenians, after they became firmly established in their habitat in eastern Anatolia and had become forged into a nation by the mingling of immigrant and local ethnic elements.[2] This process was quite rapid, so that by the time of Alexander the Great the Armenian satrapy formed one of the important provinces of the great Achaemenid realm of Iran. The capital of this satrapy was the former Urartian state capital of Van.

A fine description of the manners and customs of ancient Armenia is provided by the Greek historian, philosopher and military adventurer Xenophon, who led his Ten Thousand followers through that country in the winter of 401–400 BC. After a gruelling march north-

1 Sir Fitzroy Maclean, *To Caucasus, the End of All the Earth* (London, 1976), p. 170.

2 Charles Burney and D. M. Lang, *The Peoples of the Hills: Ancient Ararat and Caucasus* (London and New York, 1971).

wards through the wilds of Kurdistan, Xenophon's men were happy to reach Armenia, west of Lake Van. The local Armenians offered the Greeks excellent wine, strong ale, lamb, kid, pork, veal and poultry. We learn that the Armenian aristocracy used beautiful drinking cups, and reclined on couches whose legs were cased in silver. The common people lived in houses partly tunnelled underground, both for security and to keep out the bitter winter cold. During this season, the family livestock was kept inside the houses, including goats, sheep, cattle and fowls, together with their young. Such underground houses have continued to exist in Armenia and in Georgia right up to modern times.

After Alexander the Great overthrew the Persian Empire in 331 BC, the dynasty of the Orontids held sway in Armenia, until they were replaced by another ruling family, the Artaxiads, in 200 BC. In addition, there were smaller principalities and minor kingdoms in Western Armenia.

The most famous ruler of the Artaxiad dynasty was Tigranes the Great (95–55 BC), thanks to whom Armenia became, briefly, a world power. Tigranes built up an empire stretching from the Caspian Sea to the Mediterranean, and from the Pontic Alps near the Black Sea right down to northern Mesopotamia. He profited by the decay of the hybrid Greek and oriental Seleucid dynasty to take over Syria, which he ruled quite successfully for fourteen years, from 83 to 69 BC. Tigranes erected a magnificent new capital at Tigranokerta, close to present-day Farkin, in southern Turkey.

Emulating the conquerors of Assyrian times, Tigranes deported many thousands of Greeks, Jews and Syrians to populate his new capital. He grew arrogant and cruel as he got older: he used to humiliate vassal rulers by making them run along on foot beside his royal charger whenever he went out for a ride. He was so bad-tempered and superstitious that he would kill any messenger who brought him bad news, so that nobody dared to tell him the truth. Seeing the Roman general Lucullus approaching with a well trained army of ten thousand men, Tigranes uttered the famous but ill-judged witticism: 'If they are coming as ambassadors, they are too many; if as enemies, they are too few!'[1]

Lucullus sacked Tigranokerta and inflicted several defeats on the Armenians, before the severe winter, mutinies among the Roman

[1] See H. Manandian, *Tigrane II et Rome* (Lisbon, 1963).

legions, and vigorous Armenian counterattacks forced him to retreat.[1] Lucullus was recalled to Rome in 67 BC and replaced by the still more famous general Pompey. Soon Pompey brought the aged Tigranes to his knees, and the Armenian despot ended his life as a vassal of the Roman Senate. In spite of this final eclipse, Tigranes preserved Armenia's heartland intact, much as it was to remain until the Romans and Persians partitioned it between them in AD 387. The findings of archaeology, together with references in ancient authors, indicate that the land was far more verdant than it is today. Forests grew on the now barren foothills of Mount Ararat. It seems that rainfall was generally higher two thousand years ago than it is nowadays. Nomadic Kurds and Turcomans with their sheep and goats had not yet managed to turn much of eastern Anatolia into a dust-bowl, with trees gnawed away to stumps, as we also find in parts of modern Cyprus and the Balkan peninsula.

The territory of Great Armenia much exceeded in size that of England and Wales combined – it amounted to about 100,000 square miles. But much of Armenia has always been unfit for human settlement. in addition to the two great inland seas of Van and Sevan, there are mighty mountains and extinct volcanoes, some topped by eternal snow. Ravines and canyons break up the landscape, and make communication difficult. Earthquakes add to the hazards of life.

The average height of the Armenian plateau, often described as a 'natural fortress', is over 5,000 feet. Outside the Araxes valley and the plain of Van, the windswept uplands have a harsh climate, winter persisting for seven months of the year. The short, dry summer extends for little more than three months. A typical highland Armenian town, such as Leninakan, has an average winter temperature as low as 12° F, or minus 11° C.

Even more unfavourable to the development of Armenia as an independent country is the lack of convenient road and river transport, and of assured access to the sea. Armenia lies astride main invasion routes leading from Asia Minor into Iran, and from the Caucasian isthmus southwards into Mesopotamia. But the land itself is poor in trunk roads. Whereas three great rivers – the Tigris, the Euphrates and the Araxes – all have their source in Armenia, none

---

[1] Lucullus brought from Armenia to Italy the apricot (*Abricosus armeniacus*) and also the plum called *Prunus armeniaca*; from Italy the species spread all over the world.

of them is navigable for any but the smallest vessels while still flowing through Armenian territory.

Despite these natural handicaps, combined with remorseless Roman pressure, the Armenians survived remarkably well throughout the Classical period. They were helped by their strategic position and inaccessible strongholds, and also by support from the Parthians, the warlike ruling dynasty of Iran. In fact, the Roman emperor Nero invited the founder of the Armenian dynasty of the Arsacids, King Tiridates I, to come to Rome in AD 66, and solemnly crowned him in the Forum – in spite of the fact that Tiridates was himself a scion of the ruling Parthian royal family. On his return to Armenia, Tiridates built a magnificent temple in the Classical style at his summer capital of Garni. Destroyed by an earthquake in 1679, this monument has recently been re-erected by the Armenian Academy of Sciences, under the direction of Dr A. Sahinian.

During the Classical era, the Armenians laid the foundations of their rich and splendid national literature. It is true that the distinctive Armenian alphabet was not invented until after the introduction of Christianity, but pagan Armenia was far from being illiterate. From Moses of Khorene, the national chronicler, we have the texts of ancient ballads and legends, which were earlier handed down by word of mouth. Official documents and inscriptions were written in Greek or else in Iranian using Aramaic characters – an ancient form of the Semitic alphabet. King Artavazd II, son of Tigranes the Great, maintained a Greek theatre in his palace, and himself wrote dramas in Greek to be staged there. Roman legionaries brought Latin script with them, notably in the reign of Emperor Trajan, though this failed to take root among the local population.

A key event in early Armenian history was the conversion of the country to Christianity by St Gregory the Illuminator, a missionary from Parthia, during the reign of King Tiridates III. This event determined the entire future course of Armenian history. It occurred in or about the year 301, though according to hallowed legend Armenia is supposed to have been visited by the Apostles Bartholomew and Thaddeus much earlier, about twenty years after Christ's crucifixion. Armenia is thus the oldest Christian nation in the world, if we except the now vanished Christian realm of King Abgar of Edessa.

Because of continual subjection to foreign powers, the leaders of the Armenian Church have traditionally been leaders of the community at large, and this applies at the present time also.

The adoption of Christianity brought Armenia into renewed conflict with the Persians, then sworn defenders of the Zoroastrian religion. In 451, the Persian Great King Yezdegird invaded Armenia with an enormous army, including squadrons of elephants. A great battle took place at Avarayr. The Armenians were temporarily crushed, and their dead heroes are numbered among the saints of the Armenian Apostolic Church. However, the Persians were forced in the end to give up their plans for forcibly converting the Armenians to the Zoroastrian religion. Such was the importance attached by the Persian Great Kings to retaining their grip on the country that the heir apparent to the Persian Sassanian throne often bore the title of Great Prince of Armenia – just as the British heir apparent is known as Prince of Wales.

5

Between Byzantium and Islam

THE IRANIAN fire-worshippers were not the only power with which the Armenians had to contend during the period between the fourth and the seventh centuries AD. The Armenians had to defend the integrity of both their territory and their national Church against another Christian state, the Eastern Roman Empire of Byzantium, centred on Constantinople.

The basic issue at stake was that the Byzantine emperors demanded both political and religious conformity from smaller Christian kingdoms within their sphere of influence. They saw themselves as defenders of the faith throughout the whole of Christendom, and supreme arbiters of religious orthodoxy – rather like Henry VIII in England a thousand years later. This system is sometimes referred to as 'Caesaro-Papism' – which means the union of religious and political power in a single person, the Emperor.

Such an arrangement did not suit the Armenians at all. Natural individualists, they had, at great sacrifice to themselves, made Christianity their state religion several years before it was officially adopted at Constantinople. They resented the encroachments of their Byzantine 'Big Brother', and made methodical preparations to safeguard their religious and cultural autonomy unimpaired.

Such precautions were especially needful after the partition of Armenia between Byzantium and Iran in AD 387. The extinction of the Armenian royal dynasty of the Arsacids followed quite soon after this – in AD 428 – and local authority rested in the hands of the

Armenian *nakharars* or feudal princes, who were occupied to a great extent in feuds and intrigues against one another.

Political unity having been lost, the more intelligent Armenian bishops and princes realised that cultural unity must be a paramount object. Providentially, a scholar of genius was at hand in the person of St Mesrop Mashtotz, who invented the Armenian alphabet and brought it into use early in the fifth century. Following as far as possible the order of letters of the Greek alphabet, Armenian is written from left to right, though the actual shape of the letters is different from that of the corresponding Greek ones. Extra letters were added, to represent sounds which do not exist in Greek.

Originally, the Armenian alphabet was written only with large capital letters, but a more convenient everyday script was evolved later on. Alphabets were invented at the same period for the Georgians, and for the Christian Caucasian Albanians (no connection with the Adriatic Albanians of the Balkans), who lived in what is now Soviet Azerbaijan.[1]

The value of the invention of the Armenian alphabet was incalculable in terms of national survival. Inscriptions could be recorded on stone, and political proclamations and secret messages could be circulated between Armenians living under different political regimes. The Bible and other philosophical and literary works could be written down on parchment and widely circulated in the national Armenian tongue. Today, in the twentieth century, the distinctive script and literary language provide a unifying force for Armenian communities all over the world, and are an effective barrier against assimilation.

The Armenians quickly broke away doctrinally from the ruling religious ideology of the Byzantine court. In AD 451, the Council of Chalcedon officially adopted a dogma affirming and defining the dual nature of Jesus Christ, and the relation between His divine and human manifestations. The Armenians rejected this formulation of Chalcedon, and laid stress on Jesus Christ's exclusively divine nature. This doctrinal difference prevails up to the present day. During the Middle Ages, before the invention of the modern political party system, these religious distinctions had enormous importance and often determined political and military alignments.

The systematic deportation of Armenians, both by the Zoroastrian

[1] Moses Khorenats'i, *History of the Armenians,* trans. R. W. Thomson (Harvard University Press, 1978), pp. 318–23.

Persians and by the Christian Byzantine Greeks, can be traced back
to the fourth century AD. The Sassanian Great King Shapur II
(309–79) depopulated the main cities of Armenia, and transferred
the urban population to the interior of Iran – just as Shah Abbas
the Great was to do twelve centuries later. It is interesting to note
that a deposed Armenian king named Varazdat was banished by the
Romans about AD 380 to the 'Island of Thule'. This reference is
usually taken to denote the British Isles, and specifically, the north
of Scotland. Apart from any stray Armenians who may have come
over earlier with Julius Caesar or with the Emperor Claudius, this
Prince Varazdat was certainly one of the earliest Armenians ever to
enjoy British (or Scottish) hospitality.

Armenian rejection of the Byzantine-sponsored Council of
Chalcedon (451) contributed to renewed friction in the era of
Emperor Justinian the Great (527–65). Soon afterwards, in 578, ten
thousand Armenians were forcibly settled in Cyprus, laying the
foundation of the important community which exists there today.

Emperor Maurice (reigned 582–602), himself an Armenian by
birth, suggested to the Persian Great King a joint plan for deporting
the Armenians on both sides of the Greek–Persian partition line.
They were, said Maurice, a knavish and unruly nation, and best got
rid of. Maurice sent many of the Armenians living under Byzantine
suzerainty to Thrace – present-day Bulgaria – thus laying the basis
of the modern communities which flourish in Sofia, Plovdiv, Rusé,
Varna and elsewhere.

Quite apart from these unpleasant measures of coercion, thousands
of Armenians emigrated voluntarily during this period, both to Iran
and to Constantinople, where career prospects and commercial
prospects were better than in their mountainous homeland. For
instance, Prince Vardan Mamikonian arrived with a large retinue
in Asia Minor in 571, and established an Armenian colony in the
famous city of Pergamum. It was from Pergamum that an Armenian
named Bardanes (Vardan) emerged early in the eighth century, to
occupy the Byzantine throne briefly as Bardanes Philippicus (711–
713).

The Byzantine historian Procopius states that there were sixteen
Armenian generals in the armies of Emperor Justinian I (527–65), in
addition to his celebrated commander-in-chief, Narses.

The first half of the seventh century witnesses the rise of Islam.
The Arabs rapidly overran both the Persian empire and large areas

of Byzantine territory in the Near East. At this juncture, too, Armenians were much to the fore. For instance, a decisive battle between the Caliph 'Umar and the Byzantine army was fought in 636 by the River Yarmuk, a tributary of the Jordan. The Byzantine commander was an Armenian called Vahan or Baanes. The Byzantines were soundly beaten. Vahan retired from military service, to become a monk.

The victorious Arabs quickly advanced northwards into Armenia and the Caucasus. By AD 650, they had overrun most of Armenia, and they then set up an Arab viceroyalty in the city of Dvin, south-east of Erevan.

Armenia benefited economically by direct contact with the prosperous centres of the Arab caliphate, such as Damascus and Baghdad, and from integration within the Islamic monetary system. However, the Armenians suffered from time to time from religious discrimination and political repression. For example, in AD 705 the Arab viceroy Muhammad ibn al-Marwan burnt alive several hundred Armenian nobles and their families at Nakhchevan. Between 852 and 855, Armenia was ravaged by a Saracen army two hundred thousand strong, commanded by Bogha the Turk.

The period of Arab domination is depicted in picturesque style in the Armenian national epic of David of Sassoun. This epic is a cycle of heroic tales and ballads, sagas of vanished Armenian supermen of Wagnerian prowess. The Sassoun district is a highland region south-west of Lake Van. Its proud and independent inhabitants were killed or dispersed by Sultan 'Abdul Hamid in punitive campaigns during the years 1894 to 1896.

Among the Arab notables who feature in the David of Sassoun cycle is the sprightly ninety-year-old caliph of Baghdad, who marries Lady Dzovinar, ancestress of the doughty men of Sassoun. Later on, David of Sassoun's father, the mighty Meherr (the Armenian form of the name of the god Mithras) has a passionate love affair with the Queen of Egypt. The Queen gives birth to a son, Misra Melik, which is a title, meaning King of Egypt. The rivalry between David of Sassoun and his Egyptian royal half-brother runs like a theme song through the cycle. Finally, David slices Misra Melik in half, from his head to his loins, and returns home to Armenia with the Egyptian ruler's ear stuck on the end of his lance.

The ravages of Bogha the Turk were a desperate attempt to re-establish the waning Arab dominion over Armenia. A few years later, the Arab caliph began to make concessions to the reviving tide of Armenian nationalism. In 862, the Arabs granted the leading Armenian feudal grandee, Ashot Bagratuni, the title of 'Prince of Princes of Armenia, of Georgia, and of the lands of the Caucasus.'

Ashot the Great proved to be such a capable ruler that the turbulent feudal princes resolved to elect him as their king, and persuaded the caliph of Baghdad to ratify their choice and to send Ashot a royal crown. This occurred in 885, and the Byzantine Emperor Basil I (himself an Armenian by birth) hastened to follow suit.

The Bagratid kings set up their capital at the strategic centre of Ani, now very close to the Turkish–Soviet frontier. The city is situated on a triangular promontory, with two out of three sides protected by steep ravines. The population rose to close on a hundred thousand at the peak of Ani's prosperity, in the tenth and early eleventh centuries; the place was known as the city of a thousand and one churches.

There was also a rival, independent Armenian kingdom in the southern region known as Vaspurakan, centred on Lake Van, and extending eastwards into present-day Persian Azerbaijan. The ruling dynasty was the Ardsruni family, who are immortalized by their beautiful royal church of Aghtamar, on an island in Lake Van. According to the late Professor Nicolas Adontz, the able but unpopular Byzantine Emperor Leo V the Armenian (813–20) was a scion of the Ardsruni family.[1]

During this period, Armenians continued to occupy important positions, both at Constantinople and in the service of the Arab caliphate. Estimates of the number of Byzantine emperors of Armenian extraction vary from one dozen to two dozen, according to whether or not we include usurpers and short-lived pretenders, and also emperors of mixed Armenian and Greek blood. Of particular importance is the 'Macedonian' dynasty, founded by an Armenian from Bulgaria, who murdered Emperor Michael III in 867 and ascended the throne as Emperor Basil I.

These Armenian emperors of Byzantium often had chequered careers. Leo the Armenian was assassinated in church in 820 by a band of conspirators disguised as priests. John Tzimisces (reigned 969–76) – one of the ablest warriors ever to occupy the Imperial throne – was poisoned.

---

[1] Nicolas Adontz, *Etudes Arméno-Byzantines* (Lisbon, 1965), pp. 37–46.

The Armenian contribution to the intellectual and artistic life of Byzantium was extremely important. For instance, Patriarch Photius (820–93) one of the most erudite, forceful and controversial figures of the Middle Ages, was only one of many Byzantine scholars of Armenian descent. It is also significant that, when the cathedral of Hagia Sophia in Constantinople was damaged by an earthquake in AD 989, it was the Armenian royal architect Trdat who was called in to rebuild the dome in a new and improved style.

At the same period, the Muslim dynasty of the Egyptian Fatimids employed many Armenians from Edessa to embellish the city of Cairo. The gate of Bab al-Futuh in Cairo is an outstanding example of their work.

Meanwhile the process of emigration, both to Byzantium and to the Islamic world, continued. Emperor Constantine V Copronymus (a rude nickname, meaning 'dung-named') sent more Armenians to Thrace, modern Bulgaria, during the eighth century. Some of these Armenians were Paulician Dualistic heretics, and they helped to found the heresy known as Bogomilism, after the Bulgarian priest Bogomil. Other Armenians were sent as far afield as the Black Sea region of Lazistan (AD 790), Sicily (AD 792), and also Sparta in Greece (about 800) and Crete (after 961). Under Catholicos Khachik of Armenia (972–92), Armenians spread westwards to such an extent that the pontiff had to found new bishoprics in such places as Antioch in Syria and Tarsus of Cilicia.

On the other side of the frontier, many Armenians rendered faithful service to the Arab caliphs and other Muslim rulers. There was even a Muslim governor of Armenia and Azerbaijan named 'Ali the Armenian, who died in 863. In Egypt, an Armenian slave named Badr al-Jamali rose to be Chief Vazir of the Sultan in Cairo from 1073 to 1094. Another Armenian vazir in Egypt, Vahram or Bahram by name, openly professed the Christian faith while in office. In spite of this, his funeral was attended by the Sultan in person.

Within the Armenian homeland, the independent kingdom of the Bagratids did not last very long. It owed its existence to a power vacuum in the Near East, due to the decay of the Arab caliphate, dissension within Byzantium, and the failure of the Muslims (apart from the efforts of local potentates such as the Sajids) to establish a unified regime in Persia.

Soon all this was to change. The Byzantines embarked on a massive campaign to recover from the Arabs their lost lands in northern

Syria, as well as the former Armenian kingdoms of Sophene and Commagene. One of the chief Byzantine generals was an Armenian named John Curcuas (or Gurgen), who captured Melitene (Malatya) on the River Euphrates in AD 934.

The Greeks then annexed (AD 966) the province of Taron, situated in the region where the Arsanias river is joined by its tributary the Qara Su, which rises in the mountains of Nimrud Dagh to the west of Lake Van. Its capital was the city of Mush, and it contained many shrines of ancient Armenian heroes and the founders of Christianity in Armenia.

The death of the Bagratid ruler of Ani, Gagik I, took place in 1020. This event opened the final chapter in Greater Armenia's national history during the medieval period. The Bagratid domains, now reduced to the province of Shirak, were divided between Gagik's two sons, the easygoing John-Smbat III and the more dynamic Ashot IV the Valiant. Very soon the Muslim Daylamites from the Caspian region invaded Armenia (1021), while the first bands of Seljuq Turks made their appearance in Vaspurakan, around Lake Van.

Armenia's foes now included the Byzantine Empire. Instead of aiding this outpost of Christendom against Muslim incursions from the east, the government of Emperor Basil II saw this as an opportunity for territorial gain. Basil II is usually known as 'Bulgaroktonos', or 'the Bulgar-slayer'. It is worth noting that his leading foe, King Samuel of Bulgaria (997–1014), was himself of Armenian descent.[1]

After crushing the Bulgarians, Basil II invaded Georgia in 1021, and annexed several districts bordering on Armenia, notably Tao, Kola, Ardahan and Javakheti. Basil forced King Sennacherib-John of Vaspurakan to cede his kingdom to the Byzantine Empire. This kingdom comprised 10 cities, 72 fortresses and about 4,000 villages. King Sennacherib was compensated with estates in Cappadocia. Vaspurakan, briefly renamed as the Byzantine province of Basparacania, was placed under the authority of a Greek governor or catepan. Some 40,000 Armenians emigrated with Sennacherib to the regions of Sivas and Arakir, in central Anatolia.

Next to be swallowed up was the Bagratid kingdom of Armenia, comprising Ani and part of Shirak province. King John-Smbat of Ani sought to appease Emperor Basil II by designating him as heir

---

[1] Adontz, *Etudes Arméno-Byzantines,* pp. 347–407.

to the Armenian throne. When John-Smbat died childless in 1040, the Emperor of Byzantium, Michael IV, claimed the inheritance. The patriotic Armenians attempted to re-establish the monarchy under John-Smbat's nephew, who governed from 1042 to 1045 as King Gagik II. However, Gagik was ultimately bullied into abdicating, and Ani became a Byzantine outpost.

The Byzantine authorities did not long benefit by this annexation of Armenia. From 1045 onwards, the land was subject to repeated assaults by the warlike Seljuq Turks, who had swarmed out of Central Asia, and were now strongly entrenched in Persia. The trading centre of Artsn, near Erzerum, was sacked in 1048. Ani itself, now a Byzantine garrison city, fell to the Turks in 1064; the Armenians themselves were too disillusioned and disaffected to put up much resistance. The last Armenian king of Kars, Gagik-Abas, tried to save his realm by ceding it to the Byzantine emperor, but this province too was soon snatched by the Seljuqs.

The crowning disaster occurred at the battle of Manzikert (Manazkert) north of Lake Van, in 1071, when the Byzantine Emperor Romanus Diogenes was defeated and captured by the Seljuq Sultan Alp Arslan.

The Seljuq Turks swept on into Anatolia almost unopposed, and proceeded to set up a mighty sultanate based on Konia (Iconium), known as the Sultanate of Rum. The very title of the new state – Rum or Rome – proclaims the suzerainty of Islam over Christian Constantinople. Within a decade, the Seljuqs were negotiating from a position of strength with Emperor Alexius Comnenus (1081–1118) – himself one of the most resourceful, intelligent and energetic of the later Byzantine rulers.

Armenian emigration from the homeland became a flood. Demoralized men, women and children trudged westwards into Asia Minor or south-west into Cilicia, the new kingdom of Little Armenia or Sisuan. Others crossed the Black Sea and settled down in the Crimea. From the Crimea, they were later to move on into southern Russia, into Romania and into Poland.

A few local Armenian princes and minor kings struggled on in their mountain strongholds, notably the Bagratid kings of Tashir, dynasts of Lori, who were the only Armenian Bagratid rulers to strike coins in their own name. Most of central Armenia fell under the dominion of the Muslim Shah-Armen dynasty. Later, in the twelfth and thirteenth centuries, the warlike Armenian house of the

Zachariads or Mkhargrdzeli ('long-armed') ruled in northern Armenia at Ani, Lori, Kars and Dvin under the aegis of the Georgian Queen Tamar (1184–1213).

The situation took a new turn from 1236 onwards, when the whole area was dominated by warlike Mongol hordes from Central Asia.

Of particular note are the long-surviving kings of Siunia-Albania, who held out on Armenia's north-eastern borders for several generations after the Seljuq conquest. This royal house in turn gave rise to the Meliks or local dynasts of Karabagh. These Meliks come to prominence in the sixteenth century. They carried on with great bravery and resource right up to the Russian conquest of eastern Armenia early in the nineteenth century.

6

The Crusades and Links with France

THE INVASIONS of the Seljuq Turks and the consequent departure of many Armenian families for Cilicia resulted in the Westernization of important sections of Armenian society. It is a tribute to the adaptability of the Armenian character that in little more than a generation after the fall of Ani in 1064 the Cilician Armenians and their womenfolk were fraternizing, intermarrying and bickering with the Frankish knights of the First Crusade and with the members of the Crusaders' families and retinue.

Cilicia is a land of enormous strategic and commercial importance, situated north of the Gulf of Iskanderun or Alexandretta. Cilicia has several ports, notably the modern Mersin, and also takes in the great city of Adana, as well as Tarsus, birthplace of St Paul.

Following the Muslim conquest of the seventh century, Cilicia was occupied by forces of the Arab caliphs. When the Byzantine Emperor Nicephorus II recaptured most of it in AD 965, he appointed Armenians as governors of several cities and granted them tracts of land. After this, the Byzantine Greeks, and then the Seljuqs, began their encroachments against Greater Armenia, as described in the last chapter. The existing trickle of Armenian immigrants into Cilicia and northern Syria became a regular torrent.

Among Armenian feudal dynasts who set themselves up in Cilicia, pride of place belongs to Ruben or Roupen, founder of the Rupenid dynasty. He established his authority about AD 1080 at Bardzrberd, in the Cilician mountains, and his grandson Constantine I captured Sis from the Byzantines and made it his own state capital.

The Armenians of those days had no inkling of the storm which was soon to break over the Fertile Crescent in the shape of the First Crusade. We shall not go into the controversial question of whether the Crusades are to be viewed as a war of liberation, to deliver the holy places from the infidel, or whether they were simply a barbarian colonial movement, motivated by greed and bigotry directed against the relatively civilized world of medieval Islam.

Far away from Armenia – at Clermont in France – Pope Urban II made his historic speech of November 1095, called for a crusade against the infidels (specifically the Seljuq Turks) who had occupied and defiled the holy places of Jerusalem. Thousands at once took up the cry of 'Deus vult!' – 'God wills it!' Among the first zealous adherents was Bishop Adhemar of Puy, whom Urban named his legate, and appointed as leader of the holy war. It is important to note that it was on French soil that the seed had been sown. Preached in France by a pope of French descent, the Crusades started off as primarily a French – more precisely, Norman-French – enterprise. The kingdoms which they were to establish in the East, for all their cosmopolitan elements, were to be basically French kingdoms, in speech and customs, and also in their virtues and vices.

The Crusaders set off from Western Europe in the spring of 1096. After many adventures and hardships, a motley force of about 150,000 assembled at Constantinople early in 1097. Emperor Alexius Comnenus insisted on treating the Crusaders as his personal vassals, though he made it clear that he regarded them as dangerous rivals rather than as wholly welcome allies.

After crossing the Bosphorus and capturing Nicaea from the Seljuqs, the Crusaders eventually struggled south-eastwards towards Cilicia and Syria. After passing through the Cilician Gates and other passes into the world of the medieval Near East, we can imagine the pleasant surprise experienced by the exhausted warriors of Tancred and Baldwin. After coping with supercilious, suspicious Greeks, and warlike Seljuq Turks, the Franks were welcomed with open arms by friendly Armenians with their attractive ladies, bearing tasty dishes of shashlik and kebabs, and excellent local wine.[1]

Within two years of the Crusaders' arrival in Cilicia in 1097, virtually the whole of Syria and the Holy Land was in their hands, including Antioch, Tripoli and Jerusalem. The element of surprise,

[1] See Gérard Dedeyan, *Solidarité Franco-Arménienne à l'Epoque des Croisades* (Paris, 1970).

and also the superiority of Western armaments and siege machines, played a large part in this phenomenal success. However, the assistance of the Armenians, who supplied provisions and military equipment, and also guarded the Crusaders' rear, was a very material factor.

Naturally, there were some unpleasant incidents arising from military and political rivalry for domination over the newly conquered area. The Latin takeover of Edessa by Baldwin, for instance, was marked by the treacherous murder of its Armenian governor, Toros the Kuropalates ('guardian of the palace'), by a group of conspirators. Both Armenian and Western sources (for instance Albert of Aix) attest to Baldwin's connivance in the deed – despite the fact that Toros had actually adopted Baldwin and nominated him as his successor.

Later, the Rupenid Prince Toros I (1100–23) had to take up arms against the famous Tancred, who cherished ambitions of setting up a Norman kingdom in Cilicia and subjecting the local Armenians to his rule.

There was also an acrimonious interlude in 1203, when the Armenian King Levon I attacked Antioch, in an attempt to annex this principality after the death of Bohemond III.

Such alarms and excursions were part of the feudal way of life. The underlying solidarity between the Armenians and the Franks remained unbroken for two centuries. The twelfth-century Armenian chronicler Matthew of Edessa speaks with enthusiasm of the divine mission of the Crusaders to deliver the holy places from the infidel. When Edessa was recaptured in 1144 by the Muslims, the future Armenian Catholicos, Nerses Shnorhali ('the Gracious'), commemorated the city's fate in a solemn elegy.

It is significant that the Frankish law code called 'the Assizes of Antioch' has survived solely in its Armenian version. One of the main medieval authorities on the history of Mongol domination in the Near East was an exiled Armenian prince named Hetum or Hayton of Korykos. After leaving Cilicia, Hayton settled down at the Praemonstratensian abbey near Poitiers. He was a protégé of Pope Clement V of Avignon, for whom in 1307 he completed a book entitled *Flos Historiarum partium Orientis* (Flower of the Histories of the Regions of the Orient). This work was composed in French and then translated into Latin.

The Armenian nobility at the Cilician court in Sis adopted a number of European customs, such as trimming their hair and beards, wearing close-fitting European garments instead of oriental robes; they also introduced Western styles of weapons and armour, horse trappings and knightly etiquette. The seal was set on this trend at the coronation of the first king of Cilician Armenia, Levon, in January 1199. The Papal legate handed Levon a royal sceptre adorned with the French emblem of the fleur de lys. Many leading European crusading princes attended the ceremony. The Armenian courtiers gradually took on French titles, such as maréchal, connétable, chambellan, sénéchal, and comte. It was at this period that the title of 'baron' became so widespread in Cilician Armenia that it is today current among ordinary Armenians, just as 'Mr' is used in Britain or America.

Trade relations with the West played an important part in the economic life of Cilician Armenia. Trading agreements were signed in 1201 with the Genoese and the Venetians. French merchants from Marseilles and Montpellier feature in commercial records in the following century. The principal port was that of Ayas, which is mentioned by Marco Polo. Cilician Armenia became a busy outpost of Western commerce in the Levant, its strategic importance being enhanced by the fall of Acre to the Muslims in 1291. Beautiful coins, many of fine silver, were struck at Sis.[1]

From the Cilician period date the first continuous contacts between the Armenian Apostolic and the Roman Catholic Churches. It was a prime object of the Papacy to secure unity between the two churches on terms agreeable to Rome. However, this would have entailed radical changes in the dogma and liturgical practice of the Armenian national Church of St Gregory the Illuminator, which has always been a rallying point and a symbol of national independence.

Several Armenian kings, including Hetum II (1289–1305), favoured a pro-Papal policy. A synod held at Sis in 1307 sanctioned certain alterations in Armenian Church ritual, but these were strongly opposed by Church leaders from the homeland in Great Armenia.

The last century of independent Armenia in Cilicia was darkened by ecclesiastical schism and political rancour. The last Hetumid king, Levon IV, was assassinated in 1342, by Armenian nationalists who resented his *rapprochement* with Rome. The same faction promptly murdered the next king, Guy de Lusignan, a member of a distin-

---

[1] Paul Z. Bedoukian, *Coinage of Cilician Armenia* (New York, 1962) (American Numismatic Society Numismatic Notes and Monographs, no. 147.)

guished crusading family stemming from Poitou in France, but linked by marriage with the royal house of Armenia.

Later on, King Guy's nephew occupied the Armenian throne briefly as King Levon V – in 1363-4, and again in 1374-5. Being a Roman Catholic, Levon V was crowned twice, according to both the Latin and the Armenian rite.

Levon V was the last king of Cilician Armenia – indeed, the last king of Armenians anywhere in the world. He was overwhelmed in 1375 by Armenian baronial treachery combined with attacks by the Mamluks of Egypt. His faithful confessor Jean Dardel has left a moving account of the king's captivity in Cairo, followed by liberation and a royal welcome in France. In Paris, King Charles VI and all his court came out to greet an exile 'who had been disinherited and lost his kingdom in defence of the cause of Christendom'. Levon V died in 1393; his tomb in the Basilica of Saint-Denis is next to those of the Kings of France.

This special relationship between the Armenians and the French Court continued up to the 1789 Revolution and even later. Jacques Coeur (1395-1456), the millionaire merchant prince, made extensive use of Armenian commercial talent in his enterprises. Under King Henri IV (1589-1610), Armenians helped to introduce the silk-worm into France. Soon after this, an Armenian named Jean Althen began the cultivation of madder in the south of France, thus giving a mighty impetus to the French dyeing and textile industry; a statue to Althen was erected in Avignon.

Cardinal de Richelieu issued letters patent authorizing the Armenians to trade freely in France (24 June 1635). Louis XIV's minister, Colbert, reported to the French Court on the useful role played by the Armenians in extending French commercial interests. In Colbert's time, Armenians introduced coffee into general use in France, and founded the first Paris cafés.

Franco-Armenian relations also had their controversial side, as when the French Embassy in Constantinople under Louis XIV tried to spread the Roman Catholic faith among the Ottoman Armenians. When the Constantinople Patriarch Avedik of Tokat resisted, the French envoy had him imprisoned and then exiled to the island of Tenedos. The French then kidnapped Avedik and took him to France, where he suffered years of imprisonment. There is even a legend that Patriarch Avedik was the man in the iron mask.

A generation later, this proselytising movement culminated in the foundation of a Catholic patriarchal see in Cilicia. The first incumbent was Bishop Abraham Ardzivian (1740), who travelled to pay homage to Pope Benedict XIV in Rome. Benedict sanctioned the establishment of a permanent Armeno-Catholic patriarchate, officially subject to the Roman Curia (1742). A modern and most distinguished holder of this patriarchal office was Cardinal Gregory Peter XV Agagianian (1895–1971), who was at one time even considered a possible contender for the Papacy.[1]

When Napoleon invaded Egypt in 1798, he recruited into his service a number of Mamluks of Armenian descent. A score of these played a distinguished role in the French Imperial Guard, including the Emperor's personal aide Roustam, Colonel Chahine, Mir David, Jean de Chouchi and Pierre Abressof, who was aide-de-camp of Prince Eugène de Beauharnais.[2] In 1802 Napoleon issued an edict: 'The French ambassador in Constantinople should take under his protection the Armenians of Syria and Armenia.'

These historical facts prepare the way for the remarkable upsurge of Armenian studies in France which began early in the nineteenth century and continues right up to the present time. Pioneer scholars included J. Saint-Martin, Victor Langlois, M.-F. Brosset, Le Vaillant de Florival and Edouard Dulaurier. During the twentieth century, an outstanding name is that of Professor Antoine Meillet. The best scholarly journal of Armenian studies to appear in any Western language is the *Revue des Études Arméniennes*, founded in Paris in 1920. The first series ceased publication in 1933, but the journal was revived in 1964. Volume 14 of the new series appeared in 1980.

The tragic events of the First World War and its aftermath resulted in intensified contacts between France and the Armenians. After the heroic defence of Musa Dagh, immortalized by Franz Werfel,[3] it was French warships which rescued the Armenian survivors and transported them to safety. For his relief work among destitute Armenian refugees at the close of the war, the name of Colonel Édouard Brémond is remembered by Armenians with gratitude to this day.

False hopes were raised among the surviving Armenians by the

---

[1] *The Times*, Obituary column, 18 May 1971.

[2] It is sometimes asserted that Napoleon's marshal Joachim Murat, King of Naples (1767–1815), was an Armenian. However, it seems an established fact that Murat was the son of an innkeeper at La Bastide-Fortunière (Lot). Murat's Armenian ancestry seems to be a product of wishful thinking.

[3] *The Forty Days* [*of Musa Dagh*], trans. G. Dunlop (London, 1934).

entry of French troops into Cilicia at the end of 1919. The French were ignominiously ejected by the Kemalist Turks early in 1920, their garrison at Urfa (or Edessa) being entirely wiped out. (This disaster closely paralleled the loss of Edessa by the Crusaders nearly eight centuries earlier, in 1144.) Great loss of life was suffered by the Armenians of Marash, as chronicled in the outstanding book of an American eyewitness.[1]

Many thousands of Armenian refugees in Beirut, Aleppo and other cities of the Lebanon and Syria grew up under French protection between the two World Wars. They absorbed elements of French language and culture. However, French prestige underwent a serious blow in 1939, when Turkish agitation and terrorism led the French government to cede to Turkey a large area known as Hatay, in the Gulf of Iskanderun (Alexandretta). Unable to face the prospect of Turkish misrule, some 15,000 Armenians fled southwards to join their brethren in Syria. One of the conditions of the Turkish takeover of Hatay was that the Turkish Republic would come to the aid of France and England in the event of war in the Mediterranean. As is known, the Turks defaulted in their undertaking, and remained neutral until the closing stages of the Second World War.[2]

These historical circumstances help to explain the fact that the Armenian community in France is today, in 1980, by far the strongest and most numerous in Western Europe. The best available estimates place the total strength at well over 200,000 souls, of whom the majority belong to the Armenian Apostolic Church subject to Holy Echmiadzin, and smaller numbers to the Roman Catholic and Protestant faiths.

Let us take first the Armenians, close on 200,000 in number, who acknowledge the supremacy of Holy Echmiadzin.[3] Their principal church is in Paris, namely the Cathedral of St John the Baptist, Rue Jean-Goujon, established in 1904 and completed in 1906. The official title of the Armenian Archbishop of Paris is 'Apostolic Delegate of the Catholicos of All the Armenians, in Western Europe'. Four other Armenian churches are situated in suburbs of Paris, namely at Alfortville, Arnouville-lès-Gonesse, Chaville, and Issy-les-Moulineaux. There is an important church at Lyons, and smaller ones in the

---

[1] Stanley E. Kerr, *The Lions of Marash* (Albany, N.Y., 1973).

[2] G. Lewis, *Modern Turkey* (London, 1974), pp. 133–4.

[3] The following particulars were kindly compiled for me by my colleague Dr Arthur Beylerian, to whom grateful thanks are expressed.

Lyons suburbs of Décines and Pont de Cheruy; at St-Étienne there is a chapel. In Marseilles and its suburbs we find no less than nine churches functioning. There is one at Nice, and another at Valence, on the Rhône. In Paris, the Armenian Church operates a dispensary and clinic, where two doctors treat patients on two days in the week.

The Armenian Apostolic Church runs a girls' boarding school, known as the Collège Tebrotzassère, at Raincy, not far from Paris. Founded at Istanbul in 1879, its aim was to train Armenian schoolteachers. Following the Armenian massacres, this institution was transferred to Marseilles (1924), and, a few years later, to its present location. During the 1977–8 scholastic year, the school had seventy-two pupils.

The vast majority of Armenian children in France attend the excellent primary and secondary schools in the state system. During the school year, the Armenian Apostolic Church runs cultural centres, open at weekends and on Wednesdays, where Armenian children can learn the elements of Armenian language and literature. In central Paris, there are two such centres, and six in the suburbs. Marseilles, Lyons and Valence have one each. The attendance at these gatherings averages between eighty and a hundred pupils.

The long-established Armenian Roman Catholic community in France today numbers about 25,000 souls. The late Pope John XXIII, by his Apostolic Constitution of 1 July 1961, established an Armenian Catholic Exarchate in France. The Armenian Catholic cathedral, ceded by the Archbishop of Paris, is situated in the rue Charlot, Paris 3e. There are eight parishes belonging to the Armenian Catholic Church in France, namely Paris (about 5,000 souls), Sèvres, Meudon, Arnouville-lès-Gonesse, Marseilles, Lyons, Valence and Saint-Chamond.

The Armenian Catholics in France operate a secondary school (*lycée*) for boys, known as the Collège Samuel Moorat, at Sèvres. Originally founded at Padua in Italy in 1834, the college moved to Paris in 1846. The Franco-Prussian War of 1870 forced the school to evacuate its personnel and property to Venice, whence it returned in 1930 to its present home at Sèvres. During the Second World War the school was again closed down, to reopen once more in 1947. At present, there are about a hundred pupils, of whom ninety are boarders. There are three boarding schools for girls, namely the Pensionnat des Soeurs Arméniennes de l'Immaculée Conception, at

Arnouville-lès-Gonesse; the school of the Armenian Sisters at Marseilles; and the school named after St Gregory of Narek, recently inaugurated at Saint-Cyr.

Armenian Protestants in France are far less numerous than adherents of the national Apostolic and the Roman Catholic Churches, though they are active and patriotic. The Paris Protestant community, about one thousand strong, has three chapels, including one at Issy-les-Moulineaux and another at Alfortville. In Marseilles there are four chapels, with three pastors. There is a Protestant chapel at Lyons, and another at Valence. These communities are active in teaching Armenian to children of Armenian birth in their areas.

Independent of religious affiliation, the Armenians in France share a rich cultural life. They have an excellent research library – the Bibliothèque Nubarian – founded by the Armenian General Benevolent Union, or AGBU. The library possesses over ten thousand volumes in various languages, and concentrates on Armenian language, history, art and architecture. The AGBU itself, which is based in New York, maintains an important branch in France.

Also of major importance is the Union Culturelle Française des Arméniens de France (UCFAF), which arranges cultural exchanges with Soviet Armenia, and organizes lectures, exhibitions and meetings with the aim of popularizing Armenian culture in the West. The UCFAF also has a branch in Marseilles. Though primarily cultural in its activities, the UCFAF is considered to be a mouthpiece for Soviet Armenia. It maintains a youth organization, the JAF or Jeunesse Arménienne de France.

The world-wide Dashnak or Radical Nationalist movement is represented in France, on both the political and the cultural level. The French Dashnak organization is called the Fédération Révolutionnaire Arménienne (FRA) and it runs several centres termed 'Maisons de la Culture Arménienne', notably in Paris, at Issy-les-Moulineaux, at Alfortville and in Marseilles. The younger, more militant, French Armenians often join the Dashnak-sponsored 'Nor Seround' or New Generation group.

The moderate conservative Ramgavar-Azatakan Party and the social-democratic Hunchak Party are both strongly represented in France. There is also a small political organization known as the Démocrate-Arménien group, some of whose members also belong to the French Communist Party.

Such is the importance of these various bodies in Soviet eyes that the Soviet Embassy in Paris maintains an Armenian contact man on its staff, to keep an eye on comings and goings within the French Armenian community. It is his job to guide or cajole the local Armenians into a 'correct' attitude towards the Soviet Union.

Twelve Armenian newspapers and journals are published in France. The most important is the daily *Harach* ('forward'), vigorously nationalist in tone, which has been appearing since 1925. The weekly *Ashkharh* ('world') has been appearing since 1960. The French-language monthly *Haïastan* ('Armenia') is the mouthpiece of the 'Nor Seround' young Dashnak party. The *Banber* ('messenger', or 'bulletin') Armenian monthly has been coming out in Marseilles since 1922. The Armenian General Benevolent Union produces a monthly entitled *Nor Shinarar* or 'new builder'. The social-democratic Hunchaks publish a monthly which is called *Haghtanak* ('victory'). Since 1971, a French language monthly called *Arménie* has been published at Gardanne, not far from Marseilles.

Politics apart, the French Armenian community has a Société de Bienfaisance des Arméniens centred in Paris. This society runs three old people's homes, one at Montmorency and a second at Andilly (both places not far from Paris), and also a third at Saint-Raphaël, in the south of France. We find in Paris a centre of Armenian studies, with a branch in Marseilles. Armenian doctors in France have their own professional association, and there is an Armenian Red Cross society.

More than fifty separate associations unite Armenians in France hailing from specific regions of Turkey – as for instance the associations of Armenians from Mush, and from Kayseri, and a number of others. I have myself experienced the hospitality of the active Bolis or Constantinople association, based in Marseilles.

Armenians play a prominent part in the artistic and literary life of France, as well as featuring in public and official capacities.

Perhaps the best known of all Armenians in France is the singer Charles Aznavour, who can often be seen and heard on British radio and television. Also of Armenian origin is the attractive singer Sylvie Vartan. Among the young generation, the pop singers Rosie Armen, Marc Aryan, Henri Tashan and Agnes Sarkis ('The Voice of France') are widely known.

The actress Anouk Aimée is one of the glories of the French cinema. The film producer Henri Verneuil, born in Turkey in 1920, is of Armenian origin, his former name being Ashot Malakian. He has directed famous stars including Jean Gabin. In intellectual circles, Academician Henri Troyat (Tarossian) is renowned as novelist, biographer and literary historian. Born in 1911, Henri Troyat comes from a Moscow Armenian family. Several of his works, translated into English, are published in both England and America.

To end this section on an exotic note, let us record that under General de Gaulle, the governor of Djibuti, capital of French Somaliland, was an Armenian, Albert Vahé Sahatdjian, from Lyons. Incidentally, Djibuti has until recently contained a flourishing Armenian community.

While considering Western Europe, we must mention the ancient Armenian colony in Belgium and the Netherlands. In 1345, Armenians were authorized to sell rugs in front of the cathedral at Bruges, and by 1478 an Armenian hospice was established in that city. During the seventeenth century, Armenians operated on the Amsterdam bourse, and made extensive use of the Dutch fleet in their trading operations in the Mediterranean.

In the Mediterranean region, special interest attaches to the Armenian colony in Venice, where the first Armenian printed book was produced in 1512. A marine engineer and artillery expert named Anton the Armenian carried on a flourishing salvage business in Venice, clearing the port and its approaches of the wrecks which had accumulated there over the previous 500 years. This resourceful Armenian played an important part in making technical arrangements for the naval battle of Lepanto in 1571, when the Venetians and their allies, under Don John of Austria, wiped out a large Turkish fleet.[1] Such valuable services help to explain the warm welcome given by the Venetian Senate to the Armenian Catholic congregation of the Mekhitarists, when they sought refuge there in 1717.

Finally, we come to the important, long-established Armenian community in Great Britain. The origins of British–Armenian relations go back to the fourteenth century, if not to a still earlier period. In 1346, an Armenian envoy arrived in London, bearing a Bull signed and sealed by Pope Clement VI. In the year 1362, a royal tournament was held at Smithfield in London. English and Armenian knights took part in the jousting, and the Armenian horsemen 'were especially

[1] See K. S. Papazian, *Merchants from Ararat* (New York, 1979).

taken notice of by the King and Queen of England' – King Edward III and Queen Philippa. A milestone in Anglo–Armenian relations was a state visit by the last king of Armenia, Levon V Lusignan, who had sought refuge in France after the fall of Cilician Armenia to the Egyptian Mamluks. Levon arrived in Dover in the autumn of 1385, and was welcomed by King Richard II's two uncles at the head of an impressive delegation. Levon addressed the royal council in session at Westminster, and made an impassioned plea for Anglo-French unity and the launching of a fresh crusade against the Muslims. A conference was held in France in 1386, but all Levon's eloquence could not heal the political differences which at that time divided the two nations, and the projected crusade came to nothing.

From the seventeenth century onwards, the Armenians had close links with the British in India, especially after a trade convention with the Indian Armenians was signed by the Honourable East India Company in 1688. From about 1840, Armenians began to settle in Manchester, where they engaged in the textile trade. Today, there are over ten thousand Armenians in Great Britain, the majority in London. They maintain two Apostolic churches in London, and one in Manchester, show informed interest in artistic and intellectual activities, and adopt useful professions, including medicine and dentistry, carpet manufacture and distribution, and export and import trading.

7

Towards the Orient: 1

Palestine, Persia, Central Asia and Beyond

EVEN BEFORE the upheavals of the Turkish invasion and the First Crusade during the eleventh century, the Armenians had secured a firm foothold in several leading centres of the Islamic world. As traders, builders and administrators, Armenians were making a major contribution to the life of Cairo, Baghdad and the cities of Syria.[1]

A vital factor in maintaining the Armenian presence in the Near East has long been the prestige and influence of the Armenian Patriarchate of Jerusalem, which has a history extending back for well over a thousand years. Indeed, the Armenian Church hierarchy in the Holy City was already long established when the Mamluk Sultan of Egypt Malik al-Nasir formally recognized the Armenian see of Jerusalem as a Patriarchate, in 1311.

Up to the sixth century, the Armenian Christians in Jerusalem had in fact been under the jurisdiction of the Greek Patriarch of the city. All harmony was disrupted by the aftermath of the Council of Chalcedon, held in 451, which led to a bitter schism between the Greek diophysite ('double nature of Christ') Church, and those oriental churches, including the Armenian, which adhere to the

[1] A. Sanjian, *The Armenian communities in Syria under Ottoman Dominion* (Harvard University Press, 1965).

doctrine of Jesus Christ's single and undivided divine nature (mono-physites).

The persecution of monophysite Christians by the Byzantine Emperor Justinian I (527–65) and the Greek Chalcedonian Patriarch of Jerusalem forced the Armenian monks and clergy of the Holy Land to sever all ties with the Jerusalem Orthodox hierarchy. Many Armenian monks and priests fled, while those that remained formed an Armenian bishopric independent of the Greek one. From then onwards, the Greek patriarchate had authority over all Christians of the Orthodox or diophysite persuasion, while the Armenian hierarchy also protected the interests of the Syrian Jacobites, the Copts and the Ethiopians.

A number of ancient Armenian remains and works of art have come to light in Jerusalem. Greatly admired is a well preserved Armenian mosaic floor dating from the sixth century, discovered at the Chapel of St Polyeucte, near the Damascus Gate. Brownish pink in colour, the beautiful formal design incorporates peacocks and other birds, cornucopias, and a graceful and elaborate vine motif imparting unity to the whole.

The principal Armenian establishment is the Monastery of St James, which occupies the entire summit of Mount Sion, with an area of 300 acres or about 150,000 square metres. The cathedral itself stands on the spot where, according to tradition, the head of St James the Great was buried in AD 44 after the saint was decapitated by Herod Agrippa. The remains of St James the Less, the first bishop of Jerusalem, also repose within the present Armenian cathedral.

The first church built on this site goes back to the fourth century; a wall dating from this period was uncovered during restoration work carried out at the cathedral in 1957. This original structure was damaged by the Zoroastrian Persians when they sacked the city in AD 614; it was repaired in the eighth century and substantially reconstructed in the eleventh century.

The present cathedral is 24 metres long and 17.5 metres wide. Its arches resting on four massive pillars, its gilded altars and ancient paintings, the beautiful Kutahya tiles decorating the walls, and the shafts of light piercing through the high windows of the dome, all combine to impart an atmosphere of religious fervour.

The capture of Jerusalem by the Crusaders in 1099 encouraged Armenians from all over the Near East to flock there, some to take

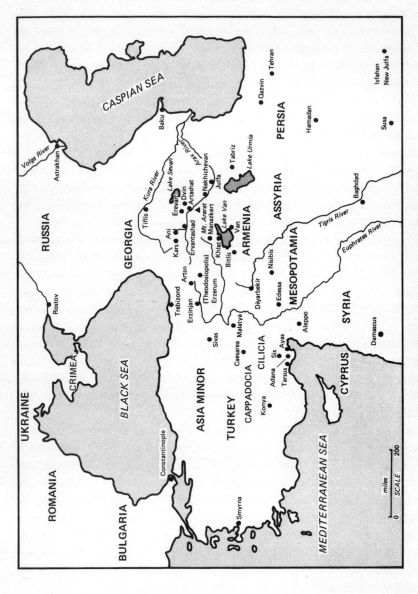

HISTORICAL ARMENIA AND ADJOINING LANDS

up permanent residence, others to perform pilgrimages. Because of this influx, and as a result of close links between the Latin kingdom of Jerusalem and the new Armenian state in Cilicia, the Armenian position in the holy places enjoyed a revival of splendour and vitality.

Jerusalem was recaptured by Saladin in 1187 and remained in Muslim hands for over seven centuries. The Ottoman Turks captured the Holy Land in 1517 and held it until General Allenby took Jerusalem in 1917.

During the Ottoman period, the Armenian Patriarchs in Jerusalem had to exercise great adroitness to maintain their position in face of powerful Catholic and Greek Orthodox interests, backed by European political patronage. Through the diplomatic skill and shrewd foresight of successive Armenian patriarchs, the community of St James has emerged into modern times as a great repository of Armenian Church tradition, education and culture, endowed with unique treasures of manuscripts and antiquities of all kinds.

Apart from the main cathedral, it is worth mentioning the Church of St Theodoros, built in Jerusalem by the Armenian king Hetum I of Cilicia to commemorate his son Toros, killed in the battle of Mari, fought against the Egyptian Mamluks in 1266. Here again we find beautiful wall decorations formed of Kutahya tiles, made by the Armenians of Asia Minor. The church also contains some old and historically important *khachkars* or tomb stones, sculpted with ornamental crosses.

Many legends attach to the nearby Convent of the Holy Archangels, the church of which serves as parish church for the Jerusalem Armenians, who number about 3,500. The precinct is known as the House of Annas, after the father-in-law of the High Priest who passed judgement on Jesus Christ. In Arabic, the foundation is called Deir al-Zeituneh, or 'Convent of the Olive Tree', so called from the remains of a tree preserved just outside the church, to which Christ was tied in the night after his arrest. The convent stands on the site of an ancient chapel dedicated to those faithful Archangels of God who covered their faces in horror, when Christ was struck by a servant of the High Priest. The present church dates from the twelfth century and was restored by the Armenian king Levon II of Cilicia in 1286, at the time when the present outer wall of the convent was built.

The Patriarchate has its own printing press; established in 1833 by Patriarch Zacharias, it was the first regular printing press in the Holy Land. The Patriarchate publishes its official bi-monthly journal in

Armenian under the title of *Sion*, the first issue of which appeared as early as 1866. The Jerusalem press provides religious and liturgical books to Armenian churches all over the world.

Also of importance for Armenian literature is the Jerusalem Gulbenkian Library, founded in 1929 by the late Calouste Gulbenkian, as a memorial to his parents. This library contains over 60,000 volumes, of which 25,000 are in Armenian and the remainder in foreign languages, mainly English and French. The Library receives about 300 different Armenian periodicals from all over the world, and has copies of the first Armenian newspaper ever published, called *Azdarar*, issued at Madras from 1794 to 1796.

The Jerusalem Patriarchate runs its own theological seminary, established in 1843, to train candidates for the priesthood. The Gayaniants Armenian school, set up in 1863, was the first girls' school established in Jerusalem by any community. The co-educational Targmanchats School, established in 1929, is attended by over 300 Armenian boys and girls.[1]

Armenian businessmen in Jerusalem and Tel Aviv compete successfully with their Israeli counterparts. Several extremely attractive Armenian air hostesses are employed by El Al airlines. There is also an ancient Armenian community in Jaffa, numbering about 300 persons.

During the present century, however, the main centre of Armenian activity in the Fertile Crescent has been the Lebanese capital of Beirut. Following the horrors of the 1915 Ottoman genocide, a massive influx took place under the protection of the French government, which obtained the mandate for the region under the Versailles settlement.

Before the present civil strife and fratricidal war in the Lebanon, the Armenians constituted 7 per cent of the entire Lebanese population. The majority live (or used to live) in Beirut and its suburbs. They include wealthy businessmen, doctors, craftsmen, farmers, and poor workers and peasants. The Catholicos of the Great House of Cilicia, the Patriarch of the Armenian Catholics, and the President of the Union of Armenian Evangelical Churches in the Middle East all have headquarters in the Beirut area.

Before the outbreak of hostilities, sixty Armenian schools – kindergartens, primary schools and high schools – and the Protestant Haiga-

---

[1] Assadour Antreassian, *Jerusalem and the Armenians* (Jerusalem, 1968).

zian College, were operating in the Lebanon. There are (or were) over twenty Armenian churches, four daily newspapers, and more than a dozen weekly, monthly and quarterly magazines. The three major political parties – the nationalist, radical Dashnaks or Armenian Revolutionary Federation, the more conservative Ramgavars, and the progressive Hunchaks – all play their role in the political, cultural, aesthetic and sporting life of the community.

The devastation of Beirut has had repercussions for Armenians all over the world. Throughout the fighting, the Armenians have sought to maintain a neutral stance, in the face of constant pressure and intimidation. However, at least 150 Armenians had been killed by 1979, and two thousand wounded. Damage to Armenian property has exceeded $200 million and several national monuments have been destroyed or vandalized. All over the world, Armenian communities are organizing relief for their stricken kinsfolk in the Lebanon, though many families have now left the country.

Another present-day Armenian disaster area is Cyprus, where Armenians have lived since the Byzantine era. In Nicosia, the Melkonian High School was bombed by Turkish planes during the 1974 invasion and largely destroyed. Its reconstruction has cost the Armenian General Benevolent Union about a million dollars. Armenians in the northern sector of Cyprus have been expelled from their homes and business premises, and beaten up. In Famagusta and elsewhere, Armenian churches and monuments have been demolished by Turkish villagers or units of the Turkish armed forces.

Elsewhere in the Near East, the situation of the Armenian communities is rather more favourable. In Egypt, the Armenian connexion goes back to the eleventh-century Fatimid Grand Vizier Badr al-Jamali, who was an Armenian and served from 1073 to 1094. During the nineteenth century, an outstanding figure was the Armenian statesman Nubar Pasha (1824–99), who handled the negotiations for the construction of the Suez Canal, and served for a time as Prime Minister of Egypt. More recently, the Cairo Armenians lost ground following the withdrawal of British power, but some are prospering today in the liberal atmosphere cultivated by President Sadat.

In Syria, Armenians are in evidence in Damascus and even more so in Aleppo. Armenian motor mechanics are the best in Syria. Aleppo was long renowned for the pioneering medical work of the Altounian Hospital, and the Armenian-managed Hotel Baron is a famous hostelry. The community at Baghdad in Iraq is also substantial. The work of Iraqi Armenian artists is regularly displayed at the Iraqi Cultural Centre in Tottenham Court Road, London.

Of great antiquity and historical interest is the Armenian community in Ethiopia. The earliest contacts between the two peoples seem to have been established in Jerusalem, where Armenian and Ethiopian pilgrims met from the fourth century onwards, and their clergy made common cause in resisting religious persecution by the Byzantine Church authorities.

Monks and hermits of the two nations also fraternized in Egypt during the Middle Ages. An Armenian holy man named St Vahram took up residence at the monastery of Deir as-Surian, a place in the Egyptian desert frequented by Ethiopian pilgrims, in the year 1074. St Vahram was later joined by a group of fellow Armenians; monks of both Armenian and Ethiopian nationality were residing at the monastery of Deir Abu-Maqar in 1374.

Both St Gregory, the apostle of Armenia, and St Hripsimé the martyr are commemorated in early Ethiopic liturgical and historical works written in Ge'ez, the Ethiopian literary language. A church on the island of Dek in Lake Tana in northern Abyssinia is dedicated to St Hripsimé.[1]

Armenian–Ethiopian church contacts were reinforced during the fourteenth century by the mission of the Ethiopian monk Ewostatewos (Eustace), who travelled all the way to Armenia around 1339. After the death of Ewostatewos, his surviving disciples returned to Ethiopia with an Armenian monk who had befriended them. Together they founded the monastery of Dabra Maryam in the district of Qohayn, and six other religious communities in the northern provinces. These are only a few of the instances of inter-church friendship which led in the present century to the appointment of the Armenian prelate Bishop Derenik Poladian (murdered in 1963) as Dean of the national seminary of the Ethiopian Church at Addis Ababa.

From the sixteenth century onwards, Armenians played a key role in the conduct of Ethiopia's foreign trade and diplomatic relations. These Armenians were well acquainted with the outside world, and knew their way around the Ottoman Empire which dominated the Red Sea littoral, Egypt and Arabia, and controlled the access routes

---

[1] R. Pankhurst, 'The History of Ethiopian–Armenian relations', in *Revue des Études Arméniennes,* nouvelle série, tom. XII (Paris, 1977), pp. 273–345; continued in tom. XIII, 1978–9, pp. 259–311.

to this largely isolated African state. So little known was Ethiopia in the medieval Christian and Muslim worlds that the Armenian envoys were sometimes arrested and beaten up, or treated as charlatans and impostors. The Ethiopian rulers came to rely on their loyalty and devotion to such an extent that in the eighteenth century Armenians were occasionally appointed to the post of Ethiopian Royal Treasurer.

Armenians brought to Ethiopia the rudiments of medical science. Several Ethiopic medical texts written down in the fifteenth century include prescriptions described as 'cures from Armenia'. Armenians from Abyssinia also contributed much to zoological knowledge in the seventeenth century, when an Armenian named Murad, acting as Ethiopian ambassador, took zebras as gifts to friendly rulers in India and the Far East.[1]

An enthusiastic tribute to the Armenian community in Abyssinia comes from the pen of Evelyn Waugh, who travelled to Addis Ababa in 1930, to report on the coronation of the late Emperor Haile Selassie.[2] During his stay, Evelyn Waugh made a trip to the monastery of Debra Lebanos, accompanied by a 'bullet-headed Armenian chauffeur', and an American scholar referred to as 'Professor W.' – in fact, the eminent Thomas Whittemore – and had a series of hilarious adventures.

On his return journey from Addis Ababa to London, Waugh spent a few days at the city of Harar, where he was befriended by an Armenian of rare character, named Bergebedgian. This gentleman owned a dubious hotel, where he sold great quantities of inflammatory home-produced liquor, and served greasy, pungent and indigestible meals. Bergebedgian spoke a queer kind of French, with remarkable volubility. Evelyn Waugh much enjoyed listening to his opinions. 'I do not think', says Waugh, 'that I have ever met a more tolerant man; he had no prejudice or scruples of race, creed, or morals of any kind whatever; there were in his mind none of those opaque patches of principle; it was a single translucent pool of placid doubt ...'

Bergebedgian noticed Evelyn Waugh's partiality for the exquisite topless ladies of Harar, and offered to fix him up with a temporary marriage for no more than four silver thalers a month, plus board and lodging – though it was possible that the parents might expect a bit

---

1 E. van Donzel, *Foreign Relations of Ethiopia, 1642–1700* (Leiden, 1979).
2 See his travel book, *Remote People* (Duckworth, London); abridged version in *When the Going was Good* (Penguin Books).

more in the case of a foreigner. Evelyn Waugh draws a discreet veil
over any romantic developments which may have ensued during his
sojourn in Harar – a veil which neither his son Auberon Waugh nor
Waugh's biographer Christopher Sykes has apparently managed to
penetrate.[1]

The Armenians who helped Evelyn Waugh during his Abyssinian
adventures inspired him with a warm admiration for their community
– 'a race of rare competence and the most delicate sensibility'. The
Armenians seemed to him to be the only genuine men of the world.
In later years, when confronted with the manifold social and financial
problems of everyday life, Waugh used to comfort himself by reflect-
ing that had he been born an Armenian all these knotty issues would
have seemed a great deal easier to cope with.

An outstanding example of ability to cope with adversity and disaster
– and even to benefit in some way from apparently hopeless situations
– is provided by the Armenians' relations with the Mongols, who
overran Greater Armenia during the 1230s. Initially, the intrusion of
the Mongols was viewed as wholly pestilent and destructive – 'ugly
progeny, engendered in sin', a medieval Armenian historian calls
them, continuing :

> What shall I write now, concerning the pain and misfortune of this
> time, of the separation of fathers and mothers from their sons; of
> the severance of affection among loved ones and close relations;
> how they took their inherited property; how the lovely palaces
> were consumed by fire, and children were immolated in the arms
> of their mothers; how lovely and gently raised youths and maidens
> were led away captives naked and barefoot ![2]

Once the Mongols, led now by the successors of Jenghiz Khan, had
consolidated their rule in Central Asia, Russia and the Near East,
they began to appreciate the services which the Armenians and other
oriental Christians were in a position to render them. The Mongols
of Persia did not adopt Islam as their state religion until 1295, and
they meanwhile found the major Islamic powers, such as the Mam-

---

[1] Mr Sykes has most courteously gone through Waugh's diaries for me, and I
thank him for his generous help.

[2] Grigor of Akanc', *History of the Nation of the Archers,* trans. Blake and Frye
(Harvard University Press, 1954), pp. 287, 305.

luks of Egypt and the Turkish Sultans of Iconium, to be the principal obstacles to their westward expansion. At the same time, the Roman Popes sent a number of embassies to the Supreme Mongol Khaqan at Karakorum in Outer Mongolia, and the Mongol rulers from time to time dangled before the noses of the papal emissaries the entrancing prospect of a wholesale Mongol conversion to the Roman Catholic faith.

Individual Armenians began to serve the Mongols as trade envoys, interpreters and soldiers. In 1245, the regent of Cilician Armenia, Constantine, placed his kingdom under Mongol protection, largely to secure protection against the Seljuq Turks of Asia Minor and the Egyptian Mamluk dynasty.

In 1253–4, the Franciscan friar and world traveller William of Rubruck undertook an arduous embassy for the Vatican, all the way to the Karakorum headquarters of Mangu Khan, who ruled from 1251 to 1259. On arriving at the Mongol ruler's court, William found that the Chief Secretary was a Nestorian Christian. Then Rubruck entered a church where he found an Armenian monk, with whom he prayed. This Armenian monk, Sargis by name, had arrived in Karakorum a month before William, and had previously lived as a hermit near Jerusalem. Sargis had travelled on foot with another Armenian, who had brought a silver cross inlaid with four precious stones. Considering that the journey from Jerusalem to Karakorum was at least five thousand miles long, and most of it undertaken in the most vile climatic conditions, we can only marvel at the endurance of the pious Armenians of those far-off medieval days.

Not long after the enterprising Rubruck, the king of Cilician Armenia, Hetum I, also came to pay homage to the Supreme Mongol Khan Mangu. The contemporary account of Hetum's journey, based on the king's own impressions, is full of valuable insights into the manners of those remote times and places.[1]

Setting off from Cilicia in 1254, Hetum cunningly eluded the vigilant agents of his overlord and enemy, the Seljuq Turkish Sultan of Rum (Asia Minor), who would gladly have detained him or even put him to death.

And because King Hetum was afraid that the nobles of Rum

[1] J. A. Boyle, 'The Journey of Het'um I, king of Little Armenia, to the court of the Great Khan Möngke', in *Central Asiatic Journal*, vol. IX, No. 3, 1964, pp. 178–9.

[Iconium, Asia Minor] would assassinate him treacherously, he spread a report that he was sending an envoy on in advance to the Mongol Khan, and that when he received his travel permit, he would set out himself afterwards. He also wrote letters to the Sultan of Rum to the same effect. But actually King Hetum set out in person together with this ambassador of his, the king being disguised in servant's dress and leading a horse. King Hetum was dressed in filthy rags, and rode on a most wretched nag. —— In this way, he passed through all the cities of Rum, and nobody knew him, until in the city of Erzinjan, a man in the bazaar recognized him and exclaimed: 'Look, there is King Hetum!'

When the Armenian ambassador heard this, he turned round towards the king as he was leading the horse, and smote him on his cheek and scolded him. He shouted to his royal master: 'You stupid fool, so you fancy yourself as a king in these parts, you encourage people to take you for a king, indeed!' —— In this way the bazaar busybody's suspicions were removed. And the king continued to wear peasant garb until he arrived at the frontier of the land of the Georgians.

King Hetum's initiative in undertaking this vast and hazardous journey was much appreciated by the haughty Mongols, who entertained the Armenians at Mangu's court for fifty days, and gave them official charters guaranteeing protection to the Armenian nation and its monasteries and churches. On his return to Sis in Cilicia, King Hetum – like Marco Polo two generations later – regaled his friends with tall stories about Mongolia and China. On the far side of China, he said, there was a country (probably Tibet) in which the women were endowed with human form and with rational powers, but the men were in the shape of dogs and devoid of reason, large and hairy in aspect. These dog-men refused to allow visitors into their country, and hunted game on which they and their women lived. When the dog-men had intercourse with the women, their male offspring were born in the shape of dogs, and the girl children were like ordinary women. An early account of yetis, the Abominable Snowmen?

As a result of the Armenians' relations with the Mongol Great Khans, an Armenian presence was established in China. In 1318, the Armenians built a church at Khan-baliq, seat of the Great Khan in China, close to the modern Peking, and placed it under the jurisdiction of the Roman Catholic archbishop there. At Ch'uan-

Chou, a great medieval port near Amoy, a wealthy Armenian lady bequeathed to the Roman Catholic missionaries a church with a residence attached, and left in her will an endowment for clergy and Christian pilgrims. This lady belonged to an Armenian merchant family settled in China, engaged in the caravan trade which operated between China and far-off Cilician Armenia, thousands of miles to the west.

The tradition of Armenian Christianity in the Far East was maintained, with interruptions, right up to the present century. There was a flourishing Armenian community at Harbin (present-day Ha-erh-pin) in Manchuria, with its own church. Harbin fell to the Japanese in 1931. Later on, the Armenian pastor Vardapet (later Archbishop) Asoghik Ghazarian was thrown into a concentration camp. Living in terrible conditions, Father Ghazarian ministered heroically to other Christian prisoners right up to the liberation in 1945.

Appointed Primate of the Armenian Church in Iraq, Archbishop Ghazarian died there, in Baghdad, in 1978. Now that Harbin is incorporated into Communist China, the Harbin Armenians are dispersed and their community life there is, for the time being, at an end.[1]

There is, however, a small Armenian colony in Hong Kong. Its best known member was the 'grand old man of Hong Kong', the millionaire cricketer and racehorse owner, Sir Catchick Paul Chater (1846–1926).

Another important zone of Armenian settlement in the Orient is Persia, where Armenians have lived since pre-Christian times. They fought for the Great Kings of the Achaemenid dynasty right up to the invasion of Alexander the Great. The Arsacid rulers of Armenia, who reigned from the first to the fifth century AD, were of Iranian Parthian origin. During the fourth century, the Persian Shah Shapur II deported the inhabitants of several Armenian towns into the interior of Persia. Although these deportees were said to be mostly Jews, there were certainly Armenian families as well.

For about eighty years in the thirteenth and fourteenth centuries, eastern Armenia was united politically with the Persian empire of the Mongol Il-Khan dynasty. Armenians were found increasingly in the great cities of north-western Iran, such as Maragha, Tabriz and Sultaniya. In 1329, under the Il-Khan ruler Abu Sa'id, the Armenians were able to enlarge and reconstruct their ancient church of

---

[1] Personal information from Archbishop Bessak Toumayan, London, 1979.

St Thaddeus, 20 kilometres from the town of Maku, in Persian Azerbaijan.[1] During the same period, the ancient Armenian capital of Ani staged a social and commercial revival, and Armenian traders made substantial contributions to the treasury of the Mongol over- lords in Iran. High-quality silver coins, with Arabic and Mongol inscriptions, circulated throughout eastern Armenia in large quantities.

By the middle of the fourteenth century, the Persian and Armenian empire of the Mongol Il-Khans had disintegrated. Eastern Armenia was carved up by rival Turcoman dynasties. At the end of the century, eastern Armenia and Georgia were ravaged from end to end by the Central Asian conqueror Timur Leng – the Tamburlaine of Chris- topher Marlowe's tragedy.

The miseries of the Armenians in the homeland were aggravated still further by the fall of Constantinople to the Ottoman Turks in 1453. Eastern Armenia was cut off from Europe, and sank back into a state of stagnation and poverty. The country was devastated in the course of destructive wars fought between the Ottoman Turks and the Persian dynasty of the Safavids, founded by Shah Ismail in 1500. By a peace treaty signed by the Turks and the Persians in 1555, eastern Armenia was divided between them into two spheres of in- fluence – much as had been done at earlier periods, in Byzantine times.

Under Persian suzerainty, the Armenians of the Araxes valley eventually managed to rebuild their shattered fortunes, and re- establish their traditional export trade. Their main emporium was Old Julfa, a city built beside an ancient bridge, on the north bank of the Araxes. Today a frontier crossing-point between Iran and the Soviet Union, Old Julfa had long been a staging-post on the route leading from Tabriz in Persian Azerbaijan northwards to Nakhchevan, and on to Tbilisi, capital of Georgia. According to an English travel- ler, the population of Old Julfa about AD 1600 amounted to ten thousand persons, dwelling in two thousand houses, 'all of hard quarry stone'. The Armenian citizens were 'very courteous and affable, great drinkers of wine'; they were successful in the international silk trade, whereby the city had waxed rich and full of money.

The prosperity of Old Julfa was abruptly cut short by the Persian conqueror Shah 'Abbas I (1587–1629). This brilliant but cruel ruler campaigned repeatedly against the Ottoman Turks, who overran

[1] Agopik and Armen Manoukian, *S. Thadeï Vank*, Milan, 1971 (Documents of Armenian Architecture, No. 4.)

much of Georgia, Armenia and Azerbaijan in 1578. The Shah resolved to depopulate most of eastern Armenia and create an empty tract or buffer zone between himself and his Turkish foes. He also hoped to exploit the mercantile talents of the Armenians in order to expand Persian international trade with India and with Western Europe.

In 1604, Shah 'Abbas forcibly transferred some 60,000 families from Old Julfa and the surrounding region to his capital at Isfahan. In spite of bitter winter weather, he gave them only three days to gather up their possessions. Then he set about destroying the town of Old Julfa and the bridge over the River Araxes. There were not enough boats to ferry the deportees over the raging torrent, and many were driven into the water by Persian troops and drowned. The operation was naturally considered a national disaster by the Armenians, who composed pathetic songs lamenting their eviction from a once prosperous area.

Shah 'Abbas the Great did something to make amends for all this, when the survivors struggled into Isfahan several months later. They were given extensive grants of land to the south of the main city, across the river Zanderood. There they built a cathedral and several other beautiful churches. These edifices look from the exterior something like the Persian mosques of Muslim Isfahan, but they are decorated inside both with stylized paintings in the oriental style and also with frescoes depicting biblical scenes and episodes from Armenian history, such as the mission of St Gregory the Illuminator, who converted Armenia early in the fourth century.

Successive Persian shahs of the seventeenth century tended to show special favour towards their local Armenian subjects, who gradually became reconciled to their new surroundings. These shahs greatly enjoyed Armenian hospitality, especially as this included liberal supplies of excellent wine, which was (nominally at least) forbidden to them in their own palace, according to the dictates of the Muslim religion. Shah Safi (1629–41) once drank and overate so immoderately at the home of a Julfa Armenian merchant that he was violently sick in the night. His host, fearing torture and execution, committed suicide, which greatly distressed the Shah, who had fully recovered by the following morning.

According to Western travellers of the time, the houses of the Julfa Armenians were 'extremely neat and well kept'. The rooms inside were covered with fine carpets and full of cushions of gold and silver brocade. The front gates of most of the Armenian mansions were kept very small and narrow, partly to prevent arrogant Persian visitors from riding in on horseback, and partly to discourage the prying eyes of Persian tax collectors and other officials.[1]

That celebrated world traveller, Jean-Baptiste Tavernier, Baron d'Aubonne (1605–89), has left a picturesque account of Armenians whom he met on his six journeys to the East. Tavernier was struck by some puritanical features of Armenian married life, and also by the sometimes tyrannical dominance of the Armenian 'heavy father':

> The Man goes to Bed first, the Woman pulling off the Man's Breeches, though she does not lay aside her Veil 'till the Candle be put out. Let it be what time in the year it will, the Woman rises before day. So that there may be some Armenians that in ten years after they are marry'd never saw their Wives' faces, nor even heard them speak. For though her Husband may speak, and all the rest of her kindred, yet she never answers but with a Nod. The Women never eat with their Husbands; but if the Men feast their Friends today the Women feast theirs the next day.[2]

Prosperous citizens and domestic tyrants at home, the Armenian merchants of New Julfa and their employees lived very differently once they set forth on their extensive business journeys. They were frugal, resourceful and highly enterprising. They believed in travelling light, apart from useful equipment, and in keeping caravanserai or hotel charges down to a minimum. Each Armenian merchant took with him his own mattress and bedding, and his own cooking utensils. They also took with them supplies of biscuits, smoked meat, hard-boiled eggs, onions, flour, wine and dried fruits. These they supplemented as they went along by lambs and kids which they could buy cheap in the hill country, or else by fishing in streams and lakes.

Long before the invention of the American Express card, the Armenian bankers and merchants evolved their own private international credit system, whereby large sums could be remitted from country to country by the intermediary of leading Armenian businessmen. Much of this business was transacted by word of mouth or by simple exchange of letters, often in code. As contracts could not be

---

[1] John Carswell, *New Julfa: The Armenian churches and other buildings* (Oxford University Press, 1968), p. 86.

[2] Quoted by Carswell, *New Julfa*, p. 87.

readily enforced in local Islamic courts, a high standard of commercial and personal integrity was maintained within the Armenian community, supported by stringent internal sanctions.

With all this energy and thrift, it is not surprising that 'there returned very few caravans into Persia without 200,000 crowns in silver, beside English and Dutch cloth, fine tissues, looking glasses, Venice pearls, cochineal, and watches, which they thought most proper for the markets in Persia and India'.[1]

By the middle of the seventeenth century, Julfa Armenian merchants were ranging as far afield as Tongking in northern Indo-China (Vietnam), Java, and the Philippine Islands. Among the commodities shipped from the Far East to Persia were cotton goods, musk, spices, and Chinese porcelain. Silk was exported westwards from Persia through Tabriz and Erzerum to Smyrna (Izmir), whence it was shipped across the Mediterranean to Venice, Livorno, Marseilles and other ports. There was also a route via Baghdad and Aleppo.

The Julfa Armenians also operated profitably in Muscovite Russia. In 1667, two Armenians from Persia obtained an *ukaz* or decree from Tsar Aleksei Mikhailovich, allowing them to import silk duty-free for sale within Russia, and also to re-export it to Europe on payment of transit duty. Up to about 1700, Armenian merchants were the only oriental traders permitted to trade in Russia north of Astrakhan. A rich Armenian from Julfa, Philip de Zagly, concluded a commercial agreement with Frederick Casimir, Duke of Courland, which was signed at Mitau, near Riga, in 1696. Zagly unfortunately became involved in international politics and was executed by the Persians in 1707.[2]

Several Armenian merchants from New Julfa passed through India to carry on business in Tibet. A certain Hovhannes Jughayetsi, or John of Julfa, arrived in Lhasa in September 1686, having crossed Nepal en route. He spent five years in Tibet, buying and selling various items of merchandise, learning the Tibetan language, negotiating with Tibetan officials, paying local taxes, and even suing and being sued in local Tibetan courts of law.

Other Armenian merchants visiting Tibet at this period pushed on even further east. Some indeed reached the city of Si-Ning, over a

---

[1] Tavernier, quoted by Carswell, *New Julfa*, pp. 4–5, 77.

[2] Roberto Gulbenkian, 'Philippe de Zagly et l'établissement du commerce persan en Courlande', in *Revue des Études Arméniennes,* nouvelle série, tom. VII, Paris, 1970, pp. 361–99.

thousand miles north-east of the Tibetan capital, and quite close to the great Chinese city of Lanchow.[1]

When Catholic Capuchin missionaries reached Lhasa in 1707, they found five rich Armenian merchants in residence. Each bore the honorific title of Khoja, and their chief was called Khoja David. Although the Armenians themselves belonged to the Armenian Apostolic Church, they were extremely friendly and helpful towards the missionaries, showing them how to make wine for celebration of Holy Communion, gaining them audiences with the local rulers, and acting as interpreters.

The Armenian community in Lhasa dwindled and disappeared between 1717 and 1720, at which period Tibet was invaded by savage hordes of Dzungars, followed by forces of Chinese, who turned the country into a Chinese protectorate.

It was not long after these events that the prosperity and peaceful existence of the Julfa Armenians was itself brought to an abrupt end. In 1722, a large Afghan army invaded Persia and besieged and captured Isfahan. The Persian Shah was deposed, after thousands of Armenian and Persian citizens had died violent deaths or perished from starvation. A few years later, the Persian Empire was restored by the megalomaniac conqueror Nadir Shah (1736–47), but he inflicted heavy taxes and fines on the Armenians, partly to finance his military campaigns in India and Central Asia. Many leading Julfa Armenians emigrated, either to Russia or to India, and also to the port of Basra on the Persian Gulf.

However, a number of Armenians remained at Isfahan and in other Persian cities, particularly Tabriz. Several played a prominent role under the Qajar dynasty, which ruled throughout the nineteenth century and during the early years of the twentieth century. For instance, we can cite the extraordinary careers of two Persian Armenians of this period: Mirza Malkom Khan, Persian Ambassador in London during Victorian times, and Yeprem Khan, security chief and guerilla leader, who played a key role in the Persian constitutional revolution from 1909 onwards.

During the half-century of the now displaced Pahlavi dynasty, the Armenians were well treated and regained much of the commercial

---

[1] L. Khachikian, 'Le registre d'un marchand arménien en Perse, en Inde et au Tibet (1682–1693)', in *Annales: Économies, Sociétés, Civilisations*, No. 2, Paris, 1967, pp. 231–78.

prosperity which they had enjoyed under the Safavi Shahs, three centuries earlier. The Iranian popular revolution of 1978–9 has, inevitably, harmed Armenian interests in international trade, hotel keeping, transport and finance. However, the government of Ayatollah Khomeini and his associates has expressed friendly sentiments towards the Armenians in Iran, who share with the Persians, the Parthians and the Medes a common Aryan cultural tradition. The expression of such sentiments has not, however, prevented the present Iranian regime from embarking on various oppressive and discriminatory measures against Armenian Christian schools and cultural associations, and also against Armenian commercial interests throughout the country. Many Armenians have already sought exit permits from the troubled land.

8

Towards the Orient: 2

Armenians in India and South-East Asia

I ONCE heard an apocryphal story about a visit paid by an Armenian businessman to the President of Bangladesh.

'How many people do you have, living in the different countries of the world?' inquired the President.

'About six million altogether,' the Armenian visitor replied.

'Is that all?' the President rejoined. 'I am surprised, I thought it was more like six hundred million.'

'Why is that?'

'Well,' said the President, 'I travel about quite a lot, and I always inquire everywhere for any of our own countrymen living locally. We Bangledeshis are about sixty million across the world. But for every single Bangladeshi I come across, I bump into ten Armenians! That is why I thought you Armenians must be six hundred million strong.'

Although Armenians are not as numerous as they were in the Indian subcontinent and the countries of South-East Asia, they can still be encountered in several of the main ports and trading cities.

The origins of Armenian settlement in India are lost in the mist of legend. According to one tradition, an Armenian merchant named Mar Thomas landed on the Malabar coast of south-western India as early as AD 780, when a certain Sheo Ram was ruler of Cranganore.

Mar Thomas found favour in Sheo Ram's eyes, thanks to which he amassed considerable riches by trading in muslins and spices.[1]

However this may be, Armenians, both clergy and laymen, were well established in this area by the fifteenth century, before the arrival of Vasco da Gama in 1498. Early Portuguese travellers and missionaries refer to help received from hospitable Armenians long established in the district. From Cochin on the Malabar coast an Italian missionary from Urbino, Father Nicolo Lancilloto, wrote in 1548 :

Here in Cochin there is a very old Armenian bishop. For forty years already he has been teaching the principles of our faith to the Christians of St Thomas who are here in this land of Malabar.

The great St Francis Xavier himself paid tribute to the pioneer work of this venerable Armenian prelate, whose name was Jacome Abuna. St Francis Xavier describes Jacome Abuna as 'a bishop from Armenia, a very old, virtuous and saintly man.[2]

We move now to the Mogul capital at Agra, famous for the Taj Mahal. The Emperor Akbar (1556–1602) was distinguished for his religious tolerance, so different from the Muslim fanaticism which disfigured the reign of his descendant Aurengzeb (1658–1707). Like his younger royal contemporary Shah Abbas I of Persia, Akbar was highly appreciative of the commercial talents and integrity of the Armenians, to whom he granted numerous privileges and considerable religious freedom.

One of the Emperor Akbar's queens was an Armenian lady, called Mariam Zamani Begum. This Armenian consort of the great Akbar had a sister, Juliana by name, who was a doctor employed to supervise the Emperor's seraglio. Juliana married an exiled French prince, Jean Philippe Bourbon de Navarre, who had been forced to flee from France after killing a relative in a duel, and was then welcomed by Akbar and taken into his service. It was the French prince and his Armenian wife who built at Agra the first Armenian church in India, consecrated in 1562.

Akbar's Chief Justice or Mir Adl was an Armenian, called 'Abdul Hai. Under the emperors Jahangir (1605–27) and Shah Jehan (1627–

---

[1] Mesrovb J. Seth, *History of the Armenians in India* (Calcutta, 1895), pp. 22–3.

[2] Roberto Gulbenkian, 'Jacome Abuna, an Armenian Bishop in Malabar (1503–1550)', in *Arquivos do Centro Cultural Português*, vol. IV, Paris, 1972, pp. 149, 164.

58), another Armenian, Mirza Zul-Qarnain (1592–1656) held a number of high offices of state.

The custom of bestowing Armenian wives on distinguished European visitors continued in India during the seventeenth century. In 1609, Captain William Hawkins arrived in Agra as envoy of King James I of England, and was cordially received by the Mogul Emperor Jahangir. By 1612, Jahangir was persuaded to allow the English East India Company to establish factories at Surat, Ahmedabad and Cambay, though the intrigues of the Portuguese Viceroy prevented Hawkins and his associates from putting the project into effect immediately. Jahangir also provided Captain Hawkins with an Armenian bride, an orphan, the daughter of a certain Mubariq Shah, who had been a distinguished military officer in the service of the late Emperor Akbar.

This lady was a person of exceptional character and charm. Through the sultry nights and boring days spent hanging around the Mogul court, Captain Hawkins was supported by his Armenian wife's affection and encouragement. In his memoirs, Hawkins declares that following his marriage to her: 'For ever after I lived content and without feare, shee being willing to goe where I went and live as I lived.'

Captain Hawkins and his Armenian wife set sail for England in May 1613, but Hawkins died at sea in his wife's arms on the passage from the Cape of Good Hope. The Honourable East India Company presented the Armenian lady from Agra with a purse of two hundred gold pieces, 'as a token of their love'. In the following year, the widow married Captain Gabriel Towerson, an old friend and shipmate of her late husband. Towerson was appointed Factor at the Molucca Islands, where he was tortured and murdered by the Dutch in 1623, during the notorious Massacre of Amboyna.[1]

The Armenian lady from Agra, whose name has not come down to us, was spared from the Massacre of Amboyna, as she was then staying with her family in India. Anonymous though she is, she deserves honourable mention in the annals of British India, as the helpmate and partner of the first Englishman to gain a trading concession in that fabulous land.

Naturally, all was not plain sailing for the Armenians under the Moguls – there were inevitably occasional clashes between the auto-

---

[1] Mesrovb J. Seth, *Armenians in India, from the earliest times to the present day* (Calcutta, 1937), pp. 96–101.

cratic Muslim emperors and their strong-willed Christian subjects. Under Jahangir, there were cases of forced conversion to Islam, which involved circumcision, performed in a brutal and painful manner.

Nor must we forget to mention the tragic fate of the naked Armenian poet and sage Sarmad. This renowned ascetic originally came from Persia to India as a merchant, but then contracted a sexual infatuation for an Indian lad, at whose door he would go and sit stark naked. Sarmad became a noted Sufi, and composed verses and quatrains in Arabic and Persian. The ill-fated Mogul Crown Prince Dara Shikoh was his disciple.

After Aurengzeb's palace revolution of 1658, the new emperor had his elder brother Dara Shikoh murdered. Under various pretexts, Aurengzeb also had poor Sarmad beheaded at Delhi in 1661, amid popular consternation. Though not a Muslim, Sarmad was buried under the steps of the Jama Musjid mosque, where both Hindus and Muslims long made offerings of flowers, lit candles, and burnt incense on the saint's grave. 'The people of India', remarks an Armenian historian, 'have not forgotten that the harmless naked saint was killed by the order of Aurungzebe because he loved Dara Shikoh and championed his cause.' [1]

The Armenian colony living in India increased in size, wealth and importance throughout the seventeenth century. When the King of Golconda seized San Thomé (Mylapore) from the Portuguese in 1662, he appointed an Armenian named Markur Erezad as Governor. A large Armenian trading community operated from the original British commercial concession area at Surat. Armenians were established in Madras by 1666, and built a church there in 1712. Armenians were instrumental in procuring from the Mogul government the rights and privileges which enabled Job Charnock to establish the port of Calcutta in 1690.

A milestone in relations between Great Britain and the Armenians was the formal agreement signed in June 1688 between the Honourable East India Company and the leaders of the Armenian community in India. One important object of this agreement was to divert Armenian trade between India and Europe from the old overland route to the new British-dominated sea route round the Cape of Good Hope.

By this agreement, the proud British afforded such recognition to Armenian national prestige as has rarely been paralleled in the dealings of European colonial nations with oriental peoples. For instance,

[1] Seth, *Armenians in India*, p. 172.

Armenians were allowed to reside and trade freely in the Company's towns and garrisons, where they could hold all civil offices and employments, equally with the British. The Armenians were allowed free exercise of their religion according to the rites of the Armenian Apostolic Church. The English even undertook to pay for the building of an Armenian church whenever forty or more Armenians resided at any of the Company's towns or garrisons.

On the whole, the 1688 agreement proved advantageous to both sides. The Armenians found that British military and political protection could save them from oppression by Indian native rulers, and flocked to take up residence at the new British cantonments and establishments, including Bombay. They were of great service to the East India Company's agents and factors in their disposal of goods imported from England, as also in providing these agents with Indian merchandise for export to Britain.

From the early period of the East India Company's operations right up to the nineteenth century, Armenians were in demand as soldiers. During the reign of William and Mary, in 1691–2, the Company's court resolved 'to engage about sixty Armenian Christians, to serve as soldiers, and to offer them a bounty of forty shillings per man, and the same pay as the English soldiers, because, professing nearly the same religion, and being, in other respects, of good character, they might be deemed almost a regular part of the Company's military establishment'.[1]

By way of variety, let us cite the remarkable career of Dr Joseph Marcus Joseph, MD (1826–86), an Armenian pioneer of the Indian Medical Service, which he joined in 1852, later rising to the rank of Deputy Surgeon-General. Born in Bombay, Dr Joseph was trained at St George's Hospital, London, and became MRCS and LRCP. He also studied in Glasgow, becoming MD of that university, which later elected him an Honorary LL.D. Dr Joseph was a Fellow of the Royal College of Physicians of Edinburgh, and a Bencher of the Inner Temple. After a useful career spanning thirty-three years, Dr Joseph retired from the Indian Medical Service in 1885, and was awarded the then very substantial pension of £950 per annum, supplemented by a special annuity of £400.

Many Armenians served with distinction in the armies of various maharajahs and other local Indian rulers. Around 1760, the Indian armament industry was largely in Armenian hands. Shah Nazar Khan

---

[1] Bruce, *Annals of the Honourable East-India Company*, vol. 2, p. 621.

(d. 1784) worked for Ahmad Shah Durrani at Lahore, and cast the famous gun known as Zamzamah, of which Rudyard Kipling later wrote :

Who hold Zam-Zammah, that fire-breathing dragon, hold the Punjab, for the great green-bronze piece is always first of the conqueror's loot.[1]

The eminent Armenian gun-maker was buried in the Armenian cemetery at Agra. An elegant Persian epitaph commemorated

Shah Nazar Khan, he whose name was world-famed and in the craft of casting cannons, he added even to the excellence of Loqman, since he was a believer in the Messiah. He went to the blue sky of Heaven to pay obeisance to Him. A voice from the unknown mournfully uttered the following verse which gives the date of his death : 'He has kissed the feet of Jesus.[2]

A contemporary of Shah Nazar Khan, Gorgin Khan, was Minister and Commander in Chief of Nawab Mir Kassem of Bengal, from 1760 until Gorgin's death in 1763. He too was a noted expert in casting guns and built up his master's artillery to formidable proportions. Gorgin Khan's real name was Khoja Gregory; he began his career as a humble Armenian stallkeeper and was murdered by Indian mutineers at the early age of thirty-three.

Equally remarkable and far longer was the career of Colonel Jacob Petrus (1755–1850), who served for seventy years in the army of Gwalior, and was still on the active list when he died at the age of ninety-five. Colonel Jacob was in command of the First Brigade of the army of Scindia, comprising 12 regiments of infantry, 4 of cavalry, and a squadron of artillery with 150 guns. In those times of 'free enterprise' arrangements, Colonel Jacob's success rested in large part on the regularity with which he paid his troops, who remained devoted to him throughout the turbulent events of those days. At his funeral, ninety-five guns were fired from the ramparts of Gwalior fort – one

---

[1] *Kim*, chapter 1.

[2] The sage Loqman, according to Persian tradition, invented guns and artillery. According to the oriental system of reckoning called *Abjad*, the word *Isa* (Jesus) has the numerical value of 1784, the date of Shah Nazar Khan's death.

for each year of the veteran Armenian colonel's life. Colonel Jacob, sad to say, was predeceased by his elder son, Major David, who led an extravagant, luxurious and licentious life, 'surrounded by notorious musicians and dancing girls'. Major David's stables of valuable horses and tame tigers were renowned at Gwalior, but he died of tuberculosis at the age of thirty-five.

The Indian Armenians made many valuable contributions to literature and learning in the Indian subcontinent, and were pioneers in introducing printing to several cities of this vast region. By 1772, a press had been set up in the business sector or Black Town of Madras by an Armenian named Jacob Shameer (Shahamirian), who in that year compiled and printed a reader for Armenian schoolchildren; in the following year he brought out a work of moral theology. Though Jacob died in 1774, the press continued up to 1783 under the management of his younger brother Eleazar. Then in 1789 the Reverend Arathoon Shumavon started a second Armenian press at Madras, which began in 1794 to issue the monthly *Azdarar*, the first ever Armenian journal.

In Bengal, Armenian printers were active in Calcutta by the end of the eighteenth century. For instance, the Reverend Joseph Stephen published in 1796 a chronicle of the primacy of Abraham III, known as Abraham of Crete, Supreme Catholicos from 1734 to 1737.

On 1 December 1815, a society was founded in Bombay to stimulate the education of Armenian youth and the members of the society undertook the translation of works of foreign literature, at the same time trying to create their own original works.

A milestone in Armenian education was the opening of the Armenian Philanthropic Academy in Calcutta on 2 April 1821. Later, this institution was known as the Armenian College; it has sent out educated Armenians to carry on useful careers all over the world.

The Indian Armenians were pioneers in evolving a modern, national theatre. As early as 1812, the Shahamirian brothers brought out an Armenian version of Voltaire's tragedy, *La Mort de César*. In 1821, dramatised scenes from Armenian life in India were presented at theatres in Madras and Calcutta. At the end of the nineteenth century, the Reverend Bessak Hagopian presented his historical drama, *Hayastan* ('Armenia'). Early in the present century, Megerditch Hagopian, a graduate of the Calcutta Armenian College, founded a dramatic society within the college, and produced the historical tragedies *Nerses the Great* and *Arshak II*. In 1908 the New Empire theatre was built in Calcutta with funds supplied by Arathoon Stephen, and provided the local Armenian actors, amateur and professional, with a regular home.

The high level of education among the Calcutta Armenians enabled them to perform creditably in the legal profession. During the second half of the nineteenth century, thirty-three Armenian advocates, attorneys and solicitors practised at the Calcutta High Court, the most distinguished being the Honourable Sir Gregory Charles Paul, KCIE. The first Armenian Sheriff of Calcutta was Seth Apcar, son of Arathoon Apcar (1779–1863), founder of the famous firm of Apcar & Company.

During the nineteenth century, the Armenian community in India produced several merchant princes and bankers whose world-wide benefactions included granting scholarships to deserving students, restoring the main shrines of the Armenian Apostolic Church, and founding hospitals for sick and aged Armenians. In 1836, the Moorat-Raphael Armenian Secondary School in Venice was established by donations from Indian Armenian benefactors; it still operates, in a magnificent palazzo which I visited in 1967. Indeed, the Indian Armenians of the last century fulfilled very effectively, on an international scale, the same aims which have been taken over in our time by the Armenian General Benevolent Union and the Calouste Gulbenkian Foundation.

Among family names often met with in the records of the Armenian community in India are Apcar (Abgarian), Gregory (Gregorian), Arathoon (Harutiunian), Pogose (Poghossian), Gasper (Gasparian), Bagram (Bagramian) and Catchick (Khachikian).

We have several interesting glimpses of Armenian social life and customs in eighteenth- and nineteenth-century India. A historian of Bombay, Mr S. M. Edwardes, noted that :

The Armenians are wearing the Persian dress, and dyeing their hair and whiskers with henna. Armenian ladies pass their time either engaged in the care of their families, or in receiving and paying visits, drinking coffee or sherbet, embroidering and making delicious confections of Hulwah [Halva] and various sweetmeats. They have very considerable influence in their families, understand business admirably, and are commonly entrusted with the full control of their property. Their condition is easy and agreeable, little restraint being placed on their conduct, a slight degree of personal seclusion being considered honourable and dignified.

In general, the Armenian residents in India were conservative in their social habits, and greatly attached to their ancient Church and national literature. They were exclusive in life and outlook. Though engaging freely with their European confrères in trade, they mixed little with them socially, and rarely married outside their own nationality. Thereby they preserved their distinctive ethos for many generations. Only in the twentieth century did they discard their national costume, apart from the clergy. A number of Armenians later intermarried with Europeans and Eurasians, and abandoned the Apostolic Church of Armenia for the creed of their wives.

The rise of Armenian business enterprise in India had been closely associated with the Honourable East India Company. The Company lost its monopoly of Indian trade by Act of Parliament in 1813, and responsibility for governing India was transferred to the Crown after the Indian Mutiny. There was little discrimination against the Armenians as such, but they suffered increasing competition from London-based international business and banking houses, some operating their own fleets of ships.

As a result of many economic and social factors, the Armenian community in India now underwent a steady reduction in wealth and numbers, so that by the 1930s the main colony in Calcutta numbered only about one thousand. There were still a few mercantile houses, and Armenians were also active in Calcutta as doctors, barristers, solicitors, authors, schoolteachers, dentists, veterinary surgeons, brokers, house and estate agents, underwriters, chemists and druggists, builders and contractors, cabinet makers, hotel and boarding-house keepers, bakers and confectioners, electricians, mechanics and motor engineers.

Matters became rather more unfavourable after the end of British rule over the Indian subcontinent. Local nationalism was added to economic pressure, and many more Armenians left for destinations as far afield as Australia and the United States of America.

Those Armenians remaining in Calcutta and elsewhere have done everything possible to keep the cultural flag flying. In March 1948, the Haygazian Artistic Society was founded in Calcutta with the aim of arousing the interest of young people in Armenian art and literature, old and new. This society maintains cultural relations with Soviet Armenia. In 1954, the society presented Shirvanzadé's play, *For the sake of Honour*, to raise funds for the reconstruction of the old building of the Armenian Philanthropic Academy. On 14 April 1956, the play *David of Sassoun*, based on Armenian national legend, was given by students in the hall of the Academy. A year later, at an evening held in the New Empire theatre, the Haygazian Artistic Society presented a comedy, *The Honourable Beggars*, based on the novel by the nineteenth-century Constantinople Armenian satirist Hagop Baronian.

In South-East Asia, the first notable Armenian establishments were in Burma. Armenians arrived at the old port of Syriam, not far from Rangoon, as early as 1612; the earliest Armenian tombstone there dates, however, from 1725. They obtained a monopoly of the valuable trade in rubies, large deposits of which are situated at Mogok, 90 miles to the north-north-east of Mandalay. By the end of the seventeenth century, the Armenians of Burma had established a small trading fleet of their own. In 1694 an Armenian sloop was captured by the King of Ava, who seized the vessel at the port of Martaban and imprisoned the crew. During the 1720s, Armenians were plying an active trade between Burma and Madras. They suffered a severe setback in 1743 when the Mons or Talaings sacked Syriam and burnt down the Armenian church there.[1]

Armenians played a leading role at the court of the unifier of Burma, King Alangpaya (Alompra), who reigned from 1752 to 1760. The king's Armenian advisers foresaw the imminence of British intervention in Burmese affairs, which threatened their own trading monopoly as much as it did the young kingdom's independence. Thus we have a rather unusual scene of acute Armenian-British hostility in Burma during the 1750s, culminating in the destruction of the British factory and trading station at Negrais and the massacre of its personnel. A leading instigator of this outrage was an Armenian called Gregory, who was 'sea-customer' (Shahbandar or Akawun) of Rangoon, and one of King Alangpaya's most influential advisers on foreign relations.

When Michael Symes undertook his two embassies to the Burmese Court of Ava, in 1795 and 1802, he attributed the many problems and obstacles which he encountered to Armenian hostility. The Armenians, Symes said, were intent on retaining the 'dictatorial power' which they wielded in Burmese government and commercial circles. Many of these Armenians lived at Amarapura, on the River Irrawaddy between Ava and Mandalay. As late as 1854, these Armenians were openly

[1] B. C. Colless, 'The Traders of the Pearl', in *Abr Nahrain*, vols 9–11 and 13–15, Leiden, 1970–5.

praying for a Russian victory against England and France in the Crimean War.

There are many references to Armenian activity in Java, Sumatra and the islands of the China Sea. Between 1770 and 1824, they were prominent in the spice trade in the Molucca Islands.

The foundation of Singapore by Sir Stamford Raffles in 1819 dramatically improved relations between the British and the Armenians in South-East Asia. Within two years, Armenians had arrived at the new commercial metropolis, where church services in Armenian were held from 1821 onwards. Three Armenian firms were operating in Singapore during the 1820s. The British administration granted the Armenians a site for a church – 'lying at the Botanical Gardens, facing the public road called the Hill Street'. Work was started on the church in 1835 and it was consecrated in the following year.

The Armenians of Singapore played a constructive part in helping to set up the independent state there in 1965, and have been loyal to the new regime. The Armenian-founded Raffles Hotel remains outstanding among the hostelries of the Orient.

A comparative newcomer to the list of important Armenian communities of the diaspora is that of Australia. Unlike the colonies in India and Burma, it dates very largely from the present century.

Among the younger Armenian communities, that of Australia is one of the most dynamic. There are 9,000 Armenians in Sydney, 3,000 in Melbourne, and 800 in Adelaide, Perth and Brisbane combined. The total is thus close on 13,000. The Armenian church in Sydney is directed by a bishop, that in Melbourne by a vardapet (learned doctor of theology).

The Armenian groups in Australia are go-ahead and energetic, and thrive in the fast growing industrial economy of that country. They publish two monthly journals and organize cultural events which are open to the Australian public. Apart from many individuals doing well in industry and trade, the Australian Armenians can muster at least six persons holding the PhD degree, two university lecturers, eight engineers, two doctors of medicine, eight senior scientific workers and five engaged in music and the fine arts. Promising students are sent for specialist study to educational institutions all over the world, including the University of London.

9

Eastern Europe and the Russian Connection

AFTER BYZANTIUM and the Near East, the oldest important Armenian settlements outside the homeland are those in Eastern Europe. We have noted that the Byzantine emperors embarked on systematic deportation of Armenians to Thrace, modern Bulgaria. Emperor Maurice (582–602) sent thousands of Armenians to the Philippopolis (Plovdiv) region, where they form an important element today. They implanted in Thrace the Paulician heresy, which in turn helped to give rise to the Bogomil movement, which proved highly disruptive throughout the medieval Balkan world.

A new phase of Armenian settlement in Eastern Europe was set off by the invasions of the Seljuq Turks during the eleventh century. As we have noted earlier, the Seljuqs captured the capital city of Ani in 1064, and went on to defeat and capture the Byzantine Emperor Romanus Diogenes at the Battle of Manzikert, fought near Lake Van in 1071. Those terrible times are evoked by medieval writers, such as Aristakes Lastivertsi, who wrote:

> Our towns are destroyed, houses burnt down, castles committed to flames, royal palaces turned into ashes, The men are slaughtered in the squares, the women carried away as captives, the skulls of infants smashed by stones, virgins publicly dishonoured, youths

killed . . . The swords of the foe grew blunt, but there was no compassion in the hearts of the enemies.

The same author describes the result of this catastrophe – widespread emigration of the native population, while Armenia itself 'lies on the crossroads of all the ways, bare and dishonoured, and passers-by devour and abuse it'. According to the historian Matthew of Edessa, the farmer's work was interrupted and there was no bread, hence famine swept through the land. 'From the blows of the enemies, all sorts of people left their country in large numbers, in thousands, in tens of thousands.' (A figure of 200,000 refugees is given by modern authorities.) Mortality spread among the refugees, and the land was covered with their corpses. These tragic events were repeated in the thirteenth century, when Armenia was invaded and devastated by the Mongols.

Many Armenians reached Cilicia, where they formed the Christian kingdom of Little Armenia.[1] Since the Seljuqs now dominated Iran, Anatolia and Asia Minor, there was little point in seeking refuge in those areas. This left only one other important escape route – across the Black Sea to the Crimean peninsula.

From the eleventh century onwards, Armenians settled in the Crimea in large numbers, at first in Kherson, and subsequently in the city of Kaffa or Theodosia at the eastern end, not far from Kerch and the Sea of Azov. Kaffa became very prosperous in the thirteenth and fourteenth centuries, and was a port and trading centre ruled by the Genoese. From Kaffa, trading caravans travelled far and wide, even as far as China, whence silk was brought back in large quantities. There was also a substantial Armenian colony in the town of Stary Krym ('Old Crimea') or Solkhat, to the west of Kaffa, about fifteen miles inland.

Many of the Crimean Armenians were descended from citizens of Ani, capital of the Bagratid kings. They were intensely patriotic, and continued the cultural traditions of that city. They built a number of churches and monasteries, in which they carried on the tradition of domed construction which had been perfected in early medieval Armenia. They were skilful at decorating the walls with finely carved sculpture. They also built several caravanserais modelled on tradi-

[1] T. S. R. Boase (ed.), *The Cilician Kingdom of Armenia* (Scottish Academic Press, 1978).

7   Old-style Armenian village priest, about 1870. *(BBC Hulton Picture Library)*

8   Antelias Cathedral, near Beirut. Seat of the Catholicos of Cilicia. *(Armenian Bishopric, Aleppo)*

9 Two Churches, one umbrella. Vazken I, Supreme Catholicos of All the Armenians, with Bishop (now Archbishop) Robert Runcie, St Albans, 1978. *(Nicholas A. Spurling)*

tional Armenian design. Several Armenian scribes and miniature painters were active in the Crimea and produced beautiful illuminated gospels, the finest examples dating from the fourteenth and fifteenth centuries.[1]

Shortly before the Ottoman conquest of the Crimea in 1475, there were between 150,000 and 200,000 Armenians in the peninsula. They formed two-thirds of the population of Kaffa, the trading metropolis, where they numbered over 40,000. The Armenians and Greeks were hostile to the ruling Genoese oligarchy of Kaffa. When the Turks besieged the city, the Armenians and Greeks staged a revolt on the fifth day and insisted on surrendering, threatening to massacre the Genoese and their families if they refused to comply.

The Turkish occupation brought the Armenians little joy. When they refused to adopt the Islamic faith, the local pasha invited many of the notables to dinner, and had them beheaded by a swordsman as they left the banqueting hall. Some Crimean Armenians were deported to Istanbul, others fled to the north-west, to swell the important colonies of Lvov and northern Moldavia. When the French merchant adventurer Chardin visited Kaffa on his way to Persia in the seventeenth century, the Armenian colony had dwindled to a few hundred families.

From the sixteenth century to the eighteenth, the Crimea was ruled by autonomous Tatar Khans, whose court attained considerable splendour. In 1777, General Suvorov invaded the Crimea on the orders of Empress Catherine the Great. One of his first acts was to disperse much of the Armenian population – then estimated at 12,600 – and resettle it in other parts of southern Russia. In 1779, Suvorov founded the city of New Nakhchevan, six miles from Rostov-on-Don, and settled it with Armenians from the Crimea. Since the transfer of population was carried out in bitter winter weather, and with inadequate provision for the needs of the new residents, many Armenians perished from cold and starvation.

In spite of these vicissitudes, the Crimean Armenians have remained there to the present day. In the nineteenth century, they produced two outstanding figures – the Supreme Catholicos Khrimean Hairik and the marine painter Aivazovsky. In spite of fierce battles which took place here between the Red Army and the invading Germans

---

[1] A. L. Yakobson, *Srednevekovy Krym* ('The medieval Crimea': Russian) (Moscow and Leningrad, 1964).

in the Second World War, several Armenian architectural monuments have been preserved, in relatively good structural condition.

From the Crimea, we pass to nearby Romania, where I was able in May 1973 to visit several of the main centres of Armenian settlement, thanks to the friendly help of the Armenian bishop in Bucharest aand his small, hard-working band of parish clergy.

The oldest Armenian colonies here are those in Moldavia, which were already long established by the middle of the fourteenth century. A manuscript gospel book copied at Jassy in 1354 can be seen in the Bucharest Armenian church museum, while the church at Botosani dates from 1350. It is interesting that the city of Botosani takes its name from Batu Khan, grandson of the Mongol conqueror Jenghiz Khan, who occupied the place during the thirteenth century. During the Middle Ages, the post of Botosani city treasurer was often held by an Armenian.

The prosperity of the Romanian Armenians dates from the reign of Prince Alexander the Good of Moldavia (1401–35), who settled them in seven of his towns. One of his first official acts, in 1401, was to found the Armenian bishopric of Suceava, then the Moldavian capital, and to assign the Armenians extensive domains at the north side of this picturesque city. The Armenian nunnery of Hagigadar, south-east of the town, was founded in 1512 and has an impressive church. It was built by merchants who wished to express gratitude for successful business trips to Turkey. People still crawl round the outside of the church on their knees and pray for divine protection on journeys, while girls wishing to find husbands crawl all the way up the nearby hill. Equally picturesque is the fortified Armenian church of Zamca to the north of Suceava. Built in the seventeenth century, it was once seized and occupied by the Polish King Jan III Sobieski (1674–96), the liberator of Vienna.[1]

The Armenians in Romania somehow managed to resist assimilation and to preserve the traditions and ritual of their own Apostolic Church. This led to accusations of heresy – as expressed in the murals of the painted churches of northern Moldavia, notably Voroneţ (1488) and Humor (1530). Here we find frescoes depicting the Last Judgement, where the Armenians in their striking oriental costumes are lined up next to the Jews and the Turks, and shown as cast down into hell among the sinners and unbelievers.

[1] L. Şimanschi, *Le Monastère de Zamca* (Bucharest, 1967).

During the sixteenth century, the Armenian community at Suceava fell foul of certain members of the ruling Raresh family. In 1551, the infamous Stefanitsa instigated vicious pogroms, in the course of which some Armenians were cast bound into tents, and burnt alive. Many of the survivors were forcibly converted to Greek Orthodoxy, others had their property confiscated. These tragic events are commemorated in the elegy entitled 'Lament of the Moldavian Armenians', by the sixteenth-century poet Minas of Tokat.

From Suceava, the Moldavian capital was moved to Jassy in 1565. Soon afterwards, in 1572, an Armenian nobleman actually became Voda or Voivoda (supreme ruler) of Moldavia. His name was John Viteazul, which means 'the brave' or 'the heroic'. However, John was betrayed by his boyars and beaten in battle by the Turks, his reign ending tragically in 1574.

In the Romanian capital of Bucharest, the Armenian episcopal church traces its foundation back to 1581, though the original building was a modest structure, which has been rebuilt several times. The present church, dedicated to the Holy Archangels, was begun in 1911 and completed in 1915 – the year of the Ottoman holocaust of the Armenians. The domes and belfries are handsome in their proportions, and recall the architectural style of the mother church at Holy Echmiadzin.

The Armenian population of Romania numbered more than 50,000 at the beginning of the twentieth century – the extensive and well-kept graveyards which I saw at Jassy and Suceava bear witness to this. However, the repressive policies of Anna Pauker and other Stalinist leaders who took over after the Second World War forced most Armenians to emigrate, and today there are only about 5,000 left.

However, the survivors continue to make a contribution to Romanian life and culture out of proportion to their numerical strength. While in Bucharest in 1973, I noted the names of two local Armenian opera singers, two theatre stars, three noted professors of medicine, and two outstanding painters. The Khanul Manouk, a famous restaurant, was formerly an Armenian merchant's home. The Romanian Minister of machine tool production was then an Armenian, as was the Director of the Universal Stores. The Zambakchian Museum was functioning in the street of that name. An Armenian historian, Dr H. D. Siruni, had just died. The weekly Bucharest Armenian newspaper, *Nor Giank* ('new life'), was, and still is, being printed in an edition of 3,000 copies, which are sent to thirty-four countries of the world.

Of considerable interest and, perhaps, of much potential value to mankind are the researches of the Romanian Armenian scientist Dr Ana Aslan, discoverer of the controversial Gerovital H3 drug, which is reputed to stave off old age as well as promoting the growth of hair in cases of baldness. Through the Geriatrics Institute of Bucharest, Dr Aslan operates three spas with a total of 1,500 beds. Although H3 has not been approved officially in every country of the world, it is sometimes taken in pill form as a vitamin supplement by members of the West German police force. Dr Aslan visited the United States of America in 1978, at the age of eighty-two. She was then reported to look much younger than this, possibly because she was one of the first persons to use her own discovery.[1]

Terrorized by the notorious Moldavian prince Stefanitsa Raresh, large groups of Armenians emigrated during the sixteenth century to the relative security of Transylvania, then an autonomous principality, and later part of the Hapsburg Empire. Further groups joined them in the seventeenth century, when they founded the once all-Armenian town of Gherla, not far from Cluj. The crests of leading Armenian merchant families can be seen still, carved over doorways in the old quarter of Gherla, where an Armenian Catholic cathedral in the baroque style was consecrated in 1748. Over the years, the Armenians of Transylvania intermarried with local Hungarians and Romanians, and have become virtually assimilated.

In Hungary and Austria too, Armenians played an important role during the seventeenth and eighteenth centuries, being noted as brave soldiers. In Vienna, the Armenian Catholics of the Mekhitarist order founded a monastery in 1811, which still operates today, though in reduced circumstances. The Mekhitarists in Vienna, like their colleagues in Venice, issue a noted scholarly journal, and have a large library and museum, and also a printing press and a picturesque church. The Armenian Apostolic congregation, subordinated to Holy Echmiadzin, has a modern church in the Kolonitzgasse, directed by a British-trained archpriest, the Very Reverend Dr Mesrop Krikorian. Several Armenian opera singers contribute to the cultural life of this musical metropolis.

We conclude the study of Armenian settlement in the Balkans and

---

[1] *The Armenian Reporter*, 28 December 1978, p. 14.

Central Europe with a survey of the important colonies in Bulgaria, which date back over a millennium and a half. During the Byzantine period, a number of Armenian noblemen, persecuted by the Persian Zoroastrians, settled in the region of Philippopolis (Plovdiv) and Adrianople (Edirné), during the reign of Leo I (457–74). At various times between the sixth and the tenth century, large groups of Armenians were transferred to Thrace from Anatolia. Many of them were militant Paulician heretics, who rejected both the Eastern Orthodox and the Armenian Apostolic Churches. The Paulicians helped to found the disruptive Bulgarian sect of the Bogomils, but eventually merged into the local Slav population; however, their presence is commemorated by several Bulgarian place-names, such as that of the small town of Pavlikeni, not far from Lovech.

The ferocious Bulgarian Khan Krum captured Adrianople in 813, and took into captivity ten thousand people, including many Armenians – among them a boy who was to become the Byzantine Emperor Basil I (867–86), founder of the Macedonian dynasty. A few decades after this event, Pope Nicholas I wrote to the newly converted Bulgarian ruler Prince Boris-Michael: 'Many Christians have come to your country from different parts, among them Greeks and Armenians.' Around the year 996, both the Duke and the Governor of Salonika were Armenians. One of the bravest medieval Bulgarian tsars, Samuel (997–1014), was an Armenian – his mother was called Hripsimé, his brothers, Movses, David and Aharon. Armenian architects and masons designed and built several early Bulgarian churches.[1]

During the eleventh and twelfth centuries, Armenian churches functioned in Sofia and several towns of Macedonia. Eight long-established Bulgarian and Macedonian towns bear names associated with Armenia – Armenophor, Armenitsa, Ermensko and so on. An Armenian monastery was established at Plovdiv in the twelfth century. In 1184, the Supreme Catholicos of Armenia sent Bishop Gregory of Plovdiv to the Vatican, to discuss with Pope Lucius III the question of Armenia's relations with the Roman Catholic Church. During the thirteenth century, and up to the Ottoman conquest of 1393, an Armenian trading community flourished in the ancient Bulgarian capital of Great Tirnovo.

Eighteen years before the Ottoman conquest of Bulgaria, the Arme-

---

[1] D. M. Lang, *The Bulgarians* (London, 1976).

nian kingdom in Cilicia had fallen to the Egyptian Mamluks (1375). For five centuries, the Bulgarians and Armenians shared a common fate as *rayas*, that is to say non-Muslim second-class citizens. They were forbidden to carry arms or ride on horseback, and suffered discrimination of many kinds. It is interesting, however, that after the Turks captured Constantinople in 1453 the Armenian bishop of Plovdiv, Joachim, was summoned to the new Ottoman metropolis and installed as Patriarch of the Armenian Apostolic Church in that city.

During the sixteenth century, Great Armenia and eastern Anatolia became the theatre of savage wars between the Ottoman sultans and the Safavi shahs of Iran. The country was laid waste, and thousands of refugees made the long journey across Asia Minor to Bulgaria, where they found a sympathetic welcome. At the same time, the bloodthirsty tyrant Stefanitsa Raresh of Moldavia was slaughtering and persecuting Armenians in northern Romania, some of whom fled southwards across the Danube to join their compatriots in Bulgaria. A further influx of Armenians into Bulgaria took place after the Turkish capture in 1672 of the city of Kamenets-Podolsky in the Ukraine. Two ships carrying Armenian deportees from this place were shipwrecked on the Bulgarian Black Sea coast. In 1675, they took over an abandoned Greek church in Plovdiv, which is in use to the present day.

The main Armenian settlements in Turkish-occupied Bulgaria were at Plovdiv, Rushchuk (Rusé) on the Danube, Sofia, Shumen, and the ports of Varna and Burgas, though a total of twenty Bulgarian towns with Armenian colonies are mentioned in the archives. Of particular commercial and strategic interest was the Danube port of Rusé, with its handsome boulevards and ornate buildings, and bridges and ferries over the river to Romania. The Rusé Armenians were intermediaries between their compatriots in Poland and Romania, and the great bazaars in Istanbul and the Near East.

By the early nineteenth century, the Armenian population in Bulgaria had grown to 140,000. A few of them were wealthy businessmen and entrepreneurs. Many were professional men and artisans, working as doctors, pharmacists, jewellers, tailors, bootmakers, masons and builders. There were also many poor labourers, whose families lived a precarious existence close to destitution. It is also worth recording that Armenian printers and publishers in Istanbul played an important part in the nineteenth-century Bulgarian renaissance.

They issued a number of works in Slavonic which helped to foster the emergent modern Bulgarian literature and thus contributed to the success of the national liberation movement of 1876–8.

At the Congress of Berlin, which worked out the final settlement after Russia's victory over Ottoman Turkey in 1877–8, the Bulgarians and Armenians both suffered as a result of the intervention of the British Prime Minister, Disraeli. The Tory leader drastically cut down the size of the new independent Bulgaria, thereby helping to create the still festering Macedonian problem; enormous areas of Turkish Armenia captured by Russian forces were restored to Ottoman misgovernment.

Whatever criticism may be levelled at the regime of King Ferdinand of Bulgaria, he certainly displayed great kindness to Armenian victims of Turkish atrocities. In 1895–6, during the 'Abdul Hamid massacres, 10,000 refugees were settled in Varna, Rusé, Shumen and Burgas. Between 1915 and 1922, about 50,000 more fled from Turkey to Bulgaria, though many afterwards left for Soviet Armenia or the United States of America.

The Armenians loyally repaid the Bulgarians for their acts of friendship. During the 1870s, the Armenian Patriarch of Constantinople, Khrimean Hairik, supported the creation of an autonomous Bulgarian Exarchate. In fact, the first secretary of this new Bulgarian Exarchate was an Armenian, Garabed Effendi, who was also the secretary of the Armenian Patriarchate. Early in the present century, Armenian revolutionaries taught the Bulgarian guerillas in Macedonia how to make and let off bombs. During the 1912 Balkan War, Armenians in Bulgaria organized a squad of volunteers 300 strong, commanded by the partisan leader Andranik, and they fought bravely alongside the regular Bulgarian army.

During five visits to Bulgaria between 1967 and 1979 I visited several Armenian colonies there to evaluate the present condition of the community, which is about 25,000 strong. Apart from the capital, Sofia, the most important groups live in Plovdiv (about 6,000), Varna (about 2,000), Rusé on the Danube, and Shumen. The well attended churches come under the authority of the Armenian bishop at Bucharest, himself subordinate to the Supreme Catholicos in Holy Echmiadzin.

At Plovdiv in 1971 I visited the Armenian school named after Stepan Shahumian, and found 600 pupils of both sexes who studied there up to the 8th class (age fourteen), when they went on to the

Bulgarian State Secondary schools. This Armenian school was taken over by the Bulgarian government in 1976 and annexed to the state system, which caused great resentment. A similar fate had already overtaken the former Armenian schools in Varna and Rusé. This appears to be part of a drive to integrate, if not to assimilate the Armenians and other minorities living in Bulgaria. During the census period, I was told, officials try to induce Armenians to adapt their names to the Slavonic pattern – for instance by turning the surname Benlian into Benlianov.

There is, of course, another side to the question. The Armenians retain the right to study their own language, alongside Bulgarian. By becoming completely bilingual, they are assured of better jobs in government service and in industry. Armenian clubs, concert halls, theatres, football teams and snack bars seem to function without much outside interference, and a number of Armenian books and periodicals continue to appear. At Rusé, I met an Armenian who is a member of the city council.

The Armenians are generally well liked by the Bulgarian public and government. They are experts in many fields of professional life and in the fine arts. They are traders, goldsmiths, watchmakers, shoemakers, technicians, photographers and lawyers. Several are renowned in Bulgaria as musicians, and I heard of more than one champion sportsman.

We have left to the last the story of Armenian settlement in Russia and in adjoining regions of Poland, despite the vital role of Russia and the Soviet Union in ensuring the corporate survival of at least part of the ancient Armenian homeland – namely the territory which comprises the modern Armenian Soviet Socialist Republic.

The origins of Armenia's connection with Russia are very ancient. Soon after the establishment of Arab rule over Armenia in AD 650, the caliphs of Damascus and then of Baghdad opened up extensive trading links with South Russia, in which Armenian merchants played a full part. The Arabs struck large quantities of silver coins in Armenia, at Dvin and elsewhere, and such silver pieces are sometimes found in hoards dug up in Russia and even further afield in the direction of Scandinavia. Around AD 944, the Russians under Varangian (Viking) leaders raided Caucasian Albania, then a province of Armenia. A medieval chronicler records with indignation:

A certain people of strange and foreign appearance called Ruzik [i.e. Russians] attacked from the lands of the north, and rushing like a tempest over the inland sea of the east, the Caspian, they reached Partaw, the capital of Albania, in not more than three days, and this city, unable to resist them, was put to the sword. They seized for themselves all the possessions of the inhabitants which took their fancy . . . The women of the town, however, devised a trick and offered the Ruzik the cup of death, but they saw through the deception and slaughtered the women and their children without mercy.[1]

During the Middle Ages, we find two large waves of Armenian immigration into the Ukraine and Poland – the first after the fall of Ani in 1064, the second following the collapse of Cilician Armenia under Mamluk attack in 1375. Russian princes of the eleventh and twelfth centuries welcomed Armenian settlers, and employed them in resisting the marauding Polovtsian steppe dwellers of 'Prince Igor' fame. The coffin of Prince Yaroslav the Wise (1016–54) is the work of an Armenian craftsman, and Prince Vladimir Monomakh (1113–25) employed an Armenian physician.

Prince Fedor Dmitrievich allowed Armenians to settle in Ruthenia and Galicia. When Prince Lev of Galicia founded the city of Lvov in 1270, he also installed Armenians there; with its cathedral and many churches, Lvov eventually became the Armenian metropolis of the Ukraine and eastern Poland. Armenians were also living in Podolia by the fourteenth century: Kamenets-Podolsky is mentioned as an important Armenian church centre in a charter of Catholicos Theodore II, dated 1390.

Many of these areas inhabited by Armenians came under Polish suzerainty during the reign of Casimir the Great (1333–70), who annexed the greater part of Galicia or 'Red Russia', and expanded Poland's international trade links, as well as proving a great protector of the cities and of the peasantry. Casimir founded the Armenian bishopric of Lvov in 1367, and allowed Armenians a large measure of self-government, including the use of the German law code. After Casimir's accidental death, Queen Jadwiga confirmed the privileges of the Armenians (1379), and her guarantees were ratified by successive Polish monarchs right up to the time of Jan III Sobieski (1674–96).

[1] Movsés Dasxuranci, *The History of the Caucasian Albanians*, trans. C. J. F. Dowsett (Oxford University Press, 1961), p. 224.

The Church of St Nicholas the Miracle-Worker at Kamenets-Podolsky dates from 1398. During the fifteenth century, Armenians fought with the Lithuanian Grand-Duke Witowt against the Teutonic Knights, and took part in the battle of Tannenberg in 1410. King Sigismund of Poland sanctioned the use by the Lvov Armenians of their own national law code, translated into Latin (1519).

Further east, Armenians settled among the Bulghars of the Volga region. In Peter the Great's time, some medieval Armenian tombstones were found in this area, and the tsar ordered them to be deciphered and studied.

During the seventeenth century, the Lvov Armenians were affected by struggles then going on between the Ukrainian Orthodox and Catholic Uniat Churches. A schism took place between the Armenian adherents of Rome and those of Holy Echmiadzin, which greatly weakened the community, although an Armenian theatre was founded in Lvov in 1668. The capture of Kamenets-Podolsky by the Turks in 1672 was a crushing blow to the Armenians resident there, many of whom were deported or killed by the invaders. Gradually, the Polish and Ukrainian Armenians lost their virtual monopoly of international trade, which was taken over by the expanding Jewish community. However, many Armenians were able to buy estates in Poland during the eighteenth century, and were ultimately assimilated into the Polish gentry class.

Armenians played a significant role in the intellectual life of Poland during the romantic revival of the nineteenth century. The poet Juljusz Slowacki (1809–49) had an Armenian mother. He died in Paris and scientific examination of his remains by anthropologists has proved that he had characteristic Armenian physical traits. In his unfinished masterpiece *Król Duch* (the spirit king) – conceived in the spirit of messianic mysticism and based on belief in metempsychosis – the poet introduces a strong Armenian element. Indeed, much of Slowacki's verse reflects the contrasting shades of the mysterious Orient.

Armenians in Poland have also distinguished themselves as painters and sculptors, and as senior ecclesiastics of the Roman Catholic Church. Some 10,000 Armenians, most of them partly assimilated, lived in Poland up to the Nazi invasion of 1939, in which many lost their lives. In recent years, there has been a revival of interest in Armenian history and culture in four Polish universities, and several interesting works on Armenia have been issued by Polish publishers.

The scene moves now to neighbouring Muscovy, later transformed by Peter the Great into the Russian Empire, and in our own time turned into the Union of Soviet Socialist Republics. The Moscow region itself was overrun during the thirteenth century by the Mongol hordes of Jenghiz Khan's successors, rendering large scale Armenian settlement there impossible. The situation changed dramatically in the fifteenth century, with the emergence of Muscovy as a world power under Ivan III, known as the Great (1462–1505). Armenian merchants gradually moved in to this new and lucrative market, and an Armenian inn was operating in the sixteenth century at an address in the 'White Town' in Moscow, not far from the present-day Dzerzhinsky Square.

This site later became the focus of an important Armenian quarter, which continues to exist today, although most residents have drifted away from the original *Armyansky pereulok* or 'Armenian lane', which still houses the Armenian SSR High Commission in Moscow.

After Tsar Aleksei Mikhailovich granted the Armenians a monopoly in the Russian silk trade (1667), they built up important depots at Astrakhan, on the Caspian Sea. In 1673, the Armenian Catholicos Hacob IV and a group of Armenian merchants appealed to Tsar Aleksei for military and political protection against their Persian overlords. The political effects of this movement were felt under Tsar Peter the Great, who saw in the Armenians valuable allies in his campaigns against the Turks and in his expansionist plans in the direction of Persia, Central Asia and India. A Karabagh Armenian named Israel Ori, who had spent many years in Europe, visited Russia in 1701 and convinced Tsar Peter of the viability of his plans for an independent Armenia under Russian protection. Peter later nominated Ori as his diplomatic agent at the Persian court in Isfahan, though he was later unmasked and expelled from Persia.

Peter the Great's large-scale invasion of north Persia in 1722 aroused great excitement among both the Armenians and the Georgians. However, the tsar's precipitate retreat from the Caspian region of Persia, due largely to Turkish diplomatic and military threats, left Russia's Christian allies in a precarious situation. The Armenians of the mountainous Karabagh region banded together under the partisan leader David Beg, and fought off assaults by the invading Turks.

Tsar Peter did not forget the Armenians, and in 1724 issued an ukase or decree according them special privileges and protection within the Russian Empire. The prosperous and enlightened Lazarev family moved to Astrakhan from New Julfa in Persia (1747), and thence to Moscow. Here they founded a cotton mill and a silk factory which prospered considerably. After Moscow was burnt down during Napoleon's invasion of 1812, the Lazarevs built a handsome college in the Armenian lane, which later became renowned as the Lazarev Institute of Oriental Languages. The Moscow Armenians had their own cemetery and memorial chapel, which still function. They worked as painters, teachers, doctors, government officials, artisans and tradesmen.

A new phase in Russian relations with the Caucasian peoples opened in 1801, when Tsar Alexander I decreed the kingdom of Eastern Georgia annexed to the Russian Empire. The Georgian capital of Tbilisi (Tiflis) had long been an important centre of Armenian settlement. An Armenian bard of the eighteenth century, Sayat-Nova, was court musician of the Georgian king Erekle II (1744–98). During the nineteenth century, the city of Tbilisi was expanded and beautified by such far-sighted Russian viceroys as Prince Vorontsov, and became a centre of trade, literature, and the theatrical and operatic arts, to which the Georgians, Armenians and Russians all contributed. The *kintos* or cockney-type barrow boys of the Tbilisi bazaar were mostly Armenians.

The Russian annexation of Georgia was followed by that of eastern or Persian Armenia, which fell to General Paskevich-Erivansky in 1827. By the Treaty of Turkmanchai, signed in 1828, the Russian frontier with Persia was fixed along the River Araxes, where it remains today. In 1836, the Tsar's government issued a regulating statute or *polozhenie*, permitting the Armenian Church to retain its lands, and Armenian schools to retain their autonomy.

Armenian hopes for a revival of their ancient national state were doomed to disappointment. The Russian authorities ruled the Erevan province like any other colonial territory in their oriental domains, and the peasantry remained very poor. An Armenian radical movement grew up, headed by Khachatur Abovian and Michael Nalbandian, both of whom died quite young in tragic circumstances.

Nonetheless, the Armenian nobility and middle classes fared very well under Russian suzerainty. General Prince Argutinsky-Dolgoruky (1798–1855) distinguished himself in the war against Imam Shamil in the mountains of Daghestan, and founded the town of Temir-Khan-Shura. A quartet of robust and able Armenians – Generals

Loris-Melikov, Lazarev, Tergukasov and Shelkovnikov – led the Russian army of the Caucasus to victory in 1877–8.[1] Several Armenian capitalists made large fortunes from exploiting the rapidly expanding oilfields of Baku, the important Caspian port and industrial centre.

During the 1880s, the favour shown to the Armenians began to evaporate. Tsar Alexander II was assassinated in 1881, and his liberal chief minister, the Armenian General Count Loris-Melikov, was dismissed by the new tsar, Alexander III. In 1884, the Russian authorities closed down the senior grades of the Armenian schools. Militant Armenians were increasingly influenced by Russian revolutionary movements and their ideologies. They founded their own Armenian Revolutionary Federation or *Dashnaktsuthiun* at Tbilisi in 1890, and pledged themselves to create a united and independent Armenia out of the territories which were then shared between the Tsarist and the Ottoman governments.

Such a programme was, predictably, as repugnant to the St Petersburg authorities as it was to the suspicious Ottoman Sultan 'Abdul Hamid. Fear of Armenian nationalism helps to explain the lack of any effective Russian intervention during 'Abdul Hamid's Armenian massacres of 1894–6. When Prince G. Golitsyn became Governor-General of the Caucasus in 1897, one of his first acts was to close down all remaining Armenian schools. In 1903, he followed this up by attempting to nationalize all Armenian Church property. When the clergy resisted, the Russian police occupied Holy Echmiadzin, seat of the Catholicos. Cossack terror led to Armenian bombings and shooting.

The 1905 Russian Revolution unleashed an upsurge of nationalism among the Georgians of the Caucasus, and terrible inter-community strife between the Armenians and the Muslim Tatars. The Governor of Baku, Prince Nakashidze, openly incited the Tatars to massacre the local Armenians, and similar excesses took place in country regions of Azerbaijan. Nakashidze was soon assassinated, but mob violence led to serious fires in the Baku oilfields. Later on, the Armenians gained the upper hand, and took revenge on the Azerbaijan Tatars.

Right up to the eve of the First World War, Tsar Nicolas II

---

[1] W.E.D. Allen and Paul Muratoff, *Caucasian Battlefields* (Cambridge, 1953), p. 546.

continued to combat Armenian nationalism. In 1912, a number of Armenian nationalists were sent to Siberia. Others joined Lenin's Bolsheviks. Among these we must name Stepan Shahumian, one of the ill-fated Baku commissars; Kamo (Ter-Petrossian), a celebrated revolutionary bank-robber; and A. I. Mikoyan, later a Soviet elder statesman. At the outbreak of war in 1914, Tsar Nicolas rather belatedly made his peace with the Armenian community in Russia, predicting a brilliant future for the Armenians in the event of a Russian victory. Such pronouncements raised false hopes, and by arousing Turkish suspicions contributed to the Ottoman holocaust of the Armenians which broke out in 1915.

For a brief period between 1915 and 1917, the Russian armies occupied virtually the whole of historical Armenia, the front line being pushed as far west as Erzinjan; the Russians also captured the Black Sea port of Trebizond. For the Armenians, this was a hollow triumph, since their erstwhile homeland had recently been depopulated with ruthless efficiency by the Young Turk junta.

After the Bolshevik Revolution of 1917, Russia withdrew from the First World War. Lenin and Trotsky signed the Treaty of Brest-Litovsk, which left the Caucasian peoples at the mercy of the Turks and their German allies. The Armenians began by forming a federation with the Georgians and the Azerbaijanis (Tartars, Azeris), but soon found themselves stabbed in the back. The Georgians even made a secret deal with the Turks, handing over the strategic fortress of Kars to the enemy.

Led by such heroic generals and partisan commanders as Nazarbekian, Dro and Silikian, the Armenians repulsed the advancing Turks at the battle of Sardarabad, to the west of Erevan, on 22–4 May 1918. The independence of the Armenian Republic was declared at Erevan on 28 May. However, the Turks bypassed the core of Armenian resistance, and captured the oilfields of Baku a few weeks before the Ottoman Empire surrendered to the Allies at the Armistice of Mudros, 30 October 1918. The Armenian partisan leader General Andranik with his division held out in the mountainous region of Zangezur until the Armistice; his services to the allied cause were acknowledged by President Poincaré, who awarded him the title of Officer of the Legion of Honour.

Independent Armenia lasted less than three years, though its symbolic importance for Armenians throughout the world was and remains incalculable. Thanks to initial British support, its territory was considerably larger than that of the present-day Armenian Soviet Socialist Republic, since it came to include Kars and Ardahan and areas of what is now eastern Turkey. But economic conditions were catastrophic. The scenes of famine and privation in the winter of 1918–19 were as bad as the horrors of 1915 in Turkey and Syria. Half a million refugees from Turkish Armenia, dressed in filthy rags or sacking, roamed the frozen land, or shivered in caves and dugouts. They were reduced to eating grass or gnawing human bones, before death released them from their misery.[1]

As they hung on desperately to their independence, the Armenians were buoyed up by the specious promises of the Western leaders as they gathered in Paris to frame the terms of the Versailles settlement. Lloyd George, Clemenceau and Woodrow Wilson vied with one another in pledging that this martyred land would never be returned to what was described as 'the blasting tyranny of the Turk'.

During 1920, the world situation changed so dramatically as to make nonsense of the promises made to Armenia by the allied powers. The war-weary British evacuated Caucasia, and the Soviets liquidated the White Russian forces of Generals Wrangel and Denikin. Broken in health, President Wilson faced a hostile Congress, bent on isolationism. The Turks under Mustafa Kemal amazed the world with their dramatic national recovery. They ejected the French from Cilicia, site of the medieval Little Armenia. Later on, in 1922, they reoccupied Smyrna (Izmir) and liquidated the British-backed Greek intervention, with great loss of life and enormous material damage.

The Turks quickly reached a secret understanding with Lenin and Trotsky in the Kremlin. In September 1920, the Turkish warlord Kiazim Karabekir Pasha crossed the old 1914 Russo–Turkish frontier, and overran the Kars district. The Bolsheviks closed in from their bases at Baku and elsewhere in Azerbaijan, and proclaimed a Soviet republic in Erevan (29 November–2 December 1920). The Armenian government, which was dominated by the Dashnak Revolutionary party, had little room for manoeuvre. Rather than embark on a futile and destructive civil war, the Dashnak leaders of independent Armenia decided to hand over power peacefully to the Bolsheviks.

Such was the doctrinaire and oppressive nature of the new regime

---

[1] Sir Harry Luke, *Cities and Men, An Autobiography* (London, 1953), vol. 2; E. St John Catchpool, *Candles in the Darkness* (London, 1966).

that the hard-pressed, starving Armenian populace staged a revolt against Soviet power early in 1921, and deposed the local soviet. But the Armenian Dashnak triumph was short-lived. In neighbouring Georgia, the Red Army conquered the local Menshevik government in February 1921. The Soviet forces then turned on Armenia once more, and Erevan was retaken from the Dashnaks on 2 April 1921. In the highland region of Zangezur, several thousand Armenian partisans continued their desperate resistance until, exhausted, they fled across the border into Persia in July.

Soviet Armenia is even smaller than independent Armenia had been, and embodies only a tenth of historical 'Great Armenia'. The cession of Kars and Ardahan to Turkey was finally confirmed by the Treaty of Kars (13 October 1921). Curiously enough, this treaty also provided that the Nakhchevan district, once an integral part of medieval Armenia but later extensively peopled by Tatar Azeris, should be attached to the Soviet Republic of Azerbaijan, based on Baku. The Nakhchevan ASSR is entirely cut off from Soviet Azerbaijan by Armenian territory and today, over half a century later, forms a much resented enclave situated between Soviet Armenia and Turkey. Similarly, Karabagh, a particularly patriotic Armenian region, was cut off from Armenia, and left as an enclave within Soviet Azerbaijan.

To wipe out local nationalism in Armenia, Georgia and Azerbaijan, Stalin merged their territories into a single Transcaucasian federation. This arrangement continued until the local leadership had been thoroughly purged by firing squad and Siberian exile. The republics did not emerge as separate entities until the promulgation of the Stalin constitution in 1936. Local nationalism was not stamped out, but only driven underground; all Soviet efforts to eliminate it have proved fruitless.

The Kremlin leadership under Stalin set out to make Transcaucasia, particularly Georgia and Armenia, a showplace. They rebuilt Armenia so that it would be a mecca for the Armenian diaspora all over the world. Foreign relief organizations, organized by high-minded individuals such as Herbert Hoover, were encouraged to accord Armenia special attention. The Leninist New Economic Policy provided a flexible framework within which the small shopkeeper and craftsman could make a modest living – until the clamp-down which attended the five-year plan campaign from 1928 onwards. Ambitious hydroelectric schemes harnessed the power potential of Lake Sevan and several rivers. Collectivization was ultimately forced

10   16th-century Armenian
lady in traditional costume.
(BBC Hulton Picture Library)

11   Armenian mountaineer in
the Caucasus, after
Vereshchagin, 1896. *(BBC
Hulton Picture Library)*

12   Armenian rural dwelling in the Caucasus, after Vereshchagin, 1896. *(BBC Hulton Picture Library)*

13 (a) and (b)   Armenian ladies in national costume, about 1910. *(D.M. Lang collection)*

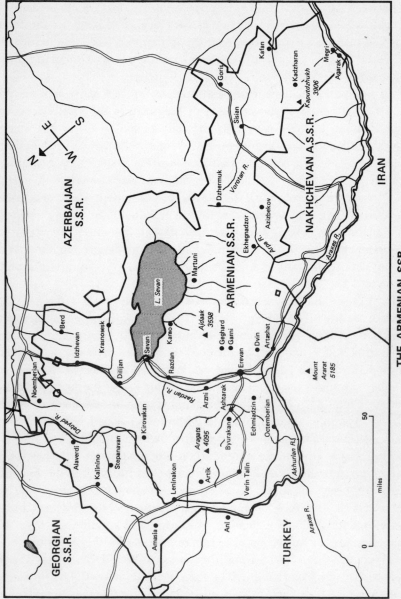

THE ARMENIAN SSR

through on the farms, and tractors and other modern machinery introduced extensively.[1]

Between 1917 and 1980, the population of the Armenian capital, Erevan, rose from a mere 34,000 to just over 1 million. In the forty years from 1940 to 1980, the overall population of the Armenian SSR increased from 1,320,000 to just over 3 million. The Armenian ethnic majority in the population is as high as 88 per cent.

An important element in the national resurgence of Armenia is the fact that Armenian is the first official language of the republic, along with Russian. Soviet Armenia is the only region in the world where official business is conducted primarily in the Armenian vernacular. The republic has a first-rate public education system. An Armenian branch of the Soviet Academy of Sciences was founded in 1935, and promoted in 1943 to the status of an independent academy. Associated with the Academy is the Byurakan Observatory, directed by Academician Viktor Hambartsumian, well known in international astronomical circles. The names of Academicians Arzumanian, Knunyants, Sisakyan and Alikhanov have also won international renown.

By Middle Eastern standards, the people are well fed, and the level of health and hygiene is high. Young people are encouraged to take part in sport and athletics. Members of the new generation are noticeably taller and better formed than their parents, who lived through the purges and the Second World War. The proportion of families owning a television set and a motor car is the highest in the Soviet Union. However, the Armenians remain devoted to their ancient Apostolic Church, and His Holiness Vazken I is certainly the most influential public figure in the entire Armenian SSR.[2]

The Soviet Union has made a colossal investment in developing Armenian agriculture and light and heavy industry. But the benefits have not been one-sided. As a group, Armenians constitute one of the cleverest and most inventive nationalities of the Soviet Union. They operate as doctors, dentists, engineers and scientists all over the country's vast territory. To take but one example, the victorious survival of the Soviet Union in the Second World War was much assisted by the remarkable MIG fighter plane, whose joint inventor was Artyom Ivanovich Mikoyan, younger brother of the veteran

[1] See the articles on the Armenian SSR in the latest *Encyclopaedia Britannica*, and in the English language *Great Soviet Encyclopaedia*, vol. 2 (New York, 1973).
[2] Mary K. Matossian, *The Impact of Soviet Policies in Armenia* (Leiden, 1962).

statesman A. I. Mikoyan. Born in 1906, Artyom Mikoyan was from 1946 onwards a pioneer of Soviet turbo-jet aviation. Such examples could be multiplied. There is no doubt that the Armenian contribution to Soviet technology is incalculable, and goes a long way towards repaying the cost of building up the Soviet Armenian homeland.

Another benefit which accrues to the Soviet government from its development of the Armenian SSR as a national homeland is good will among the majority of the widely scattered Armenian diaspora. Virtually alone among the émigré communities having a home base inside the USSR, Armenians abroad consistently remain on good terms with the organs of Soviet power. Seldom do Armenians, even in the United States, voice fundamental criticism either of communist ideology or of Soviet foreign policy. Rich Armenians, however capitalistic their attitudes and business methods, vie with one another in making gifts to the national shrine at Holy Echmiadzin, or to such institutions as the Erevan Matenadaran Manuscript Library and the Historical Museum of Armenia. They contrast the self-respect with which an Armenian can conduct himself in the Soviet Caucasus with the furtive, cringing manner which an Armenian in Turkey has to adopt in order to avoid jail or worse. They also contrast Stalin's vigorous 1945 campaign to recover some of the lost Armenian lands in eastern Turkey with the conduct of the United States and Great Britain when the Turks launched their assault on Cyprus in 1974.

Most Armenians realise that, without the iron ring of the Red Army protecting their small homeland, the Turks could overrun Soviet Armenia in a matter of hours. There may be a small and vocal dissident movement within Soviet Armenia, making capital out of the lack of certain elements of individual freedom, as this is understood in the liberal West. However, the current uncertainties of life in such traditional centres of Armenian settlement as Iran, Syria and the Lebanon make Soviet Armenia increasingly attractive as a haven to which the weary traveller is glad to return. A major preoccupation is shortage of living space – in the shape both of housing and also of agricultural land in this beautiful but largely infertile upland region.

The bustling activity in industry, agriculture, construction and cultural life in the Armenian SSR is in marked contrast to the deathly hush which prevails in the 90 per cent of historical Armenia still under the domination of the Turk – a region deliberately kept barren, depopulated and waste, a telling memorial to man's inhumanity to man.

10

Armenians in the New World

NEXT TO the Armenians of the Soviet Armenian homeland, the most important and dynamic community today is undoubtedly that of North America – the United States and Canada combined. It is one of the newest communities of any size, and certainly the richest. Since the Second World War, the colony in North America has almost trebled in numbers – from just over 200,000 to a figure between half a million and 600,000. The Armenians of North America provide political muscle and financial sinews to sustain the institutional life and the morale of hard-pressed Armenians throughout the world today.

So far as we know, the Armenians played no part in evolving the vanished civilization of the Aztecs, nor did any Armenians stow away in the ships of Christopher Columbus – although with Armenians one must always be prepared for surprises.[1] The earliest recorded Armenian settlers came over to America from 1607 onwards, in the wake of the pioneer colonist of Virginia, Captain John Smith (1579–1631). They were experts in the manufacture of such items as silk, tar, and

[1] One such surprise was contained in a letter from Mr James H. Tashjian of Boston, Mass., dated 15 December 1976, in which he referred to a manuscript journal written by an Armenian bishop of the fifteenth century, and preserved in the Bibliothèque Nationale in Paris. This bishop 'seems to have accompanied Columbus on his second voyage to the New World'. When the journal is published, we shall be able to evaluate this startling claim.

also glass beads and trinkets suitable for bartering with the local Indians. Records of Virginia around 1620 refer to the death of a certain Zorobabel – presumably, Zohrab Abel – and also to the business affairs of a tobacco-grower called Martin the Armenian.

Later in the seventeenth century, in 1653, the English Puritan governor of Virginia, Edward Digges, invited two Armenians over from Turkey to advise his planters on the culture of the silkworm. Digges had learnt of the Armenians' skill in sericulture from his father, who served as British Ambassador in Russia. So successful was this venture that in December 1656 the Assembly of the State of Virginia passed a resolution in the following terms :

> That George the Armenian for his encouragement in the trade of silk and to stay in the country to follow the same have 4,000 pounds of tobacco allowed him by the Assembly.

A poet named John Ferrar had written some verses to celebrate the arrival of the two Armenian silk growers :

> But noble Diggs carries the Bell away.
> (Lass ! want of eggs made small the great essay);
> His two Armenians from Turkey sent
> Are now most busy on his brave attempt,
> And he had stock sufficient for next yeare
> Ten thousand pounds of Silk would then appeare
> And to the skies his worthy deeds upreare.[1]

It is satisfying to learn that the enterprising Puritan Digges and his two Armenians made such a solid contribution to the prosperity of Virginia – a contribution which helped to inspire rhapsodical rhymes like the following :

> Where Wormes and Food doe naturally abound
> A gallant Silken Trade must there be found.
> Virginia excels the world in both –
> Envie nor malice can gaine say this troth !

Diligent search fails to unearth any traces of significant Armenian activity in America during the eighteenth century.

The picture changes abruptly after the arrival of American missionaries in Turkey from 1831 onwards. Originally hoping to convert the Muslim Turks to American Protestantism, the missionaries soon found

[1] Quoted with permission from James H. Tashjian, *The Armenians of the United States and Canada* (Boston, 1947), pp. 6–7.

this aim to be both impracticable and dangerous. The Muslim Turks almost to a man scornfully rejected all American missionary blandishments, and any stray convert was promptly stoned to death by a fanatical mob led by furious mullahs.

The American missionaries soon turned their attention to the Christian minority peoples of the Ottoman Empire, such as the Maronites, the Greeks and the Armenians.

Among the Turkish Armenians, the American Board of Foreign Missions found a fertile soil awaiting cultivation. A literary and educational renaissance was in progress among the Constantinople Armenians, as it was soon to be among their kinsmen in Russian Armenia to the east. Many Armenians were unsettled and restive following the successful Greek War of Liberation, which had done nothing towards freeing the Armenian homeland itself. Young Armenians resented the inferior status of native Christians in the Ottoman Empire, and the continuing supremacy of the Constantinople Armenian patriarchate, with its supporting clique of conservative, prosperous, largely pro-Turkish *amiras*, as the notables were called. Thus young Armenians found American democratic, go-ahead ideas rather congenial, and listened with interest to stories about the Declaration of Independence and the Rights of Man.

From modest early beginnings sprang a network of American colleges and schools scattered throughout the Ottoman Empire. Among the best known of these was Robert College at Constantinople, the American college at Smyrna, and Anatolia College at Marsovan.

As often happens in such circumstances, these missionary efforts encountered resistance, and aggravated latent racial and sectarian tensions. Very many Armenians, even today, consider that membership of the Armenian Apostolic Church centred on Holy Echmiadzin and on Antelias in the Lebanon is the essential factor in being a genuine Armenian. Some would go so far as to think that any Armenian who quits the Apostolic Church should be thrown out of the community as a renegade. (Hence the traditional Armenian opposition to mixed marriages.) The Armenian Church hierarchy in the Ottoman Empire felt itself threatened by the self-confident American newcomers, and reacted to their overtures with open hostility. The Americanized Armenian for his part could become alienated from his traditionalist kinsmen, and, even more, from the backward indigenous Turkish population.

Let no one underrate, however, the great value and importance of the Protestant contribution to the modern Armenian revival. Few today would dare assert that the Protestant Armenian is a jot less patriotic than his Apostolic counterpart. The Armenian Missionary Association of America, now centred at Paramus, New Jersey, supports many worthy Armenian causes throughout the world, including Haigazian College, one of Beirut's leading university institutions.[1]

To revert now to the era of the 1830s, the pioneer American missionary efforts soon resulted in a trickle of Armenian visitors and permanent immigrants to the United States. Outstanding among these was Khachadour Osganian, a pupil of the missionary school near Constantinople. Osganian graduated from the City College of New York, which has itself, one and a half centuries later, become an active centre of Armenian intellectual life in America. Osganian became a feature writer on the *New York Herald-Tribune*, and was ultimately elected President of the New York Press Club. He had connections with Columbia University, and was appointed Custodian of the Library of Jurisprudence there. Osganian's articles introduced the Armenians to American readers as the 'Yankees of the Near East', while other articles of his, printed in Constantinople, enlightened the Turkish reader on the unfamiliar world of American life and thought.

Armenians soon began attending other leading American universities, including Princeton and Yale, also the Union Theological Seminary. The future physician and inventor Christopher Der Seropian entered Yale in 1843, and is credited with inaugurating the 'class book' system at that university. It was Der Seropian who discovered and patented the black and green dyes used today in manufacturing American paper currency. The US Treasury was plagued at that time by a wave of counterfeit banknotes produced by nimble forgers, so Der Seropian's patent dye process was bought up by the American government, though it paid him a ludicrously small sum for his important invention.

Between 1850 and 1870, several scores of Turkish Armenian families came over to settle in the United States, while other Armenians came as migrant workers and then returned home to Anatolia. The Armenians made their contribution to the Union war effort during the American Civil War. Thirty Armenians fought in the Northern armies, while three Armenian doctors tended the wounded in hospitals at Philadelphia.

[1] See G. H. Chopourian, *The Armenian Evangelical Reformation: Causes and Effects* (New York, 1972).

Hagop Mataosian, who built up the largest printing house in the Ottoman Empire, came over to America at this period to learn modern methods of printing from American experts, and then returned to Constantinople to put this specialist knowledge to practical use.

By 1894, the period of Sultan 'Abdul Hamid's first Armenian massacres, an estimated 5,000 Armenians had arrived in the United States. They were centred at first in the New England area and around New York, and only later settled in large numbers in the Detroit region of the Middle West. To give some idea of the makeup of those early communities, we may note that in Boston in 1885 there lived just nine Armenians – two students, an artist, a storekeeper, a rug merchant, a machinist, a copper worker, and a jewellery worker and his wife.

The early migration of Armenians to the Far West is largely associated with the Californian city of Fresno, birthplace of William Saroyan, which I visited in 1965. Situated in the heart of the San Joaquin Valley, Fresno was laid out as a township in 1872, when the railroad came through the country. Its climate, subtropical in the summer months, is ideal for fruit and vine growing.

An Armenian from the east coast, Hagop Seropian, visited Fresno in 1881 when travelling in California for health reasons. He wrote home with enthusiasm to his kinsfolk at Marsovan in the depths of Anatolian Turkey about the wonderful fruit and vegetables he found growing there – grapes as big as eggs, ten-pound eggplants, and boat-sized watermelons. It was not many months before a team of hardy Armenian husbandmen descended on the young town of Fresno, having sailed the Atlantic and travelled rough over the entire North American continent. They set out to make Fresno a veritable Garden of Eden, and it is in large part due to Armenian expertise that the district has prospered from that day to the present time. The centenary of Armenian settlement in Fresco is being celebrated in 1981.

The stability and self-confidence of the budding Armenian community in America were enhanced by the foundation of the first Armenian Apostolic Church establishment in the country – built in Worcester, Massachusetts, in 1891. The pastor of the church, Father Hovsep Sarajian, came from Holy Echmiadzin, and was the first Armenian clergyman in America to head a permanent parish community. Only seven years later, in 1898, the Armenian Apostolic Church of America became a separate diocese, with its own bishop, having authority over thirty separate church communities.

Worcester was also the site of the first Armenian Protestant church, called the Church of the Holy Martyrs, set up there in 1892. From these modest beginnings sprang a many-faceted religious organization, today numbering several Apostolic archbishoprics and episcopal sees, and well over a hundred churches and chapels of several denominations, all spread over the United States and Canada, not to mention the vigorous and fast-growing Armenian church organizations of various countries of South America.

A new era of American sympathy for the Armenian cause, accompanied by organized Armenian immigration into the United States, was triggered off by the savage massacres perpetrated by Sultan 'Abdul Hamid between 1894 and 1896. The reign of terror inaugurated by this sadistic ruler made it clear to many Armenian families that their only salvation lay in quitting the Anatolian homeland once for all. In 1899, however, the Sultan prohibited any further Armenian emigration from Turkey, and this embargo continued until the Young Turk revolution of 1908. Emigration was then resumed, until the outbreak of the First World War in 1914.

Immigration records tell us that during the two periods in question, namely 1895–9 and 1908–14, a total of 70,982 Armenians entered the United States. This is by far the most concentrated era of Armenian immigration into North America. The customs and attitudes of the American Armenian community continue to this day to be dominated by the traditional ways of Armenian old-timers from the Anatolian homeland, whose grandchildren now occupy posts of responsibility in the American community.

Several thousand Armenians served with the American armed forces during the First World War, while Armenians in the Middle East formed a special brigade to help General Allenby in his struggle against the Turks in the Levant. The pioneer plastic surgeon, Varaztad Kazanjian (1879–1974), jointed the Harvard Medical Unit in 1915. His success in reconstructing the shattered features of wounded and disfigured allied soldiers earned him the British order of Companion of the Order of St Michael and St George (CMG). Lieut.-Colonel H. Malejian was another of the American army's outstanding surgeons.

Between 1915 and 1922, the Young Turk dictators and their successors, the Kemalists, virtually completed the work begun by Sultan 'Abdul Hamid. At least a million and a half Armenians had perished during the genocide organized by Interior Minister Talaat Pasha. The survivors fled as best they could, some to what is now Soviet Armenia, others to Iran, Syria and the Lebanon. The Arab

Middle East, then under British and French mandate, proved rather attractive to displaced Armenians, who built up a new homeland centred on Beirut.

This fact, combined with the new restrictions on immigration imposed by the US Congress in 1924, helps to explain the rather small scale of Armenian immigration into the United States immediately following the First World War. Between 1920 and 1931 only 26,146 Armenians are recorded as permanent entrants to the USA, of whom 4,770 went to Massachusetts, others to New York, Detroit, Chicago, and to California.

The first generation immigrants of the period between 1895 and 1925 were mostly bewildered and distressed victims of persecution. They were handicapped by poor knowledge of English, and of American go-ahead manners and ideas. They had to struggle to survive, and achieved success and recognition the hard way.

Armenians soon proved themselves to be skilled and conscientious workers, and gained employment in shoe factories, woollen mills, and in the fast-growing automobile plants of Detroit, Pontiac and Flint, Michigan. They manufactured such diverse articles as shirts, aluminium goods, candy, wire and machine tools, as well as working as miners in the Pennsylvania coalfields. Armenian business aptitude showed itself in the establishment of numerous stores, some selling Near Eastern foods and spices, others oriental carpets.

During the 1920s a period of isolationist reaction set in throughout North America. The much canvassed plan for an American mandate over the former Turkish Armenia had come to nothing.[1] The Kemalists staged a spectacular comeback, and inflicted humiliating reverses on French, British and Greek invading forces.

Within the United States, the generous impulses of the Wilson era gave way to a phase of provincial petty-mindedness, of which such enactments as the immigration quotas and the self-righteous prohibition laws were typical symptoms. Congress and the public joined in spurning the League of Nations. President Harding entertained his lady friends in the White House itself, while his aides outside profited from shady deals such as that of the 'Teapot Dome' concession.[2] Those in the know enriched themselves by speculating on Wall Street,

[1] James B. Gidney, *A Mandate for Armenia* (Kent State University Press, Ohio, 1967); Gregory L. Aftandilian, 'The American Committee for the Independence of Armenia, 1918–1927' (unpublished thesis, Dartmouth College, 1979).

[2] See the memoirs of Harding's last mistress, quoted in British Sunday newspapers.

until the crash of 1929 brought their house of cards tumbling to the ground. In far off Istanbul, the vain and opportunistic US High Commissioner Admiral Mark Bristol was cultivating the favour of the new Kemalist regime, and denouncing the dispossessed Armenians and Greeks as troublesome agitators.

The 1920s were a period of hardship for underprivileged immigrant groups in America, especially those from Near Eastern countries. The Armenians were regarded with resentment in cities like Fresno, where they formed a sizeable and long-established element. Old-timers have told me distressing stories of incidents in Fresno schools of that period, when Armenian boys – sometimes called 'Black Armenians' – were assaulted, kicked around and otherwise made to feel thoroughly unwelcome. In some cities, Armenians were obliged to live 'beyond the railroad tracks', and condemned to a ghetto existence.

During the 1930s, under President Roosevelt's New Deal administration, the mood of the country improved. The struggle for jobs became less acute, and hostility towards recent immigrants abated.

The Armenians were by now in a stronger position than in the immediate post-war era. Many families had risen in the social scale from being factory or farm workers to occupying professional and business positions. A new generation of English-speaking, college-educated Armenians was making its voice heard in the counsels of the American Armenian community. Political parties which had been largely extirpated by the Young Turks and the Russian communists revived in the democratic atmosphere of America, and founded branches in New York, Boston and California. Newspapers and magazines were by now regularly appearing, both in Armenian and in English.

One man in particular created a revolution in American attitudes towards Armenians. That man is William Saroyan, born in Fresno in 1908, and still going strong. While one or two members of the Armenian intelligentsia abroad, such as Michael Arlen, Sr., tried to conceal their Armenian past, Saroyan gloried in it. His whimsical stories and plays frankly and constructively tackled the pressures faced by members of a small, exotic immigrant community, and came up with a message of hope that all would be well in the long run. Saroyan's work and personality played a great role in popularizing the Armenian community not only in America but also internationally.

The same can be said of that prodigious film director and drama producer Rouben Mamoulian, born in 1897. The sight of Mamoulian's name blazoned all over Hollywood and Broadway was a great boost to community self-confidence. The fact that an Armenian director produced one of Greta Garbo's best films, *Queen Christina*, was a major event in Armenian cultural history.

Armenian participation in America's Second World War struggle was on a greater scale than it was during the First World War. (Armenian bravery was a material factor in the success of Soviet arms between 1941 and 1945.) At least 20,000 Armenian men and women wore the uniforms of the US army, navy and air force, and about five hundred lost their lives. The first American soldier to die in the invasion of North Africa was an Armenian, Lieutenant Koushnarian. Armenians died at Omaha Beach, in the crossing of the Rhine, and in the drive through Germany in 1945, while others perished in the fight against Japan. Lieutenant Ernest Dervishian was awarded the Congressional Medal of Honour. Several Armenians distinguished themselves as air force pilots.

The highest ranking Armenian-born soldier in the US army during this war was Brigadier General Haig Shekerjian (1886–1966), who served as Commanding Officer of the Chemical Warfare Training Center at Camp Sibert. A noted expert on poison gases, Shekerjian was an effective orator, and often spoke in support of the American war effort. It is worth quoting from a speech which he made in June 1945, at a War Bond rally in Chicago:

Armenians who have come to this country have become fine Americans – they have upheld the doctrines of this nation – they have shown that they possess the true feeling of Americanism. Our late President, Franklin D. Roosevelt, once said that Americanism is not a matter of race or creed, but a matter of the heart. That is the human denominator by which all men, great and small, rich and poor, are reduced to a level of equality – one enjoying the same privilege as the other – each feeling his right to freedom and his access to justice. Americanism is not necessarily in the man who carries the biggest flag or in the man who is most lavish in his charities, but in the individual who, like you, feels in his heart the importance, and the pride, and the privilege of being an American.[1]

It was characteristic of Brigadier General Shekerjian that after the conclusion of hostilities he accepted the post of chief European repre-

[1] James H. Tashjian, *The Armenian American in World War II*, p. 159.

sentative of the Armenian National Committee to Aid Homeless Armenians. Between 1948 and 1951, working at his headquarters near Stuttgart, Shekerjian managed to resettle the majority of the 3,500 displaced Armenians who had been stranded in Germany at the end of the war. Almost three thousand of these found haven in the United States, while others went to South America and the Near East.

Since the Second World War, the Armenian community in the United States and Canada has almost trebled in numbers. In professional status and in wealth and influence, the advance has been even more noteworthy. In 1947, Mr James Tashjian listed some sixty Armenians in America whom he considered deserving of *Who's Who* status – they included physicians and surgeons, atomic scientists, industrialists, administrators, actors and singers, writers and scholars, vintners, restaurant owners, painters and sculptors.[1] If Mr Tashjian were to update his Armenian *Who's Who* today, he would have to include several hundred entries to do justice to the talent available.

To begin with medical science, we may note that Armenians in the United States have fully maintained that eminence which they earlier attained in Ottoman Turkey, Persia and Russia. Dr Varaztad Kazanjian, whom we mentioned as tending disfigured soldiers in the First World War, ended his career as a past president of the American Association of Plastic Surgeons and Professor Emeritus of Plastic Surgery at Harvard University; he died full of honours in 1974, at the age of ninety-five. Kazanjian's humanitarian tradition of public service is carried on by such surgeons as Dr John S. Najarian (born 1927), Chairman of the Department of Surgery at the University of Minnesota Medical School. Dr Najarian's pioneering work in kidney transplant surgery has given new life to hundreds of sufferers, saving them from painful degeneration and early death.

This is also the place to mention the experimental work of Dr Raymond Damadian, a native New Yorker, who had headed the science group at the State University of New York in Brooklyn. In 1973, it was announced that Dr Damadian was on the way to evolving a new diagnostic technique for cancer. In his view, nuclear magnetic resonance (or NMR) might replace X-ray and the pictorial anatomy which it provides, supplying instead a type of chemical anatomy of the body. Already this NMR method can be used to detect cancer in surgically excised tumours. Since early diagnosis is vital for successful treatment of cancer, the value of NMR lies in the hope which it holds

1 James Tashjian, *The Armenians of the United States and Canada*, pp. 29–35.

out for the detection of a malignant tumour just when it is forming.

Apart from medicine, Armenians are strongly represented throughout American scientific and technical institutions, research organizations and university departments. They excel, as they do also in Soviet Armenia, in the fields of mathematics, computer sciences, physics and nuclear physics, chemistry and biochemistry. An Armenian physicist, Dr G. K. Daghlian, lost his life through exposure to radiation when working on America's atomic energy research programme. Vazken Parsegian of the Rensselaer Institute is author of many important physics papers. Armig Kandoian served as Director of the US Office of Telecommunications. Emik Avakian, though handicapped by cerebral palsy, made valuable contributions to the field of computer systems.[1]

Armenians are quick to make use of scientific research for commercial and industrial progress. Outstanding in this respect is Mr Alex Manoogian, President of the Detroit MASCO Corporation, and Life President of the Armenian General Benevolent Union, who has already given away more money for charitable purposes than most millionaires make in their entire lifetime.

Also important are the Sarkes Tarzian electronic factory in Bloomington, Indiana, and the Mardigian Corporation in Detroit. Harry Kuljian of Philadelphia built up a large firm engaged in plant designing and the building of chemical and industrial processing works. In 1950 Mr Kuljian invented a revolutionary machine for spinning rayon. He celebrated this success by endowing two open scholarships at the School of Humanities and Social Studies of the Massachusetts Institute of Technology.

A link between the industrial world and that of popular entertainment is provided by the Zildjian family of Quincy, Massachusetts, who manufacture cymbals for the international music market. I recently had evidence of the popularity of these cymbals when I found myself sitting in a London public house opposite a pleasant young man wearing a T-shirt with the inscription: 'Avedis Zildjian: Genuine Turkish cymbals. Made in USA.' The cymbals are made by a secret metallurgical process, and are esteemed equally by symphony orchestras and jazz musicians all over the world.

The Armenians have a long tradition of ballad singing and musical improvisation. In the Middle Ages, there were many travelling

[1] Arra S. Avakian, *The Armenians in America* (Lerner Publications, Minneapolis, 1977), p. 65.

minstrels of great talent, called *gusans* and *ashughs*.[1] This heritage has been put to effective use in contemporary American show business.

A true modern *ashugh* is Cathy Berberian, who is both an accomplished mimic and a versatile, talented singer. In the field of television, we may cite the names of Arlene Frances (Kazanjian), Cher (Sarkisian) of Sonny and Cher, and Kay Armen (Manoogian). The television personality Mike Connors is in fact an Armenian named Krekor Ohanian, from Fresno, California. For many years he played the part of Joe Mannix in a 'private detective' series which had the longest continuous run of any comparable programme.

The versatile David Hedison (Heditsian) is equally in demand for television and film engagements. One of his big breaks came when Sir Michael Redgrave engaged him to play in Turgenev's *A Month in the Country* at the Phoenix Theatre, London. He is currently under contract to 20th Century Fox.[2] Among Hollywood film makers, Richard C. Sarafian occupies a prominent place. He is still going strong, in 1980, though his latest production, *Sunburn,* set among the wealthy socialites of Acapulco, had only moderate notices after its London première. We reserve discussion of Rouben Mamoulian's unique contribution to drama and the cinema for the chapter, 'Armenians and the Arts World-wide'.

Being a highly articulate people, Armenians excel in the mass media, including journalism and literature. Roger Tartarian became Vice-President of United Press International, before taking up the post of Professor of Journalism at California State University, Fresno. Barry Zorthian served as President of Time-Life Cable Communications. The bold, crusading articles of Ben Bagdikian, formerly of Providence, Rhode Island, have been widely syndicated.

When we turn to public service and administration, we should first mention Paul R. Ignatius, who served as Secretary of the Navy from 1967 to 1969. Steven Derounian (New York) sat in the House of Representatives from 1963 to 1964, as has Adam Benjamin (Indiana) from 1976 onwards. Several Armenians have become successful deans and provosts of leading American universities.

Armenians possess a natural aptitude for the law, having both astute brains and a love of eloquence and argument. Charles Garry of San Francisco (born 1909) has defended many well-known clients, as well

---

1 D. M. Lang, *Armenia, Cradle of Civilization*, pp. 253–5.
2 *Armenian Weekly*, Boston, 9 Feb. 1980, p. 9.

as providing legal counsel for groups active in social struggles. Robert Mardian served in the Justice Department during the ill-fated Nixon administration. When attending an Armenian Church convention at Detroit in 1978, I met several Armenian judges and attorneys regarded as successful members of the American legal profession. Currently, in 1980, George Deukmejian is Attorney-General of the state of California.

Some Armenians have had several careers in a single lifetime – as, for instance, the multi-millionaire Kirk Kerkorian, who started as operator of a charter airline, then went in for real estate, and now controls Western Airlines, as well as the MGM studios in Hollywood.

Achievement in sport is a sure route to acceptance in American society, and here the tough and wiry young Armenians have been markedly successful. All over the country, Armenians play an active part in football, athletics, swimming and baseball. Armenian patriotic associations organize summer camps for students and schoolchildren of various ages, in which outdoor pursuits play a large part. Fitness is the order of the day. A shining example has been given by the football trainer Ara Parseghian, from 1963 to 1974 head coach of the Notre Dame football team.[1]

Some old-timers in the United States and Canada regret that many young Armenians no longer speak Armenian at home, and have ceased to read or even understand their native language fluently. They fear that the Armenian community is rapidly becoming assimilated into the general fabric of American society, and will eventually lose its characteristic ethnic flavour and traditions.

However, visits which I have paid to Armenian communities in America and other parts of the world lead me to a different conclusion. During the early days of Armenian immigration into North America, it was considered of prime importance to become integrated into the dominant English-speaking community. Possession of a foreign accent and addiction to alien ways and ideas were frowned upon. Obviously, the shocked and wretched survivors of the 'Abdul Hamid and Young Turk massacres were happy to seek refuge in America on any terms whatever, and were anxious to shed as soon as possible the quaint Near Eastern characteristics which marked them out as recent immigrants from a rather despised and backward part of the world.

[1] More details, with a photograph of Parseghian, in Avakian, *The Armenians in America*, p. 66.

Over the past twenty years, there has been a dramatic change of attitude towards the ethnic groups which make up much of American society. It is now considered natural, indeed praiseworthy, to take pride in one's remote ancestors – the cult of 'Roots' is almost universally accepted, and not only among the Black community. The idea that a person may be a loyal American and simultaneously a committed member of a national group – be it Polish, Hungarian, Greek or Armenian – is taken for granted. This new attitude is well typified by the book *Passage to Ararat* (1975) written by Michael Arlen Jr, in which he relates how he came to identify himself with his forebears and accept with pride his national heritage.

The American Armenians now constitute the largest community outside the Soviet Armenian homeland, and have excellent growth prospects. They have acquired US passports and citizenship, and make their voices heard in Congress, in the Administration in Washington, and via the mass media of press and television. At the federal capital, there is an all-party pressure group called the Armenian Assembly, which keeps the national question a live issue in Congress and the counsels of the government.

Now that they are quite rich, Armenian patriotic organizations can do much to support education in the national medium. Two main groups – the Armenian General Benevolent Union of New York and the radical Hairenik Association of Boston – support a chain of voluntary schools, in which a sound general education is combined with instruction in Armenian language, history and culture. In 1978, I spent a morning at the Alex Manoogian school in Southfield, Michigan, where a high level of general education is maintained, along with a strongly motivated interest in the national heritage.

The Armenian community has also had success in sponsoring study programmes in leading universities, including Harvard, Columbia, Pennsylvania, Ann Arbor, and the University of California at Berkeley and Los Angeles. The university posts are mostly filled by ethnic Armenians, and rather too little effort has been made to encourage non-Armenian historians and linguists to interest themselves in this important field of study. At the moment, it is definitely a situation of 'jobs for the boys'.

Armenian journalism in both North and South America has continued to expand during recent years. We see a shift of the concentration of the Armenian press in the diaspora, until recently centred in the now trouble-torn Lebanon. Today, twenty-four newspapers and magazines – in either Armenian or English, and sometimes both – appear in the USA, as against only nine in the Lebanon. Thirteen of these are issued in the Los Angeles area.[1]

Major Armenian language dailies are *Baikar* (Watertown), *Hairenik* (Boston), *Asbarez* (Los Angeles) and the semi-weekly *Nor Or* (Los Angeles). The most important English-language papers are the *Armenian Weekly* (Armenian Revolutionary Federation, Boston), *Armenian Reporter* (Independent, New York), *Armenian Mirror-Spectator* (Democratic Liberal, Boston), *Armenian Observer* (Los Angeles), and *California Courier* (Los Angeles). There has recently been an upsurge of Armenian journalism in Canada, with the English-language weekly *Horizon* (Armenian Revolutionary Federation) and the Armenian-language weekly *Abaka* (Democratic Liberal).

Whether this proliferation is wholly advantageous to the community at large is debatable. Some Armenian journalists engage in polemics and partisan skirmishes with one another, and the long-term interests of the Armenian diaspora might be better served by fewer but better organs. On the other hand, local Armenian newspapers have a valuable role to play in announcing community events, publicising cultural activities, and the like.

Healthy though the general picture is when we look at the North American Armenian situation, it would be much improved if there were some prospect of national unity. In spite of recent setbacks in Iran and the Lebanon, the divisions and rivalries within the community are at best only papered over.

The split is seen most clearly when we examine the structure of the Armenian Apostolic Church in North America, which is at present divided into two hostile hierarchies – although they profess exactly the same religious doctrine. The larger and older hierarchy pays allegiance to the Supreme Catholicos of all the Armenians resident at Echmiadzin in Soviet Armenia. The newer, smaller but fast-growing hierarchy adheres to the Catholicos of the Great House of Cilicia, now residing at Antelias, a suburb of Beirut. Out of an estimated ninety Apostolic churches in the USA and Canada, I have been informed that about sixty acknowledge the supremacy of Echmiadzin and thirty that of Antelias.

The origins of this schism go back over more than half a century, to the invasion of Independent Armenia by the Red Army in 1920, the

[1] Serge Samoniantz, 'An Overview of the Armenian press in the Diaspora', in *Armenian Weekly*, Boston, 9 Feb. 1980, p. 4.

fall of the local Dashnak Radical-Nationalist government, and the subsequent persecution of the Armenian Church by Stalin and Beria's League of Militant Godless. The American Dashnaks (Armenian Revolutionary Federation) were justifiably unhappy with the situation in the communist-dominated mother church of Echmiadzin, whose head was murdered by the Bolsheviks in 1938. A leading Armenian cleric was also murdered in New York, by an Armenian nationalist fanatic.

As a climax to this unrest, the Dashnak Party of America helped to provoke a split in the Armenian Church in 1956, by fostering the election as Catholicos of Cilicia resident in Antelias of the subservient Bishop Zareh of Aleppo. This 'election' was marked by widespread intimidation and 'dirty work'. After this, the Armenian Liberals and the Manoogian interests which dominate the Armenian General Benevolent Union remained loyal to Holy Echmiadzin, where the Armenian Bishop of Romania, Vazken, assumed office as Supreme Catholicos in 1955. Such was the rancour and bitterness unleashed by the Dashnaks and their foes that Catholicos Zareh had a heart attack and died in 1963, at the early age of forty-eight. 'Stop us eating one another!' exclaimed an elderly Armenian when I visited Aleppo in Syria in 1979. I promised to try, but there was little I could do, seeing that I was myself ejected from the AGBU Club a few hours later, through a bomb scare apparently organized by local Armenian Dashnak hooligans.

From 1956, the Armenian Revolutionary Federation (Dashnaks) have been encouraging adherents of Holy Echmiadzin to transfer their allegiance to the Cilician Catholicosate at Antelias. The situation is rather like that of the Roman Catholic Church during the Middle Ages, when there were two rival popes, one in Rome, the other at Avignon. The split is intensified by the fact that the Armenian Church is traditionally a social club as well as a place of worship – there are classrooms for Sunday school, gymnasiums for athletic activities, and halls for meetings of the church community, often serving refreshments. Thus the schism has taken on a political and even a class aspect, with the more solid, conservative elements favouring the Church based in Soviet Armenia, strange to say, and the young radicals backing Antelias.

While friends of Armenia must regret the tense atmosphere resulting from the mutual boycott of each other's activities imposed by the rival congregations, there are two important points to be made. The first is that the existence of a well-organized alternative focus of the

Apostolic Church in the Lebanon must be a powerful deterrent to the Kremlin anti-God officials, any time they may contemplate repressive action against the Armenian Church in the Soviet Caucasus. Secondly, such is the self-centred and materialist outlook of some sections of the US Armenian 'establishment' that the prevailing competition on the religious and social front may administer a healthy jolt to their complacency.

Better disciplined and less quarrelsome than their Apostolic brethren are the Armenian Protestants and Catholics in North America, where four Catholic and twenty-six Protestant churches currently operate. These two groups have an excellent record of church attendance and an exemplary standard of intellectual attainments and pride in the national heritage.

In addition to the North American contingent, there exist substantial colonies in South America, particularly in Uruguay, Venezuela, Brazil and the Argentine Republic. The total is estimated at about 120,000, and is on the increase as immigrants arrive from strife-torn Lebanon and Iran. These Armenians rapidly learn Spanish or Portuguese as their second language, and have many churches, including Protestant and Catholic ones. They issue several newspapers and magazines.

I I

Armenian Cooking

A S A RESULT of the world-wide dispersion of the Armenian people, it is now possible for non-Armenians also to enjoy Armenian cooking in many parts of the world. Excellent Armenian restaurants exist in Beirut and Teheran, in London and Manchester, and in several American cities, including Boston, New York and Los Angeles. In Armenian Church communities all over the world, ladies of Armenian mothers' guilds band together to produce national delicacies for consumption at receptions, weddings, religious festivals, children's outings and other occasions.

It is sometimes easier for the foreigner to sample Armenian cooking in the diaspora than in the national homeland in the Armenian Soviet Socialist Republic. The Armenian in his native land is second to none for hospitality, but it is not always possible for the average tourist to arrange to be invited into private homes, either in Soviet Armenia or elsewhere. In Erevan, capital of the Armenian SSR, the expert chefs of the Armenia and Ani hotels are perfectly capable of laying on a banquet in national style. But such is the relentless pressure from the Intourist organization that they are often forced to serve busloads of jaded travellers with tasteless chunks of Soviet meat, fried in large batches, and garnished with insipid Soviet chips.

There are one or two fine Armenian restaurants in Moscow itself. Often they are closed down, ostensibly for repairs and redecoration. When they are functioning, the excellence of the cuisine is such that the Muscovites themselves queue up outside the doors in large numbers, and you have to exercise great patience and diplomacy to secure admission.

Authentic Armenian cooking depends on the availability of a number of basic, health-giving natural food products, including fresh vegetables, fruit, herbs and meat. Armenia has been noted from ancient times for the high quality of its home-bred lamb, providing material for shashlik and kebabs of exceptional flavour and succulence. Apricots and cherries both originated in Armenia. In modern times, cucumbers, melons and tomatoes flourish in the Araxes valley.

Archaeological excavations enable us to take the history of food production in Armenia back into prehistoric times. At Shengavit, close to Erevan, partly charred stores of mixed wheat and barley grain have been recovered from buildings which were burnt down in Antiquity. This scorched grain is about five thousand years old, and dates from the Early Bronze Age.

Other excavations, in Armenian sites occupied by the Urartians around 700 BC, have uncovered remains of coarse-milled flour, plums, apples, pomegranates, and also water-melon seeds. Finds of cut apples and raisins show that dried fruit was already being preserved for winter use. All Urartian citadels had enormous wine stores, with large earthenware vessels buried up to their shoulders in the cellar floor. At one military centre, Teishebaini, close to Erevan, there were three wine cellars, with total capacity for as much as 170,000 litres of wine.

It is interesting to read the classic description of Armenian food given by the Greek soldier of fortune Xenophon, who led his Ten Thousand through Armenia in 401–400 BC. The local Armenians treated the Greek troops very well, and they enjoyed loaves of wheat and barley, and dishes of lamb, kid, pork, veal and poultry. There were plenty of raisins and beans. These delicacies they washed down, so Xenophon tells us, with old wines with a fine bouquet and with barley wine, which they drank through straw tubes.

Thus, modern Armenian cooking is rooted in ancient traditions of food technology, gastronomy and hospitality characteristic of the Caucasian and Anatolian region, the scene of the original Armenian homeland. The original nucleus of local recipes has been greatly enriched over the centuries, as Armenians have settled in the cities of the East, of Western Europe, and even further afield. Particularly fruitful was the influence of Georgian cuisine, which Armenians have got to know during the hundreds of years during which they have made up a large element of such Georgian cities as Tbilisi (Tiflis), Gori and Akhaltsikhe.

The industrious Armenian population of the Ottoman capital at Constantinople attained a high level of sophistication in catering.

They owned and ran the Tokatlian Hotel there. Since the Seljuq Turks overran Great Armenia as early as AD 1064, it is hardly surprising that Armenian and Turkish cooking overlap to a great degree and it is a waste of time to inquire too closely as to who invented which familiar dish, and who borrowed what from whom. There is also considerable interaction between Armenian and Syrian Arab cuisine, as I discovered when visiting Damascus and Aleppo in November 1979.

If one travels around the Balkans, one also finds many dishes – kebabs, yogurt, cucumber dishes and various salads, and also baklava pastry dessert – which remind one of Armenia. Here again there is a long tradition of cultural and culinary intermingling, as Armenians were settled in Bulgaria, as well as in Cyprus, by the Byzantine emperors over a thousand years ago. The same applies to Greece. There is in London a restaurant in Camden Town, run by an Armenian from Cyprus, Mr H. Melikian, where Greek and Armenian dishes co-exist in complete harmony.[1]

Nearly a quarter of a million Armenians live in Iran. This helps to account for the Armenians' expert use of pilaf rice dishes, often garnished with almonds and seasoned with saffron and other delicious ingredients. The sophisticated use of rice greatly enhances the attraction of kebabs and related meat dishes, which can easily become monotonous when eaten on their own.

I have always found genuine Armenian cooking exceptionally refined and delicate in flavour. Armenians like to serve their food in a fresh and appetizing manner. No Armenian restaurant or private house would serve up the coarse, lukewarm stuffed vine leaves swimming in grease which we find in cheap Greek restaurants, or the spongy, oft reheated, bright pink doner kebabs which we see revolving endlessly, like outsize babies' bottoms, in grimy Turkish kebab takeaways all over North London and elsewhere.

The golden age of Armenian cooking was the second half of the nineteenth century, when an industrious and intelligent population of over two million dwelt in the six Armenian *Vilayets* or provinces of eastern Turkey, where they provided the backbone of the Ottoman merchant class and government officialdom. Eventually, many of these Armenians were driven into exile between 1894 and 1896 by Sultan 'Abdul Hamid II, who also put many of them to death; the survivors were finally rooted out by the Young Turk dictators in 1915.

[1] Ararat Armenian Restaurant, 249 Camden High Street, London, NW1.

Earlier, many of those Armenian families had attained a high standard of living, though too often the poorer peasantry lived on little more than bread, cheese, herbs and sour milk. The novelist and poet Vahan Totovents (1889–1937) recalls in his autobiography the miserable life of hungry Armenian farm-workers in the Turkish province of Kharput :

At midday, they would sit down to a 'meal' under the tree on the farm with the most widespread branches. They would eat bread and onions, sometimes a boiled potato, and very occasionally a boiled egg. And when the dry bread refused to slide down their throats, they would stretch out and, lying on their chests, they would drink from the icy water of the brook, and would wipe their soaked moustaches with a tattered corner of the rags they wore.[1]

It was primarily the middle-class Armenian families of the towns of Anatolia and Asia Minor who developed and took with them into exile the incomparable cuisine which lives on today in many parts of the world. Particularly notable is the revival of authentic Armenian cooking which is going on in the United States of America. The Armenian population of North America is above the half-million mark and is increasing rapidly as Armenians seek security of emigrating from trouble-spots such as Iran and the Lebanon. Thanks to enthusiasts like Sonia Uvezian, Alice Antreassian, and the ladies of the Armenian General Benevolent Union,[2] even non-Armenians can prepare for themselves a wide range of Armenian dishes in their own homes, and gain some idea of the food enjoyed a century ago in prosperous Armenian homes in such cities as Van, Kayseri, Izmir and Constantinople.

Basic among foodstuffs is bread, and here the Armenians have a choice between the thin, flat oriental style of bread known as *lavash*, and the crusty loaf called *pideh*. As in Georgia and Iran, *lavash* is often baked in Armenia in a large open oven called a *tonir* (Georgian : *toneh*). I have seen bakers at work in old Tbilisi, slapping flat blobs of dough on to the heated inner sides of a huge *toneh*, heated from below

[1] Vahan Totovents, *Scenes from an Armenian Childhood*, trans. M. Kudian (Oxford University Press, 1962), p. 74.

[2] S. Uvezian, *The Cuisine of Armenia* (New York, Harper & Row, 1974); A. Antreassian, *Armenian Cooking Today* (New York, 1975); Detroit Women's Chapter of the Armenian General Benevolent Union, *Treasured Armenian Recipes*, 23rd printing (New York, 1976).

by a charcoal brazier. As the discs of bread are baked, they fall to the bottom of the oven and are retrieved with a shovel and long tongs.

Loaves of the *pideh* type, on the other hand, can be baked in a conventional European oven, and are often brushed with milk and sprinkled with sesame seeds before baking. There are several varieties of breakfast or afternoon tea roll, including a roll called *simit*, which contains eggs, milk and butter.

Lavash bread when soft is excellent for wrapping round kebabs, onions or slices of cheese. Armenia produces several varieties of cheese, made from the milk of cows, sheep, goats and even water buffaloes. From sheep's milk is made the popular white cheese called *brindzé*. Of special quality is an Armenian Roquefort-style green cheese called *muklats banir*. I recall eating this during my first meal in Armenia, which I enjoyed at Delijan in 1966 in company with an Armenian novelist, the late Garegin Sevunts.

An Armenian dinner, or extended lunch, can be a formidable affair. It is customary to offer guests a wide variety of *meza* (*mezés*) or appetizers, which could form a feast in themselves.

With cocktails, one may enjoy olives and *basterma*, which are little slices of spicy dried beef. Fried almonds also go well with drinks, as do savoury *boeregs*, made of several layers of wafer-thin pastry folded into rolls or triangles and stuffed with savoury meat or cheese mixtures. Mixed pickles (*titvash*) also precede almost every meal.

At the table, popular *mezés* include the cosmopolitan humus, a chick-pea paste; red kidney beans in sauce or *garmir lupia* (Georgian : *lobio*); and the internationally relished taramasalata – carp or cod roe dip. Fried or stuffed mussels are popular among Armenian communities with access to the sea. A distinctive Armenian sausage, usually made in October, makes a winter standby; after being cooked, it can be hung up for weeks or even months in a garage or shed until required at the table.

In summer, we can expect a wide variety of salads. Armenian farmers will eat a whole head of lettuce fresh from the fields, and give one to their children as well. They consider that such eating habits contribute to health, and to attaining a ripe old age.

Armenian mixed salad is excellent, being made with lettuce, tomato, cucumber, and green peppers, seasoned with chopped mint, basil, and parsley, and mixed with a little olive oil and lemon juice. Cucumber and tomato salad is also popular and tasty. There are many other combinations, including cucumber and yogurt salad, known as *jajik* –

this being also available as a refreshing cold soup. More unusual are white bean salad, asparagus and egg salad, spinach and yogurt salad – and there are a number of other variants on this theme.

During the winter, when salads are out of season, Armenians can start their meal with one of a wide selection of soups or broths. The range of Armenian soups extends from the rich vegetable and meat soups from Transcaucasia, called *bozbash*, to simple meat, fish or vegetable broths. Tomatoes and saffron are used to impart colour and flavour. Herbs are employed in a skilful manner, these including tarragon, mint, parsley, basil and coriander – and also garlic and onion, sometimes sautéed in butter. Little bread cubes, fried or toasted, are common garnishes for broths and clear soups.

At the heavy end of the soup list, we may single out Echmiadzin *bozbash* – a mixture of vegetables, meat and herbs, adding up almost to a regular stew, and traditionally associated with Holy Echmiadzin, seat of the Supreme Catholicos of the Armenian Apostolic Church. Another winter standby is dumpling broth, while meatball soup with rice or with cracked wheat is a meal in itself. There are several recipes for lentil soup. An unusual soup called *targhana* makes use of a form of dried dough made with yeast, flour and cracked wheat. A distinctive soup, found also in Georgia and other regions of the Caucasus, is *chikirtma*, the main ingredient of which is chicken stock, but this is strongly flavoured with egg and lemon sauce. This soup is often sprinkled with coriander. There is also a variety of *chikirtma* made from lamb stock.

For a country as land-locked as is Great Armenia, it may come as a surprise to learn that fish plays an important part in the national cuisine. Lake Sevan in Soviet Armenia produces a kind of trout called *Ishkhan*, which means 'prince'; it has reddish flesh and silvery scales. In Armenian rivers and lakes we also find salmon, carp and bass. In Antiquity, the princes and nobles built large artificial tanks for edible fish to breed and swim about in.

Several ancient ways of preparing fish have come down to us virtually unchanged. These include brushing with butter and roasting whole on a spit, or else stuffing, and gilding with saffron.

There is a national fish dish called *kutap,* made from trout, which is traditional among the Caucasus Armenians. The trout's backbone is broken in several places, and the intestines are scooped out and discarded. The fish's roe, heart and liver are retained and chopped for stuffing. Then the fish is stuffed with this chopped roe and other ingredients, including also boiled rice, melted butter, raisins and ginger, then curved into a ring. The fish's tail is inserted into its mouth, and the dish baked at about 350° and garnished with parsley before serving.[1]

Other characteristic fish delicacies include fried fish balls, fish grilled on skewers, fried stuffed mackerel, shrimp and prawn pilaf, and baked stuffed bass. Armenian national fish recipes taste equally good when made with fish caught in the rivers and seas of Western Europe, or in the Atlantic – as the many Armenians living in or near Boston, Massachusetts, can testify.

When we pass to game and poultry, the picture is equally varied. Armenia is rich in species of native birds, both wild and domesticated, including partridge, pheasant, quail, woodcock, and also the usual chicken, duck, goose and turkey. For outdoor functions, there is nothing more delicious than a bird rubbed with lemon juice and melted butter, and then roasted on a spit or barbecue over wood embers. Chicken pilaf is a great favourite, and may be served with various kinds of savoury rice, as is also the practice in Persia and Azerbaijan; raisins and toasted almonds make the pilaf extremely tasty.

The centrepiece of any full-blooded Armenian banquet is usually some national meat dish, usually based on lamb, though veal, beef and pork are also appreciated. Armenia is situated in the archetypical home of the shashlik or shish kebab – an area which takes in the vast Caucasus region, from which the dish has spread all over the world.

Shashlik is a modern development from the campfire feast of the ancient warrior or huntsman, who would cut up whatever animal he had managed to slay during the day and roast it on the end of his sword or pike, usually in the open-air surroundings of some wild mountain or forest. Something of this authentic flavour is preserved in the 'Kars shashlik', named after the fortress city of that name, now in Turkish Armenia. This Kars shashlik is made from large slices of boneless lamb, alternating with pieces of fat from fat-tailed sheep, threaded together on a large spit. The spit is fixed vertically in such a way as to rotate slowly in front of a tiered charcoal broiler. As the meat becomes cooked on the outside, thin slices are cut off and allowed to fall into a pan at the bottom of the spit. This process is continued until the centre is reached, and the meat is served with chopped onion and various herbs.

[1] See Sonia Uvezian, *The Cuisine of Armenia*, pp. 81. 91.

Climatic conditions in most of Armenia are extremely severe in winter months, when livestock have to be kept under cover to stop them from being engulfed in huge snowdrifts. Until the invention of the deep freeze and the modern supermarket, fresh tender lamb was not available in Armenia during much of the year, so that ordinary mutton and preserved meat had to be used in various ways. Pounding the meat ready for cooking was a major task in traditional Armenian households. Ground or minced meat is still widely used, and when skilfully prepared with rice, herbs and various vegetables – including aubergine – can be served up in kebab form as a dish fit for a king. The ground meat equivalent of and substitute for shish kebab is Luleh kebab, and this is almost as popular internationally as the original Shashlik recipe made with cubed lamb. Also available are recipes for a wide variety of stews and hot-pots.

There are several regional meat specialities, associated with ancient centres of Armenian settlement in the Caucasus and Anatolia. The Caucasian Armenians like to prepare fried lamb ribs, flavoured with apples and cinnamon. Armenians in the mountainous Karabagh region are fond of pork with either pomegranate sauce or fried quince. The villagers of Ashtarak – a beauty spot not far from Erevan – have an unusual ground meat dish called Ashtarak *kololik*. This consists of a small whole boiled chicken stuffed with a hard-boiled egg, the chicken being then enclosed inside a large meatball, which is wrapped in cheesecloth and cooked in broth.

From now extinct Armenian colonies of Asia Minor come such delicacies as Harput (Kharput) *keufteh*, which are stuffed lamb and wheat balls served with tomato broth; also Izmir *keufteh* (Smyrna meatballs), which may be served with egg noodles or spaghetti.

A general favourite is baked eggplant, stuffed with ground lamb, onion, tomato and green pepper. These characteristic Armenian stuffed vegetables are called *dolma*, and many regional varieties survive. Tomatoes, squash, onions, or even melons, are stuffed with minced or chopped meat combined with rice, *bulghur* (cracked wheat), herbs and other ingredients.

For picnics, or as a snack to be eaten *en route* for the station or airport, an unbeatable Armenian and Near Eastern food is a sort of pizza called *missahatz* or *lahmajoon*. This is made from a savoury meat and vegetable mixture, spread over slices of hot, doughy oriental bread and then baked in a hot oven for about twelve minutes, or until lightly browned. The meat mixture is not unlike the contents of a Western shepherd's pie. The flavour may be enhanced with garlic, paprika and lemon juice freshly strained. I have seen small Armenian boys sitting in a car near Damascus airport and demolishing slices of *lahmajoon* bigger than their own heads.

Armenian meat dishes are often served with specially prepared sauces, which have nothing in common with Western ketchups or other bottled concoctions. Armenian sauces and relishes are made to order, from selected ingredients. Thus, Armenian tomato sauce is made from fresh tomatoes, garlic, parsley, bay leaf and salt and pepper, with butter and onion; it is cooked over low heat and then strained through a food mill or sieve.

Various kinds of yogurt or *madzoon* are used as a sauce, being sometimes flavoured with garlic or cinnamon. An egg and lemon sauce called *terbiyeh* imparts an individually tart flavour to certain soups and meat dishes. Fish and fried vegetable recipes are improved by tarator sauce, which is prepared from garlic and crushed nuts – almonds, hazelnuts, walnuts or even pine nuts will serve.

For a 'sweet and sour' effect, try Armenian pomegranate syrup known as *narsharab*, or else a sweet syrup prepared from grapes, which is called *roub* – the same as the Turkish *bekmez*. These sweet sauces are perfectly compatible with pork, lamb, fish or fried eggplant.

An Armenian lunch or dinner party will often conclude simply with fresh fruit and Armenian coffee – served in delicate, demitasse cups from a traditional long-handled brass or enamel pot, as used in Turkey and the Arab and Iranian Near East.

Guests with healthy appetites may like to enjoy an Armenian dessert pastry. Perhaps the most famous of these pastries is baklava, which also ranks as an international delicacy. Baklava comes in several varieties; it is made from many layers of paper-thin crisp dough, stuffed with crushed nuts or sometimes with cheese or cream. After it is baked, baklava should be liberally drenched with syrup or honey before serving.

Closely allied to baklava is the Armenian sweet known as ladies' fingers. Here the crisp dough is wrapped round a central core of finely chopped walnuts, sugar and cinnamon, and baked in a preheated $350°$ oven for about 25 minutes. The fingers are then dipped in a syrup made from sugar, honey, lemon juice and sliced orange, before being placed in racks to cool.

Caucasian Armenians make a special variety of walnut pastry. Popular throughout the Middle East are the light and delicate Armenian butter cookies known as *kurabia*, traditionally served on large trays at weddings and at Easter and Christmas. There is a variety of rolled pastry with nut filling known as *bourma*, which can be moulded into decorative shapes, as, for instance, the form of snails or little animals.

Of distinctive appearance and texture is a dessert pastry known as *tel kadayif*, which looks very much like shredded wheat. It is drenched in syrup, and can be served with the special cream topping called *kaymak*.

Armenian Christmas pudding is very different from the familiar English variety – it is called *Anooshabour* or *Anush gorgodaboor*. The ancient recipe, which has been used for centuries, includes skinless whole-grain wheat, dried apricots, seedless raisins, vanilla, sugar, chopped walnuts and blanched almonds. The pudding may be flavoured with cinnamon if desired, or with apricot liqueur.

Armenians are fond of sweetmeats and candies. They enjoy the cosmopolitan halva, which is consumed throughout the Near East and Central Asia. This sweetmeat is prepared with different varieties of flour combined with crushed nuts or sesame seeds, and mixed with butter and sugar. Formed into a stiff paste, the confection is pressed into blocks and cut into chunks or slices.

There is another Armenian sweetmeat which is recommended only to those with strong teeth and robust digestions. This is called in Turkish *sudjuk*; in Georgian, *churchkhela*; the national Armenian name is *yershig*. It is made by stringing walnuts or other large nuts on heavy thread or thin string, and dipping them into a thickened grape juice solution. When the paste has congealed, the strings are hung up for several weeks to dry through. They develop a thick skin or outer coating, and are later rolled in powdered sugar. This confection is useful as a kind of iron ration for those cast up on a desert island; it tastes very much like candied glue, and is virtually indestructible. Those with dentures or gold fillings are recommended to stick to Turkish delight, which is served with Armenian or oriental coffee in many Armenian homes.

Armenian meals are usually graced by excellent aperitifs, wines and brandies. The Book of Genesis records that one of Father Noah's first actions after landing in the Ark on Mount Ararat was to climb down the slope and plant a vineyard, the excellent products of which eventually made him rather drunk. In Ottoman times, the Armenian paterfamilias returning from office, factory or farm would be served ceremonially with a few glasses of arak – a fiery spirit – after which he would wipe his moustache thoughtfully, and the womenfolk would prepare to serve the evening meal.

Soviet Armenia has a large acreage of vineyards, but the produce does not always reach the table in the form of red or white wine, or as muscat-type sweet wine. It is earmarked for the Armenian cognac factories, the products of which are exported all over the world, and command a handsome premium on the liquor market in Moscow. I once visited the central Erevan cognac factory, the tasting-room of which is reached by climbing down a steep ladder. Half a century ago, this room was visited by a group of fraternal Russian writers, several of whom were unable to climb up the ladder after the tasting, and had to be carried home. Maxim Gorky and Mayakovsky finished up by writing on the cellar wall: 'Comrades, respect the power of Armenian brandy! It is easier to climb up to heaven than to get out of here, when you have taken too much on board!'

On this festive note, we close this survey of some highlights of Armenian cuisine, recommending our readers to study one or more of the excellent guides now on the market. Among these are the concise and business-like *Treasured Armenian Recipes*, issued by the Armenian General Benevolent Union of New York; Mrs Alice Antreassian's *Armenian Cooking Today*, also published in New York; and Mrs Sonia Uvezian's *The Cuisine of Armenia*, which also contains some of the author's own culinary inventions.

I 2

As Others See Us: The Armenian Image in Literature

FAMILIAR AND often misleading stereotypes of national character have built up over the years in fiction, drama and the cinema – the brash American, the strong, silent Englishman, the voluble Italian, the hand-kissing Frenchman, the pedantic, boring German, the permissive Swede, and so on. In the Orient we encounter the noble bedouin Arab, the acquisitive Jew, the subtle Persian, the mysterious, inscrutable Chinaman, and a number of other types brought to life by master storytellers such as Joseph Conrad, John Buchan, Agatha Christie and Somerset Maugham.

In view of the people's long history and wide distribution throughout the world, we might expect a standard Armenian stereotype to have emerged in the pages of literature. However, the Armenian image seems nebulous, variable and rather hard to define. This may be due in part to the comparatively small world total of the Armenian people (between six and seven million), the closed, exclusive nature of their social organization, and the way in which they manage to adapt themselves and blend into any society where they happen to find themselves.

It seems, in fact, that we must come to terms not with a single Armenian literary image or stereotype but with several widely differ-

14   Millionaire philanthropist Calouste Sarkis Gulbenkian, 1869–1955,
aged 24. *(Calouste Gulbenkian Foundation)*

15   The Armenian Holocaust – massacred children, Turkey, 1915. *(BBC Hulton Picture Library)*

16   Massacred children, 1915 – detail. *(BBC Hulton Picture Library)*

ing, if not mutually contradictory, ones. In literary works of different lands and periods, it is possible to encounter such interesting types as the noble, patriotic Armenian; the oppressed, suffering Armenian; the comic Armenian; and the astute entrepreneur. Leaving out of account for the moment travel books, scholarly monographs, and books written by Armenians, we are concerned here with the image or impression created by Armenians on *odar*, non-Armenian, creative writers of different periods and countries. Some of these images are complimentary, others rather negative. One must take the rough with the smooth.

We begin in medieval times, on a romantic note, with a tribute to the beauty and fidelity of an Armenian princess. Though of a less 'Classical' type than her cousins the Georgians and Circassians, the Armenian girl with her lustrous dark eyes and raven tresses is one of the glories of the East. Nowhere are the results of her fascination more evident than in the Persian romance of Khusrau and Shirin.

Khusrau is Khusrau II Parviz, one of the Sassanian rulers of Iran, who reigned from AD 591 to 628. Shirin is a beautiful Armenian princess, whom the king espies bathing naked in a river pool. The story of their undying love has been related by Nizami of Ganja (1140–1209) in a verse romance completed in AD 1180, justly considered an immortal classic of Persian poetry. The bard had such a high conception of Shirin's grace, beauty and steadfast character that he liked to compare her with his own beloved wife.

Although Shakespeare does not seem to have had much knowledge of or interest in Armenia, there are a number of references to Armenians in English and French drama of the seventeenth century.

The most important dramatist of that era to deal with Armenian subjects was Pierre Corneille (1606–84), the founder of the French classical theatre. Although his best known play, *Le Cid*, is set in Spain, Corneille constantly showed a well informed interest in Byzantium, Parthia, Asia Minor and Syria, and liked to site his tragedies in this region, during the Greek and Roman period. In his Christian tragedy of *Polyeucte* (1643), Corneille sets the scene at Melitene (Malatya), Roman headquarters in Western Armenia, about AD 250. The hero is an Armenian Christian nobleman, married to the daughter of the local Roman governor, Felix, a careerist official of the Pontius Pilate type, and a fanatical pagan.

Polyeucte sets his allegiance to the Christian faith higher than conjugal affection and life itself, and suffers martyrdom rather than abandon his religion.

Less successful than *Polyeucte* but still full of interest is Corneille's play *Nicomède* (1652), which features a semi-imaginary queen of Armenia named Laodice, as attractive as she is dignified and virtuous.

Few people today, even in France, are aware that Corneille's very last tragedy, *Suréna, général des Parthes* (1674), has a strong and arresting Armenian content. On the basis of authentic material taken from the Classical historians Plutarch and Appian, Corneille presents a brilliant tableau of great power politics in the Near East following the catastrophic defeat of the Roman general Crassus by the Parthians in 53 BC. There is well informed discussion of the Roman-Parthian rivalry at the court of the Armenian king Artavazd II, son of Tigranes the Great. The play's heroine, Princess Eurydice, is portrayed as daughter of King Artavazd, and thus a granddaughter of the famous Tigranes. As depicted by the veteran Corneille, the Armenian princess is in every way worthy of her exalted lineage. Her love for the victorious Parthian general Suréna brings about his murder, and her own death from shock at this tragic loss.

Particularly striking in *Suréna* is the contrast between the perfidious, scheming jealousy of the Parthian king Orodes, and the high-minded fidelity of the Armenian princess and her lover, the heroic but ill-fated Suréna. When news is brought of Suréna's assassination by order of the Parthian king, the Armenian princess is asked why she is not weeping over her bereavement. Princess Eurydice's answer is unsurpassed for its classical restraint and dignity. She replies :

> Non, je ne pleure point, Madame, mais je meurs.
> (I shed no tears, My Lady, but I die.)

The beauty and pathos of these three tragedies place Corneille at the head of those French writers who have made use of themes connected with Armenian history. It is worth noting that in the following century the prophet of the French Revolution, Jean-Jacques Rousseau (1712–78), used to dress up in what he imagined to be authentic Armenian costume – much to the vexation of his jealous rival, Voltaire.

In the early nineteenth century, an outstanding figure in the portrayal of Armenian life and customs was James Morier (1780–1849), creator of that immortal rogue, swindler and humbug Hajji Baba of Isfahan. Morier was an official British diplomatic representative at the Persian Imperial court of Fath 'Ali Shah in Teheran between 1810 and 1816. He knew Armenia well, and published two serious and detailed accounts of his explorations in Persia, Armenia and Asia Minor.[1]

Morier's fame rests on the inimitable mock-autobiographical adventures of Hajji Baba, published in 1824, which have been described by the Comte de Gobineau as 'the best book written on the temperament of an Asiatic nation'. Lord Curzon once claimed that if all the scholarly literature about Persia were to be burned by the common hangman, *Hajji Baba* would suffice to replace it.

Six chapters of *Hajji Baba* are devoted to Armenia. Hajji Baba, as assistant to the Persian chief executioner, takes part in hostilities then raging against Tsarist Russian forces, which had taken over Georgia and were about to invade and overrun Persian Armenia. In a rare mood of decency and compassion he befriends an Armenian refugee named Joseph (Yusuf) and his wife Mariam, and enables them to take refuge in Russian-occupied territory.

Morier works in many interesting anecdotes which illustrate the desperate hardships of Armenian life in those days. He describes how the Persian Sardar or governor of Erevan, Hassan Khan, would attack Armenian villages by throwing hand grenades down the ventilation shafts which were let into the roofs. When looking at this Muslim autocrat of Persian Armenia, Morier says that 'it was difficult to say whether the goat or the tiger was most predominant; but this is most certain, that never was the human form so nearly allied to that of the brute as in this instance'. The Sardar is portrayed as a confirmed homosexual, and a wine bibber of no small capacity.

No bolder drinker of wine existed in Persia, except, perhaps, his present companion, the executioner, who, as long as he could indulge without incurring the Shah's displeasure, had ratified an eternal treaty of alliance between his mouth and every skin of wine that came within his reach.

To be fair, Morier is not much more complimentary when describing the Supreme Catholicos of All the Armenians, or 'caliph', as Hajji

---

[1] Published in London by Longmans, 1812 and 1818.

Baba terms him. In Morier's time, the dignity was held by Yeprem I, who occupied the See of Echmiadzin from 1809 to 1830. Entirely under the thumb of the local Persian tyrant, the Armenian pontiff is described as a heavy, coarse man, of a rosy and jovial appearance. The Catholicos cuts a sorry figure, but is perhaps more to be pitied than blamed.

Morier indicates clearly that any faults characteristic of the Armenians under Persian Qajar rule stemmed primarily from the oppression to which they were subjected by their Muslim overlords. The young Armenian couple, Joseph and Mariam, are idealized figures – Joseph, brave, handsome and resourceful, and Mariam heroic in her fidelity and devotion. They are perhaps the most attractive figures in Morier's book.

Another British friend of the Armenians was Morier's contemporary, Lord Byron. Byron lived in Venice from 1816 to 1819, and established a close relation with the Armenian Mekhitarist Fathers, a Roman Catholic congregation who possess a fine library in their island monastery of San Lazzaro.[1] He spent many weeks studying Armenian with leading scholars at the monastery, and translated into English two apocryphal letters from St Paul to the Corinthians, the text of which has been preserved in an Armenian version. Byron also financed the publication of an English and Armenian grammar, for the use of Armenian speakers. On a visit to Venice in 1967, I was shown the writing table at which the poet sat as he studied in the monastery garden.

A series of letters from Byron to his publisher, John Murray, bear witness to the poet's deep interest in the Armenians and their civilization. In one of them, Byron sternly declares : 'You must not neglect my Armenians!' 'These men', the poet wrote of the Mekhitarist Fathers, 'are the priesthood of an oppressed and a noble nation, which has partaken of the proscription and bondage of the Jews and of the Greeks, without the sullenness of the former or the servility of the latter.'[2]

Another nineteenth-century English writer to show interest in the Armenians was George Borrow (1803–81), an amazing polyglot, world traveller and expert on gypsy lore. In his semi-autobiographical

---

[1] See D. M. Lang, *Armenia, Cradle of Civilization*, 3rd edn (London, 1980), pp. 277–8.

[2] Mekhitarist Congregation, *Lord Byron and the Armenians* (Venice, n.d. (about 1970)).

Lavengro (1851), Borrow tells of his friendship with an Armenian financier and patriot whom he frequently visited in London, after saving him from having his wallet stolen by a pickpocket. This Armenian gentleman's ambition was to amass a fortune of £200,000 – an aim which he achieved. Struck with Borrow's mastery of the Armenian language, the Armenian offered to finance a translation into English of a collection of Armenian fables, similar to those of Aesop. Before Borrow could set to work, the Armenian had vanished – seized with the crazy idea of liberating eastern Armenia from Persian domination by means of his newly acquired riches.[1]

In *Lavengro*, George Borrow conveys very effectively the mixture of business ability, avarice, patriotic attachment to the culture and soil of Armenia, and sheer lunacy which characterizes this individual, who comes vividly to life. Unlike Byron, George Borrow and his Armenian friend are highly critical of Roman Catholic attempts to win over the Armenians from allegiance to their national Apostolic Church. Mount Ararat, Borrow maintains, is higher and more beautiful than the seven hills of Rome.

After Byron and George Borrow, references to Armenians in nineteenth-century English and Western European literature are few and far between. Before the massacres of 1895, most Armenians lived in a fairly confined corner of the world, locked away in north-eastern Turkey and southern Russia. It took the atrocities perpetrated by Sultan 'Abdul Hamid and the protests of public figures like Gladstone to focus the attention of the Western nations on this ancient Christian people. It was only through the tragic blood-baths and mass emigration that European writers came into contact with individual Armenians, and began to make creative use of their often colourful personalities.

Perhaps the best known of modern writers to introduce an Armenian character into his writings is D. H. Lawrence (1885–1930). The work in question is one of his later short stories, 'Mother and Daughter'. In this tale, an Armenian gentleman of mature years and outwardly unattractive appearance features as the unlikely suitor of a mother-dominated spinster, doomed apparently to a lifetime of subtle matriarchal tyranny.

The suitor is an Armenian widower from Bulgaria, Arnault Bouyoumjian by name, who has come to London for important busi-

---

[1] Literary research by Christopher J. Walker, Esq.

ness negotiations. Arnault was rather stout, and 'he sat, with short thighs, like a toad, for a toad's eternity'. His complexion was a dirty sort of paste colour, his brown eyes glazed under heavy lids. But his thick white hair, which stood up on his head like a brush, had a curiously virile look about it. His presence was soothing and reassuring. He was a man tired yet unconquered by the struggles of life, still possessing enough energy and persistence to overcome any resistance which the heroine, Virginia Bodoin, might have opposed to so incongruous an admirer. With subtle irony, Lawrence convinces us that Virginia will be far happier with her elderly knight errant than she could ever have been in the stifling, overprotective atmosphere in which her mother had enveloped her for so long.

It has been suggested that D. H. Lawrence partly modelled Arnault on the fashionable novelist Michael Arlen (Dickran Kouyoumdjian), whom Lawrence met while living in Florence.[1] Michael Arlen may indeed have described in conversation the characteristic type of old-time Balkan or Anatolian Armenian patriarch. But it is hard to conceive that the squat, oriental type of Armenian represented by Arnault could have anything in common with the dapper, cosmopolitan Michael Arlen Sr, who did all he could to merge into Western high society, and be accepted by it on equal terms.

The image of the benevolent Armenian sugar-daddy appears again, though offstage, in the chilling play *Der Besuch der alten Dame* by the Swiss dramatist Friedrich Dürrenmatt (born 1921). This play, first produced in 1956, has since become quite popular in England, under the title *The Visit*. Claire Zachanassian, widow of the richest man in the world, revisits her native town, a narrow-minded community from which she had been driven many years ago after being seduced and betrayed by a local man. To survive, Claire had become a prostitute in Hamburg, where she was befriended and then married by the Armenian multi-millionaire Zachanassian – a character perhaps suggested by the half-legendary figure of Mr Calouste Gulbenkian.

Armed now with the unlimited financial resources of her late husband, Claire Zachanassian waves a cheque for a million dollars in front of the bemused townspeople of Gullen – the cheque to belong to anyone willing to murder her erstwhile seducer. These townsfolk are, to a man, all high-principled citizens to whom crime and vice

---

[1] Leo Hamalian, 'Through a Glass Lightly', in *Ararat: A Decade of Armenian-American Writing*, ed. Jack Antreassian (New York, 1969), p. 331. See the enlarged version of this essay in *Burn after Reading* (New York, 1978).

are thoroughly repugnant – as Claire has long since learnt to her cost. But a million dollars can alter any situation quite radically : the cheque does not have to wait long before being claimed and put to grim and effective use. . . .

If we turn now to the astute entrepreneur type of Armenian, the prince of this genre is surely Mr Krikor Youkoumian, a central figure in Evelyn Waugh's prophetic novel *Black Mischief*, first published in 1932. Influential proprietor of the Emperor Amurath Café and Universal Stores in Matodi, commercial capital of Azania (really Abyssinia), Mr Youkoumian is modelled on the Harar hotelier Mr Bergebedgian, who befriended Waugh on his visit to that city in 1930. In the same way, Basil Seal, the clever and dissolute Mayfair adventurer who attempts to introduce modern ways into backward Azania, is (at least in part) Evelyn Waugh's own *alter ego*.

The story of *Black Mischief* revolves round the ill judged efforts of the young and enthusiastic Emperor Seth of Azania to reform his antiquated African realm, and drag its people forcibly into the twentieth century. Having been educated at Oxford, Seth enlists the help of his disreputable college friend Basil Seal, whom he appoints Minister of Modernization. The Ministry's Financial Secretary and general factotum is none other than the Armenian hotelier, commercial genius and universal fixer, Mr Krikor Youkoumian.

Mr Youkoumian is not only an astute Armenian – he is a richly humorous, well-rounded figure, possessed of infinite resource. Nothing gets him down. One minute he is nearly hanged by traitors, the next he is supplying the barefooted Azanian army with a thousand pairs of cut-price boots, which are promptly cooked and eaten by the starving soldiery. He produces 'instant vintage Champagne' for every court function, and happily lays on the necessary contraceptive devices for Emperor Seth's ill-fated birth control campaign.

When Seth devises the establishment of a national museum Youkoumian is naturally put in charge of collecting exhibits – 'work for which early training and all his natural instincts richly equipped him'. Apart from the usual brass pots, tanned human scalps, and some sacramental vessels stolen by Nestorian deacons, Mr Youkoumian manages to acquire the French Ambassador's Masonic apron (purloined by the Embassy butler), as well as a vast monolithic phallus borne in by three oxen from a shrine in the interior of the country. The Trustees of the British Museum have nothing on Mr Youkoumian.

A new Nubar Pasha, Mr Youkoumian is well on the way to becoming Prime Minister of Azania when revolution breaks out. Feudal reaction triumphs over modern progress and technology. Emperor Seth is deposed and dies a sordid death in the jungle; Basil Seal inadvertently eats his girl friend in a cannibal stew before returning to his West End haunts; and the Azanian empire is taken over by the League of Nations and turned into a Franco-British protectorate.

Here again, Mr Youkoumian shows his native genius for survival and for adapting himself to changing circumstances. He now supplies the British military commander both with fruit salad and with a fresh consignment of army boots for the native levies. In his café, Youkoumian zealously co-operates with the British police in enforcing British licensing laws. Assuming the genial but firm demeanour of a British publican, our Armenian friend tactfully ejects the last customers at closing time and proclaims: 'Very sorry. New regulation. No drinking after ten-thirty. I don't want no bust-ups.' At this point, the curtain falls on an African scene in which Mr Krikor Youkoumian and also his long-suffering and much battered wife play an unforgettable role.

The next fictional Armenian on our list, the barber Mnemjian of Lawrence Durrell's Alexandria Quartet, is an astute entrepreneur of a very different type. Evelyn Waugh's Youkoumian was the sort of man with whom one could spend a convivial evening, drinking Armenian Scotch whisky and swapping yarns about Azanian celebrities such as Viscount Boaz, Black Bitch, Sir Samson Courteney, Madame Fifi and the rest. Mnemjian, on the other hand, is a sinister creep, from whom a normal man would run a mile. He is a dwarf, with violet-coloured eyes, a hunchback with a 'small wheedling voice'. The Greek Hospital in Alexandria employs Mnemjian to shave and lay out its deceased inmates before they are committed to the undertaker – 'a task which he performs with relish tinged by racial unction'.[1]

Mnemjian is a procurer, who provides his clients with sexual partners guaranteed to be 'young, cheap and clean'. Mnemjian is also a gigolo – he visits several elderly Egyptian ladies, the wives and widows of pashas, for whom he provides sexual relief for an appropriate fee and also collects from them titbits of information useful to a blackmailer. In one sordid sequence, we come upon Mnemjian in the very act of copulation – the details of which Durrell relates with considerable zest.[2]

[1] L. Durrell, *Justine* (London, Faber & Faber, 1961), p. 36.
[2] *Justine*, pp. 186–190.

During the Second World War, Mnemjian comes into his element as a freelance intelligence agent. His barber's shop becomes a central clearing house for any general information concerning the city and its inhabitants. He patiently copies out his intelligence summaries in triplicate and sells copies to any secret service which will buy them.[1]

Mnemjian cuts a dashing figure in *Clea*, the last volume of the Alexandria sequence. Clad now in a dazzling silver suit, spats, and a pearl tiepin, with his fingers heavily ringed, he declares himself the richest barber in the whole of Egypt, with three salons and twelve assistants. Mnemjian's shops are cutting the soldiers' hair before they go out to the field of battle – provoking one of his clients to make the ghoulish witticism : 'Now you are shaving the dead while they are still alive.' Not an Armenian to be proud of : in fact, a thoroughly nasty piece of work.

While we are plumbing the lower depths of the Armenian literary underworld, we can hardly avoid mentioning the rascally Armenian doorkeeper at the Hotel X in Paris, as described by George Orwell (1903–50) in his autobiographical work, *Down and Out in Paris and London*.

This individual, who remains anonymous, was responsible for paying the wages of the junior employees, and also for searching them on their way home, to make sure they had no stolen food in their pockets. The Armenian doorkeeper swindled Orwell out of his over-time bonus and pocketed it himself. His behaviour provoked Orwell to conclude his account of the episode with the following bitter comments :

> He called himself a Greek, but in reality he was an Armenian. After knowing him I saw the force of the proverb, 'Trust a snake before a Jew and a Jew before a Greek,' but don't trust an Armenian.'[2]

After this excursion into Armenian literary low life, it is a relief to turn to some writings which present Armenians in a more congenial light. Several twentieth-century historical novels fulfil this function very effectively.

We can begin with the earliest recorded period of Armenian

[1] *Justine*, p. 170.
[2] Penguin edition, pp. 64–5; literary research by Miss Elizabeth M. Lang.

national history, the sixth century BC. Harold Lamb's historical novel *Cyrus the Great* features two Armenian warriors, father and son, who serve the Median king Astyages. The father is called Harpaig, the son, Vartan. Both are portrayed as brave and intelligent warrior-philosophers. When Cyrus the Great overthrows Astyages, they transfer their allegiance to Cyrus and help to launch him on the road to world domination. Vartan discovers the secret of the Golden Fleece in Colchis (western Georgia), but is afterwards murdered and dismembered by a sex-crazed member of an Amazon tribe.

When we move on to the early Christian era, an outstanding Armenian character is the slave Sahak in the historical novel *Barabbas* by the Swedish writer Pär Lagerkvist, who won the Nobel Prize in 1951. Barabbas is the thief freed by order of Pontius Pilate in place of Jesus. The book is an imaginary account of Barabbas's later life, culminating in his execution in Rome.

At one point, Barabbas is re-arrested and sent to work in the dreaded copper-mines of Cyprus. There he is shackled to the Armenian Christian Sahak – a saintly, emaciated figure, with snow-white hair and a ravaged face, scorched and shrivelled by his years of suffering. Sahak teaches Barabbas the rudiments of the Christian faith, and is eventually himself crucified by the Roman authorities. Sahak is presented as an example of the finest type of early Christian believer, ready to accept martyrdom willingly rather than renounce the Lord Jesus Christ.

To bring our survey back to the early twentieth century, we turn now to an epic masterpiece devoted entirely to Armenian themes, namely *The Forty Days of Musa Dagh* by Franz Werfel (1890–1945). This book, part historical reconstruction, part novel, appeared in 1934 (German original, 1933), and deals with the courageous stand of a party of Armenians besieged by superior Turkish forces near Iskanderun (the Alexandretta) during the First World War.

Against the background of these heroic events, Werfel sets an imaginary, fictional element – the struggle between Gabriel Bagradian, a sophisticated Armenian from Paris, and the Russian Armenian anti-hero, Sarkis Kilikian. Bagradian regards Kilikian's attitude as defeatist and a threat to the continuing resistance of the beleaguered Armenians, so he ultimately kills Sarkis Kilikian with his own hand.

The plucky Armenians were, in real life, rescued by a French battleship and their descendants dwell in the Lebanese village of Anjar. Repeated attempts to turn Werfel's book into a film were blocked by the Turkish government, which exerted pressure on interested Hollywood studios through a subservient U.S. State Department. There are indications that today, in 1980, Armenian organizations in America will soon succeed in preparing the way for a film version, after nearly half a century's delay.

The Turkish attitude towards the Armenians and their sad history is aptly summed up by Rose Macaulay in her novel, *The Towers of Trebizond* :

> He knew also a little Armenian, but aunt Dot told him that this language was a mistake with Turks, and only vexed them, as they had long since pronounced *delenda est Armenia* over this so unfortunately fragmented people, and did not care to hear them referred to.

This brief survey by no means exhausts the supply of Armenian characters who feature in world literature. We may cite the gentle Armenian prostitute Vera in a story by the Soviet Jewish writer Isaac Babel, who was liquidated by Stalin's order; the strong Armenian element in *Devil's Yard,* by the Yugoslav Nobel Prize winner Ivo Andric; and the sympathetic portrayal of Armenians by Greek authors of the stature of Elia Kazan, Nikos Kazantzakis and Vasilis Vassilikos. Among American writers of note, both Ernest Hemingway and Henry Miller mention individual Armenians with understanding and sympathy derived from personal observation.[1] More recently, the veteran British novelist David Garnett (born 1892) has included an Armenian mountaineer in his novel of Caucasian life, *The Sons of the Falcon* (1972).

The foregoing account seems to confirm the view expressed earlier – that there is no single Armenian literary stereotype. The heroic, the self-sacrificing, the humorous, the astute, even the villainous Armenian brightens up the pages of literature to a surprising degree. For the most part, they are colourful figures, outsize in personality if not in physical stature. They are among nature's individualists, and they have had to learn how to survive – usually the hard way. These imaginary Armenians may be eccentric, exasperating or even dishonest, but they are scarcely ever boring. They have added a little spice to our lives, for which they and their creators deserve our sincere gratitude.

[1] Details in Leo Hamalian's article, 'Through a Glass Lightly', in *Ararat*, ed. Antreassian, pp. 321–45; enlarged version in *Burn after Reading* (New York, 1978).

13

The Armenians and the Occult

TO MANY people, the Armenians seem the embodiment of shrewd practicality and business acumen. Yet this practicality goes hand in hand with a deep religious sense, often combined with a leaning towards mysticism. Armenians have made important contributions to philosophy and metaphysics. At a less sophisticated level, the Armenian peasant of today, especially when remaining within the ancient homeland, clings to folk beliefs and traditions which have their roots in bygone pagan times. At Holy Echmiadzin, for instance, priests will bless animals which are then ritually slaughtered for a communal meal – a relic of pagan sacrificial rites.

Since the Armenians have been without kings or (apart from some brief intervals) independent government of their own for more than six centuries, the leadership of the nation has passed to the Armenian Apostolic Church. The elite of the intelligentsia has tended to enter the priesthood. Until quite recently, education among the Armenians was a Church monopoly. Armenians in all parts of the world still make the building and consecration of a church a top priority, and this church will serve the community as a religious and social centre, a focus for patriotic and charitable effort, and often as a congenial type of club.

Alongside the official doctrines of the Armenian Apostolic Church, which assumed their definitive shape fifteen centuries ago, all kinds of pagan beliefs, heresies and esoteric cults have flourished. Sometimes these movements have come into violent conflict with the

Armenian Church establishment; sometimes they have gone underground; occasionally they have managed to coexist peacefully and have even entered the tolerated area of folklore and hallowed tradition.

From the sixth century BC the Armenians were under the sway of the great empire of Iran. Thus it was only natural that their ancient, pre-Christian pantheon closely followed the Iranian Zoroastrian pattern.

Mightiest of all gods was Aramazd, whose name is the Armenian form of Ahura-Mazda, creator of heaven and earth in the cosmogony of the Indo-Iranians. The god of war was Vahagn, this being the local Armenian form of the name of Verethragna, Iranian deity of valour and victory. Vahagn may also be equated with the demigod Hercules. Vahagn's queen-consort was the lovely Astghik, goddess of love, the Armenian Venus. The god of knowledge, arts and letters was Tir, who acted as recording angel and scribe to Aramazd.

A special place was and still is assigned to Anahit, mother of the Armenians, goddess of fertility and protectress of the nation. She is the same beneficent deity as the Anahita of the Avesta, who purifies the seed of all males, cleanses the wombs of all females ready for giving birth, makes all females bear with ease, and gives mothers milk in their breasts at the right season. In both Iran and Armenia, the goddess was relied on to multiply both herds and lands. The Armenian Anahit is called the golden mother, and massive gold statues were dedicated to her. At her temple in Akilisene, temple prostitution was practised. It was thought that virgins who were initiated in the rites of love at this shrine would later turn into fertile wives and model mothers of families.

More cosmopolitan in character was the cult of Mithras, which spread from Iran as far afield as northern England, where I have visited a Mithraeum which has been excavated beside Hadrian's Wall. Mithras was especially venerated in Armenia, as an archangel, a power of light fighting on the side of Aramazd.

Several ancient deities live on today in the form of Armenian personal names. Thus, Anahit and Vahagn are popular Christian names for girls and boys respectively. The name of Tiridates or Trdat, the first Christian king of Armenia, derives from that of the god Tir. Mithras figures, in the form Mher or Meherr, in the national saga of David of Sassoun.

An important aspect of the Zoroastrian religion is worship of the sacred fire, and this cult was strongly developed in ancient Armenia. The chronicler Moses of Khorene mentions a fire-altar at Bagavan. Upon this altar, King Ardashir, son of Sasan (224–40), ordered the sacred fire of Aramazd to be kept burning and unquenched, after the Persian reconquest of Armenia.[1] At another site, close to a temple of Aramazd and Astghik, there was 'a house of fire, of insatiable flame, the god of incessant combustion'.

It is interesting that the elements of water and fire were regarded in ancient Armenia as brother and sister – water being the masculine principle. Concerning this belief, one text records: 'They took the sacred brazier and dashed it in the water, as into the bosom of its brother, according to the saying of the false teachers of the Persians.' Many rivers and springs were sacred, and endowed with beneficent virtues. The ancient Armenians offered horses as sacrifices to the River Euphrates, and made prophecies by watching its waves and foam. Transfiguration Sunday in the Armenian Church was interwoven with an unmistakably pagan water festival, during which the people diverted themselves by throwing water at one another.

The pre-Christian Armenians paid homage to the sun, the moon and the stars. Horses were sacrificed to the sun, as recorded by Xenophon about 400 BC. In the earliest Armenian calendar, the eighth month and also the first day of every month were consecrated to the sun, whereas the twenty-fourth day of the month was sacred to the moon. The lunar deity was considered to be 'the nurse of the plants'. Moreover, it was a popular belief that a sorcerer could bring the sun or the moon down to earth by witchcraft.

Evil spirits, monsters and dragons abound in ancient Armenian traditions. Acute dread was inspired by the *vishaps* or serpent monsters, whose effigies are carved on megalithic standing stones found on hills in Armenia and Georgia.[2] The stone *vishaps* are thought to have been guardian deities protecting ancient irrigation systems, but popular superstition ascribed to them a sinister role. *Vishaps* were able to enter into human beings; their breath was poisonous; they could ride and hunt on horseback, or fly in the air; they liked sucking milk from cows, and carrying off grain from the threshing floor.

Their allies were the *nhangs,* originally thought of as akin to

---

[1] Moses Khorenats'i, *History of the Armenians*, trans. Robert W. Thomson (Harvard University Press, 1978), p. 225.

[2] N. Y. Marr and J. Smirnov, *Les Vichaps* (Leningrad, 1931).

alligators and crocodiles. These *nhangs* lurked in rivers, and took on the shape of seals or of mermaids. They would catch swimmers by the feet and drag them to the bottom; then they would use their victims to satisfy their own sexual lust, suck their blood, and leave them dead on the river bank.

Also very potent were the *devs*, often portrayed as tyrants possessing seven heads. When they wrestled together, it was like the shock of mountains in collision, and lava would pour forth from volcanoes. They could hurl enormous rocks a great distance, and they dwelt in deep caverns or thick forests. Female *devs* were about the size of a hill; they went around with their left breast thrown over their right shoulder, and their right breast over their left shoulder, otherwise their bosoms would make deep holes in the ground.

The *devs* were very rich, and owned horses of fire on which they travelled vast distances in a single moment. In view of the forbidding appearance of their own females, the male *devs* much preferred girls of the human race, to whom they granted anything they asked in return for enjoying sexual intercourse with them.

Right up to modern times, Armenians have believed in witches and also in 'spirits of disease'. These spirits are small in stature and wear triangular hats. They hold in their hands a white, a red and a black branch. The spirit may strike someone with the white branch, in which case he will fall ill, but soon recover. If it is with the red one, then he will have to stay in bed a long time. But if the spirit strikes with the black branch, the victim is doomed to die and nothing can save him.

Not all supernatural beings were unfriendly. Thus we find reference to benevolent *shahapets*, or protectors of the homestead, who would shield the olive trees and vineyards from evil forces. It is also a traditional Armenian belief that every child has from its birth a guardian angel, who protects him or her against evil spirits. The angel's duty includes cutting the child's nails, and amusing it with the golden apple which the angel holds in his hand. When the child is old enough, the guardian angel returns to heaven, while the child smiles at him and stretches out its little arms.[1]

The Armenians, especially those of Anatolia and Transcaucasia, made great use of prayer scrolls, embodying magical talismanic formulae. These talismans were carried on the person, to protect the

[1] M. H. Ananikian, *Armenian Mythology* (Boston, 1925).

bearer against the evil eye, slander, the wrath of enemies, witches and wizards, impure love, snake-bite and other accidents or temptations. The talismans also served to conciliate kings, lords, officials and brigands.

The official adoption of Christianity in Armenia, credited to St Gregory the Illuminator, is usually dated to AD 301. The early Fathers of the Armenian Church had no easy task. On the one hand, they had to contend with the Great Kings of Sassanian Iran, who wished at all costs to reimpose Mazdaism on the Armenians; on the other, they had to combat the surviving adepts of the pagan idols as well as sinister groups such as the terrible sect of 'finger-cutters'. This latter grim fraternity infested Caucasian Albania, the modern Soviet Azerbaijan, and its members carried on their evil practices in association with 'witches, sorcerers, heathen priests, and poisoners'.[1]

A serious danger to the established Church, both in Byzantium and in Armenia itself, was presented by the large-scale heresy of the Paulicians, a Dualist sect, which in Anatolia assumed the character of a protracted military rebellion. Basically, the Paulicians followed the teachings of the Persian seer Mani, who taught that there are two opposing principles in the world, namely Matter, represented by darkness and evil, and Spirit, identified with God, Who is Light. The Paulicians were strongly opposed to the cult of images, and also rejected marriage and even sexual intercourse, which propagate the human body, viewed by them as intrinsically evil.

The Paulician movement, which numbered both Greeks and Armenians among its adherents, had many secret, occult features. Its adherents were divided into an inner hierarchy of 'Elect' members, and a broadly based body of 'Hearers'. Both categories were encouraged to masquerade as adherents of the established Church and to infiltrate its hierarchy; a secret network of underground cells was built up, in preparation for a general religious and social revolution. The Paulician revolution set much of Anatolia in turmoil throughout most of the ninth century. The unrest was crushed by the Byzantines only with great difficulty, the Paulician leader Chrysocheir being defeated in AD 872.

When the Byzantine emperors crushed the Paulician movement

---

[1] Movses Dasxuranci, *The History of the Caucasian Albanians*, trans. C. J. F. Dowsett (London, 1961), pp. 29–32.

17   Some who survived – an Armenian refugee camp in Syria, 1918. *(BBC Hulton Picture Library)*

18 Martiros Sarian – group of self-portraits, 'Three times of life', 1942. *(Novosti Press Agency)*

19 Yousuf Karsh, world-famous photographer of international celebrities, self-portrait. *(Karsh, Ottawa)*

in central Anatolia, its adepts promptly took evasive action, by regrouping both further west and further east.

In the west, the Paulicians found a ready welcome among numerous Armenian colonists in Thrace, the present-day southern Bulgaria, particularly at Philippopolis, the modern Plovdiv. Their oriental dualist heresy was revived and revitalized by the Bulgarian priest Bogomil, who lived in the tenth century. The Bogomil heresy developed distinct radical, even socialist, features, and caused enormous trouble both to the Bulgarian tsars and to the Byzantine emperors, notably Alexius Comnenus (1081–1118).

From Bulgaria, the Bogomil doctrines spread further west into Bosnia, and then Italy and southern France, where they gave rise to the Albigensian movement. The Albigensians in turn caused widespread religious and political disruption in France and had to be suppressed by a special series of crusades, with terrible atrocities and enormous loss of life. Thus it can be said that the Armenians of Anatolia and of Bulgaria contributed to the rise of one of the most dynamic movements of the Middle Ages – a movement which continues to arouse international interest, as witness the enormous success of Professor Ladurie's recent book on Montaillou, that heresy-ridden village in the south of France.[1]

To turn now to Paulicians in the east, we find them staging a comeback in the ninth and tenth centuries under the name of Tondraketsi, or Tondrakites, after the village of Tondrak, where their local leader had his headquarters. They formed religious fraternities of a partly occult character. In the absence of political parties in those bygone days, the Tondrakites provided an outlet for the argumentative, anarchical spirit which dwells within so many Armenians. Secular authorities backed the Church in persecuting the Tondrakites, but remnants of the sect survived for a long time.

Also of great interest, though less politically disruptive, was an Armenian sect known as the Arevordians, or 'children of the sun'. Some scholars regard them as colonies of Armenian Zoroastrians or fire-worshippers, who somehow escaped the attentions of St Gregory the Illuminator and his disciples, though this is by no means certain. A fourteenth-century authority wrote :

There are some Armenians by birth and language who worship

---

[1] Emmanuel Le Roy Ladurie, *Montaillou: Cathars and Catholics in a French village, 1294–1324*, translated by Barbara Bray (London, Scolar Press, 1978).

the Sun, and are called Sons of the Sun. They have neither writing nor literature. Fathers teach children by tradition what they have learnt from the Mage Zoroaster, the chief of the fire-temple. Whichever way the sun goes, they worship him in that direction, and they reverence the poplar, the lily, the cotton plant, and all the other plants which turn towards the sun. They make themselves like those flowers in faith and action, high and fragrant. They offer sacrifices for the dead, and they pay taxes to the Armenian priests. Their chief is called Hazrbed ('Head of a Thousand'), and twice or oftener every year all of them, men and women, sons and daughters, gather in a very dark pit.

There is a quaint Armenian quatrain which runs:

> A woman feels no disgust towards
>   A Son of the Sun;
> Nor towards a Turk or an Armenian;
> Whomsoever she loves, he is her faith.

This account of the older mystery and occult faiths of Armenia may serve to sketch in the background to the career of one of the most remarkable sages and spiritual teachers of modern times – Georgi Ivanovich Gurdjieff (1877–1949). Unquestionably, Gurdjieff is among the most intriguing men Armenia has ever produced. Yet the Armenians have been slow to claim him as one of their own, and his name appears in few reference books connected with Armenia.

According to Gurdjieff himself,[1] his father came of a Greek family whose ancestors had emigrated from Byzantium after the conquest of Constantinople by the Ottoman Turks in 1453. At first, the family moved to central Anatolia, and from there eventually to Georgia in the Caucasus. The name Gurdjieff gives some colour to this account, since 'Gurji' in Persian means 'a Georgian', and the Russian-style surname Gurdjieff would mean 'the man from Georgia'. However, the late John G. Bennett, who knew Gurdjieff intimately for many years, believes that Gurdjieff's father was called John Georgiades.[2]

Not long before the Russo-Armenian war of 1877–8, Gurdjieff's father moved to Aleksandropol in Armenia, the modern Leninakan. There he married a local Armenian girl and settled down; Gurdjieff the thinker was their eldest child.

---

[1] G. Gurdjieff, *Meetings with Remarkable Men* (London, 1963), pp. 40–2.
[2] John G. Bennett, *Gurdjieff: Making a new World* (London, 1976), p. 15.

Gurdjieff senior soon lost all his fortune in an outbreak of cattle plague. The family moved to Kars, where the young Georgi Gurdjieff was befriended and educated by the Dean and clergy of the Russian Orthodox cathedral. Gurdjieff senior seems to have become assimilated to his new Armenian surroundings, and won renown as a bard and poetic narrator (*ashugh*), under the pseudonym of 'Adash'.[1]

However sophisticated the message imparted by Gurdjieff in later years to his disciples at Fontainebleau, we can still detect the earthy tone of some of his father's adages, as recollected in tranquillity many years afterwards :

> Without salt, no sugar.
> Ashes come from burning.
> The cassock is to hide a fool.
> He is deep down, because you are high up.
> A man is satisfied not by the quantity of food, but by the absence of greed.
> Happy is he who sees not his own unhappiness.
> Truth is that from which the conscience can be at peace.
> No elephant and no horse – even the donkey is mighty.[2]

Indeed, some of these aphorisms anticipate the gnomic utterances which Gurdjieff had inscribed in a secret script high up on the walls of the Study House at the Fontainebleau Institute for the Harmonious Development of Man during the 1920s.

Gurdjieff's face, as it looks out at us from the frontispiece of several of his books, is typical of an Armenian gentleman of the old school, with perhaps a slightly Balkan element thrown in. The bald, high-domed cranium surmounts eyes full of reflection and, in the last photographs, sorrow at the perversity of the human race. In all likenesses which I have seen, Gurdjieff wears a bushy, bristling moustache, turned up at the ends, somewhat in Macedonian or Bulgarian fashion.

In his youth, this pioneer of transcendental meditation was quite a scallywag, as he tells us in his *Meetings with Remarkable Men*; he made a living at Aleksandropol as a craftsman and odd-job man, as well as by rather dubious financial deals. He showed an early interest in the supernatural. Once he attended a seance where a group of people sat around a three-legged table; when someone asked the age of each person present, the table tapped out the numbers with one leg. He witnessed more than one apparent miracle. In one instance, a paralytic man visited the shrine on Mount Djadjur, and was instantly

---

[1] Gurdjieff, *Meetings with Remarkable Men*, p. 32.
[2] Gurdjieff, *Views from the Real World* (London, 1976), pp. 273–6.

cured as if by magic. On another occasion, at a time of terrible drought, an archimandrite from Antioch visited Kars bearing a miraculous icon, and prayed for rain with such skill and speed that everyone for miles around was soaked to the skin by a torrential downpour!

Gurdjieff tells us that he was for three months an acolyte of Father Yevlampios in the Armenian monastery of Sanahin, in the far north of the country. With his friend Pogossian, Gurdjieff visited Holy Echmiadzin and admired the relics in the cathedral treasury. He spent some time at Ani, carrying out clandestine amateur excavations and unearthing some ancient parchment manuscripts. Later he accompanied Pogossian to Smyrna, and sailed with him to Alexandria. Gurdjieff himself went on to Cairo, while Pogossian carried on to Liverpool, became a qualified mechanical engineer and finished up a very rich man.

During the 1890s, Gurdjieff seems to have acted as a secret agent for one or other of the Armenian revolutionary parties. In later years, the British government compiled an enormous dossier on Gurdjieff, whom it regarded as an international spy and agitator.[1]

About 1900, Gurdjieff left the Caucasus for Central Asia, accompanied by an enterprising Russian lady named Madame Vitvitskaya. He did not surface again until his reappearance in Moscow in 1913.

Gurdjieff and his disciples in later times gave tantalizing glimpses into his life and adventures during those 'lost' years. According to his associate A. R. Orage, Gurdjieff's Institute at Fontainebleau was really a continuation of a society called 'Seekers after Truth', founded in 1895 by a group of doctors, archaeologists, scientists, priests and painters, whose aim was to collaborate in the study of supernatural phenomena. Members of the society went on expeditions to Persia, Afghanistan, Turkestan, Tibet and India, investigating ancient records and all kinds of psychic manifestations.[2]

Gurdjieff refers in his autobiography, rather vaguely, to 'our perilous expeditions into the depths of Asia, Africa and even Australia and its neighbouring islands'. He is more specific about his various business enterprises in Central Asia, which included government contracting, building roads and railways, and carpet and antique dealing.

---

[1] Bennett, *Gurdjieff: Making a new World*, pp. 90, 97, 127.
[2] C. S. Nott, *Teachings of Gurdjieff. The Journal of a Pupil* (London, 1961), p. 1.

Elsewhere he claims that he went to Tibet, where the Dalai Lama appointed him his agent to collect dues from the various Buddhist monasteries there. By 1913, Gurdjieff says, he had amassed a fortune of a million roubles, as well as collections of rare carpets, porcelain and Chinese cloisonné.[1] A film about Gurdjieff's adventures has been made by Peter Brook, and was shown in Britain and America in 1979.

The story of Gurdjieff's pioneer years near Moscow as a hypnotist, spiritual leader and philosopher is a fascinating one. From 1913 onwards, his reputation was steadily on the increase, and he built up a group of disciples. Under pressure of the 1917 Bolshevik Revolution, they all escaped to the Caucasus. They set up their Institute for a time in Tbilisi, then capital of independent Georgia.

After a spell in Constantinople, the Gurdjieff group eventually arrived in Western Europe. There is rich documentation on Gurdjieff's visits to America in 1924 and again in 1930, following the establishment of the Institute for the Harmonious Development of Man at Fontainebleau. Life at this long-vanished sanctuary is vividly remembered by a few surviving disciples still alive today.[2]

All this foreign travel coupled with great international renown might well have led Gurdjieff to forget his Armenian roots. This is far from being the case. Ample proof of this is found in the massive book on which Gurdjieff worked for a quarter of a century, namely *Beelzebub's Tales to his Grandson*.[3]

The original text of this work, 1,238 pages in length, was written out by Gurdjieff in pencil, in Armenian. 'Armenian is essence,' he could declare; 'the Armenian of our childhood, when we spoke from essence.'[4] According to Gurdjieff's disciple Orage, 'Gurdjieff had written it in Armenian; it had then been translated into Russian by Mme Galumian, an Armenian pupil, and then into English by some not very literate English pupils.'[5]

Beelzebub's Tales are an extraordinary compendium of wisdom,

[1] *Meetings with Remarkable* Men, pp. 254, 270.

[2] In London, in 1977, my wife Mrs Janet Lang met Madame Anna Butkovsky-Hewitt, who was born in Russia in 1885, and still most alert. Madame Butkovsky-Hewitt is the author of an interesting book, *With Gurdjieff in St Petersburg and Paris* (London, Routledge & Kegan Paul, 1978).

[3] First published in 1950, the year after Gurdjieff's death, by the London firm of Routledge & Kegan Paul.

[4] Nott, *Teachings of Gurdjieff*, pp. 125, 127. cf. *Beelzebub's Tales*, pp. 10, 12–13.

[5] Nott, *Teachings of Gurdjieff*, p. 92.

satire, reflections on human destiny, quaint anecdotes, profound moral teaching. They range over every facet of human life and experience with complete absence of inhibition. Sometimes, *Beelzebub's Tales* invite comparison with James Joyce's *Ulysses* (it is interesting to note that James Joyce included scores of Armenian words in *Finnegan's Wake*);[1] at others, they recall the philosophical passages in the novels of Henry Miller.

Central to Gurdjieff's programme is the struggle against the maleficent organ Kundabuffer, which has been implanted in man by a hostile agency, to make him see and sense reality upside down. It is this accursed, philistine Kundabuffer which inhibits human progress, and induces in mankind mechanicality, lack of will-power, and inability to make any effort to raise human civilization to a higher plane. One of Gurdjieff's main aims was to enable his disciples and mankind generally to rise above inherited taboos and fulfil their human potential – which would lead to the eventual destruction of Kundabuffer and all it stands for.

Gurdjieff's terminology is, intentionally, mysterious and allusive. It is full of allegories. Strange, phantasmagorical figures and concepts abound. Like Tolkien's Hobbits, these figures gradually grow on the reader and assume compelling reality.

In building up his cosmic system, Gurdjieff draws extensively on the folklore of Armenia and Anatolia. One of his favourite sources is the body of tales and adages attributed to the legendary Mullah Nasr ed-Din, who is equally popular in Turkey, Iran and Armenia. Quite early in *Beelzebub's Tales* (pp. 45–50), we come across an amusing though long-winded anecdote about a great friend of Gurdjieff, a richly humorous Armenian railway worker – 'that precious jewel, the extremely sympathetic Karapet of Tiflis'. It is also worth noting that Gurdjieff and his exponent A. R. Orage maintained that the name of Beelzebub's spaceship, Karnak, was Armenian in derivation, being connected with the Greek idea of the body being the tomb of the soul.[2]

Gurdjieff had a typically Armenian knack of sizing up everyone he met, and seeing the strong and the weak points of every nation and every individual he visited. *Beelzebub's Tales* even include a

[1] V. Nersessian, 'Armenian in Finnegan's Wake', in *A Wake Newslitter*, vol. XIII, no. 3, July 1976, pp. 48–51.

[2] Nott, *Teachings of Gurdjieff*, p. 128.

hilarious 'take-off' of the Germans, with a parody of a German drinking song :

> Blödsinn, Blödsinn,
> Du mein Vergnügen,
> Stumpfsinn, Stumpfsinn,
> Du meine Lust.

> (Barmy bloody-mindedness,
> You are my pleasure;
> Blessed dim-wittedness,
> You are my joy.)

In the very next sentence, Gurdjieff cites a characteristically down-to-earth Armenian maxim (ascribed to Mullah Nasr ed-Din !) : 'The very greatest happiness consists in obtaining the pleasurable with the profitable.'[1]

With the passage of time, G. I. Gurdjieff, Armenian international prophet and guru, offspring of nineteenth-century Aleksandropol and Kars in the forsaken lands, attracts ever-increasing interest, as one of the most stimulating and unorthodox influences of the twentieth century. This interest is by no means impaired by intermittent attempts to 'debunk' him – attempts which the resilient sage continues to resist with undiminished posthumous vigour.

A final glimpse of Armenian mastery of the occult arts is provided in the imaginative novel, *A Hundred Years of Solitude,* by the Colombian writer, Gabriel García Marquez. Here, the leading character encounters a group of gypsies who are plying their trades in a South American village. Among them was a taciturn Armenian, who in Spanish was hawking a syrup guaranteed to make one invisible. This Armenian drank down a glass of the amber substance, and promptly 'turned into a puddle of pestilential and smoking pitch'. Eventually the group dispersed, attracted by other amusements, and 'the puddle of the taciturn Armenian evaporated completely'.[2] Perhaps this is a fitting conclusion to this brief survey of Armenian contact with the supernatural powers.

---

[1] *Beelzebub's Tales*, p. 661. Compare the following passage, however : 'One of the great illusions consequent on the organ Kundabuffer is that the pursuit of happiness as an aim in itself is good. If we have a real aim, then we may obtain happiness as a by-product' (Nott, *Teachings of Gurdjieff*, p. 145).

[2] Spanish original, published in Argentina, 1967. English trans. by Gregory Rabassa, 1970, p. 21. Literary research by Elizabeth M. Lang.

14

Armenians and the Arts World-wide

IT IS REMARKABLE that a small nation like the Armenians, scattered all over the world, and never numbering more than seven million in aggregate, should distinguish themselves in so many branches of artistic creation. Sometimes this creation takes the form of original folk arts and crafts – stone and wood carving, ceramic ware, and production of hand-woven rugs and carpets, or of delicate silver filigree work. Sometimes the creative drive is applied to enriching the Western literary and artistic experience, as in the case of the writers William Saroyan, Michael Arlen and Henri Troyat, the film director Rouben Mamoulian, or musical virtuosi and opera stars such as Manoug Parikian and Sona Ghazarian. Sometimes again the Armenian genius is applied to giving pictorial expression to life wherever the artist may happen to find himself, whether in his homeland or in a distant country far from his native land.

Modern Armenians are heirs to ancient local traditions of art and culture which had been practised by their forerunners long before the Armenians themselves appeared on the world scene. From the Early Bronze Age onwards, the Hurrians and other inhabitants of the eastern Anatolian area were at the forefront of ancient technological development, notably in ceramics and metallurgy. The burnished pottery of the Kuro-Araxes culture (from 3000 BC) is decorated with elegant geometrical designs, particularly spirals. By about 1500 BC, many branches of advanced metal processing were perfected in Armenia, including forging, chasing, cutting, stamping, grinding and polishing, as well as jewellery inlaying.

From around 1000 BC, the Urartians centred on Lake Van further developed these useful arts. They produced unusual bronze shields, decorated with animal figures, and cauldrons with distinctive handles, which were purchased by several peoples of the ancient world, including the Etruscans. The Urartians were adept as goldsmiths and workers in ivory; they manufactured furniture of sophisticated design.[1]

Urartian architecture was highly inventive. Much of it was military in character, but there were elaborate temple buildings dedicated to the chief gods. The Urartians were experts at carving large blocks of stone which fitted neatly together without the use of mortar. They excelled at constructing aqueducts, sewers and tunnels.

An important contribution to architectural science was the sloping roof with triangular pediment and surrounding colonnade. These features occur at the Urartian temple of Musasir – a shrine looted and destroyed by the Assyrian king Sargon II in 714 BC, and then depicted in Assyrian reliefs of Khorsabad palace. After extensive use in Classical Greece and Rome, the design occurs in the main façade of the British Museum. The interior walls of many Urartian public buildings were adorned with coloured frescoes.

Between the fall of Urartu soon after 600 BC, and the conversion of Armenia to Christianity in AD 301, art in Armenia had a somewhat derivative, provincial character. However, we find beautiful silver gilt rhytons or drinking horns, while the silver coins of King Tigranes the Great (95–55 BC) are masterpieces of numismatic art. The Classical temple at Garni, now restored by Professor A. Sahinian, is noteworthy for its harmonious and beautiful outline, and its spectacular siting on a high rocky promontory.

The architects of early Christian Armenia took over the Classical basilica, probably via Syria, and also created original variants, such as the Ereruk basilica (fifth and sixth centuries). Armenian master masons were also great experts in domed construction. The seventh-century circular cathedral at Zvartnotz, near Holy Echmiadzin, is now in ruins, but it was one of the architectural marvels of early Christendom.

An art in which the Armenians have long been highly skilled is that of manuscript illumination. Sometimes stylized, sometimes naturalistic,

---

[1] Guitty Azarpay, *Urartian Art and Artifacts, A Chronological Study* (University of California Press, 1968).

but always colourful and graphic, the miniatures in medieval Armenian manuscripts constitute a major treasure of the Christian world. Many of these illuminated manuscripts can be found today in libraries throughout the world, including the Chester Beatty library in Dublin, the Walters Art Gallery in Baltimore, the British Library, the Bibliothèque Nationale, and the Armenian Patriarchate in Jerusalem.[1]

Both instrumental and vocal music have a long history in Armenia. Five thousand years ago, simple melodies were being played on pipes and flutes fashioned from bone and horn. The Urartians are known to have sung cheerful songs to keep up their morale. In early medieval Armenia, *gusans* or minstrels played a central part in social life – much to the disgust of the puritanical clergy. At important feasts, these minstrels were accompanied by drummers, pipers, trumpeters and harpists.

When at Erevan in 1978, I was shown a wide selection of traditional instruments which are still manufactured and widely used in Armenia today. Stringed instruments which I saw comprised the *kanun*, a type of Egyptian harp or trapezoidal zither; the spiked fiddle or *kamancha*; and a kind of lute, not fretted, with bent neck, called the *oud*. Another popular stringed instrument is the *tar*. Also characteristic are two percussion instruments, the *dap*, which is a small drum like a tambourine, and the medium-sized drum called *dohol* or *davul*. There is also an extensive range of wind instruments, including a local variant of the shawm (ancestor of the oboe), pan-pipes, and a sort of bagpipe.

As Armenians moved around the world, they took their creative expertise with them, and practised their skills wherever their destiny might take them. When the dome of Saint Sophia Cathedral in Constantinople was damaged by an earthquake in 989, the Byzantine authorities sent to far-off Ani to summon the Armenian royal architect Trdat, whose new dome still stands upright almost a millennium later. In Cilicia, the Armenians designed a number of castles, such as that of Anazarba, which withstood repeated sieges during the turbulent era of the Crusades. The Frankish Crusaders were in turn influenced by what they saw of Armenian national architecture, which contributed elements to the decorative figure sculpture of Romanesque churches. The circular domed churches of Armenia were copied in France, and also in the familiar Round Church, opposite St John's College, Cambridge. A representation of the circular cathedral of

[1] Lydia A. Dournovo, *Armenian Miniatures* (London, 1961).

Zvartnotz is among the biblical reliefs adorning the Sainte-Chapelle in Paris, although these are now thought to be mainly nineteenth-century additions.

The architecture of Seljuq and, later, of Ottoman Turkey incorporated several Armenian elements. Thus, the circular tomb towers or *kümbets* of Anatolia, with their pointed roofs, look as if they had been sliced off the top of Armenian churches, and then set up on platforms at ground level. It is worth mentioning that Sinān, court architect of the Ottoman Sultan Sulaiman the Magnificent (1520–66), is reputed to have been of Armenian descent. In Iran, at New Julfa close to Isfahan, the seventeenth-century Armenian community created a wonderland of churches and dwellings in which the Armenian national style is cleverly fused with that of Safavi Iran.[1]

In recent times, a world-wide reputation was enjoyed by the late Édouard Utudjian of the Rue Saint-Lazare, Paris, who ran an establishment called Le Monde Souterrain and issued a regular bulletin. Monsieur Utudjian was an international consultant on all forms of underground construction, including railway tunnels, mines, piped water supply and drainage systems.

In painting, there has been a veritable explosion of Armenian talent during the past century or so. A pioneer of modern painting was Hacop Hovnatanian (1806–81), who flourished in Tbilisi during the middle of the nineteenth century. Hovnatanian was unsurpassed in his day as a portraitist, specializing in painting members of the Armenian middle classes and aristocracy. His eye for character is unerring, and his meticulous depiction of costume and hair style provides valuable material for the social historian. His portraits of the Russian Viceroy General Golovin and of the Armenian Catholicos Nerses V are classics of their kind.

Later in the century, a dominant position in Russian marine painting was held by Ivan Konstantinovich Aivazovsky (1817–1900), born at Theodosia in the Crimea. Aivazovsky is a consummate master of all the varying moods of the sea, ranging from the terror of the storm to calm, sultry nights in romantic ports in the Bosphorus or the Mediterranean.

Among Soviet Armenian artists, popular favourites were the late Hakop Kojoyan (1883–1959) and the lamented Ervand Kochar (1899–1979). Kojoyan was a master of vivid colour and painted with

1 John Carswell, *New Julfa. The Armenian churches and other buildings* (Clarendon Press, Oxford, 1968).

uninhibited verve and a strong sense of the fantastic and the grotesque; he excelled as a book illustrator. Ervand Kochar was a likeable and many-sided personality, equally talented as a painter and as a sculptor. His equestrian statue of the legendary Armenian hero David of Sassoun rears up in front of Erevan railway station, as if to protect it from attack by unscrupulous capitalists.

The greatest Armenian painter I ever met was Martiros Sarian (1880–1972), who became a legend in his own lifetime. Sarian's career began at the turn of the twentieth century, and his early works include evocative scenes from the Muslim Near East. Looking at these pictures of hot, dry countries, you can hear the mangy dogs quarrelling in dusty lanes, taste the dates on the palms, and itch from the prickly heat from sand blown across the desert. Sarian was invited in 1921 to take charge of rebuilding cultural and artistic institutions in recently established Soviet Armenia.

From then on, Sarian devoted himself to the artistic regeneration of devastated Armenia, both by his inspiring leadership and in his own creative work. He excelled in many genres, including landscapes and still life, and painted portraits of leading Soviet personalities, including some future victims of the Stalin-Beria purges of the 1930s. The man of the soil and the intellectual were blended in him – and without any self-conscious effort. His sense of colour and form was uncanny. It is useless to argue that Sarian was an Impressionist, or a Post-Impressionist, or whatever. His inner spiritual world blended with the outer world around him, and he produced a seemingly endless stream of canvases, imbued to the highest degree with technical mastery and humanistic integrity.[1]

Another high spot of twentieth-century Armenian art is the original, disconcertingly unorthodox work of Alexander Bazhbeuk-Melikian (1891–1966). Bazhbeuk-Melikian lived in Georgia and belonged to the same Tbilisi school of Armenian painters which had produced the portraitist Hovnatanian. He was a close friend of his younger contemporary and neighbour, the Georgian painter Lado Gudiashvili, and some of his canvases could be mistaken for Gudiashvili's. Bazhbeuk-Melikian's paintings are redolent of the old Tbilisi *vie de bohème*, and his beautiful, scantily clad women have more than a touch of some oriental Folies Bergères, or of the harems of the Arabian Nights.

Bazhbeuk-Melikian was ignored and persecuted by the Soviet

[1] Martiros Sarian, *Iz moiei zhizni* (autobiography : Russian), (Moscow, 1970).

artistic establishment. He lived with three other members of his family in a single room which served as studio, kitchen, and bedroom combined. So sensitive was he to the ostracism and ridicule which his idiosyncratic art attracted that he made little or no attempt to sell or exhibit his wonderful pictures. When his family needed more living space, he would take a few canvases outside at night and burn them. Only after his death did the Soviet cultural bureaucracy realise that a painter of international stature had been working for half a century unrecognized in its midst. A similar fate befell another talented Tbilisi Armenian painter who adopted the pseudonym of Giotto, and died at the age of seventy. His brilliant but mildewed paintings were rescued in the nick of time from a sordid, rat-infested basement in Tbilisi, and now occupy a place of honour in the Erevan Museum of Modern Art.

Hardship and personal tragedy also dogged the life and career of the most influential of all modern Armenian painters, Arshile Gorky (1904–48), who worked in America. His real name was Vosdanik Manuk Adoian, but he later assumed the name Gorky, which is Russian for 'bitter'. By the time he began his schooling, the Turks had massacred all his four grandparents, six uncles and three aunts. He himself had survived a 150-mile forced march across mountains and desert, after which his mother died of starvation in his arms. By some miracle, the young Gorky gained admission to America in 1920, when he was fifteen years old – he was also 6 foot 4 inches tall, an exceptional stature for an Armenian.

By 1925, Arshile Gorky was installed in his first Greenwich Village studio, on Sullivan Street, New York. The Depression proved a hard time for him, and poverty became a way of life. He taught at the Grand Central School of Arts, and later moved to a studio at 36 Union Square. In 1935, he began his monumental Newark Airport murals, comprising ten panels covering 1,530 square feet – a great technical achievement. Later, the murals were painted over, but they are now being uncovered and restored. Gorky's picture *The Artist and his Mother*, based on an old photograph taken in Van in 1912, established his reputation on its completion in 1936. Hailed as a *magnum opus* of the twentieth century, it hangs in New York's Whitney Museum.

In 1943, the French *avant-garde* painter and philosopher André Breton, then living in New York, befriended Gorky. By the time Gorky had his one-man show at the Julien Levy Gallery in New York in

1945, he was already considered an important member of the Surrealist movement. Probably through the influence of André Masson and Joan Miró, Gorky developed an *art informel* style, though he always worked objective shapes into his pictures. Gorky is the connecting link between the European Surrealists and the young Americans, to whom he demonstrated the actual technique and working out of Automatism.

During the mid-1940s, Arshile Gorky was working with ferocious energy in his 'Glass House' studio in Sherman, Connecticut. Early in 1946, the studio caught fire and all his paintings and books kept there were destroyed. He also underwent an operation for cancer. His marriage was under strain. In June 1948, when Gorky was a passenger in Julien Levy's car, his neck was broken and his right arm paralysed in a serious accident. Next month his wife and two daughters left him. On 21 July 1948, his body was found hanging in a shed at Sherman. In white chalk, on a nearby picture crate, was written: 'Goodbye My Loveds'.

Arshile Gorky's influence on young American artists was and is enormous. He is a great emancipator. He breaks through the rigid structuring of Cubism to a pure poetic imagery, with free-flowing space, constantly moving forms, improvisation and spontaneity. This explosive impetus came partly from his need to express what was Armenian in his own background, the emotional freedom and immemorial splendour of rural antiquity in the region of Van and of Ararat. The Armenian past saturated his consciousness, as if the links with his homeland had never been broken.

Arshile Gorky was passionately interested in the aesthetic principles of art. He could not understand how a revolutionary country like the Soviet Union could ape Western governments by maintaining such a reactionary posture in its official attitude to art. Socialist Realism he dismissed as 'poor painting for poor people'. In his painting as in his principles, Gorky was a major, important artist, whose influence was direct, clear and lasting.

Although Armenia has never since produced an artist of Arshile Gorky's stature, the traditions of Armenian painting are kept alive today by many talented exponents, in the Lebanon, Egypt, Italy and the United States of America. Particularly vigorous is the French school of Armenian painters, one of the senior representatives of which was Zareh Mutafian (1907–80). Mutafian is noted for his love of vivid colours, and he excels in landscapes and in marine subjects: between

1933 and 1976, he held no less than thirty one-man exhibitions in different countries of the world.[1]

Even better known internationally is the French Armenian Surrealist painter Garzou or Charzou, pseudonym of Garnik Zulumanian, also born in 1907. His career culminated with election in 1978 to the Académie des Beaux-Arts, and his evocative, thought-provoking paintings hang in many of the leading galleries of the world. Also highly esteemed is Jansem, whose real name is Jean Semerjian. Born in Asia Minor in 1920, Jansem is well known as a book illustrator, while his oil paintings (some of them considered rather traditional in style) are regularly exhibited in Paris at the Garnier Gallery.

The prince of Armenian book illustrators in modern times was Edgar Chahine (1874–1947), that most stylish of engravers, whose incomparable, imaginative work adorns some of the best editions of French writers such as Flaubert, Barrès, Colette, Huysmans and the Goncourts. Chahine's father was from Akn, in eastern Turkey; his mother Nemzik was from the Armenian community of Suceava, Romania. Edgar himself was born rather casually at Vienna, when his parents were passing through on their way to a cure at Carlsbad. His mother had not realized that she was pregnant, such was the genteel ignorance of the facts of life then prevalent among some Armenian brides.

Until he was eighteen Edgar Chahine lived with his parents in Constantinople. Then he left for Venice, where he studied at the Accademia di Belle Arti and at the Armenian College, run by the Mekhitarist Fathers. In 1895, Chahine and his mother moved to Paris. The young artist enrolled at the Académie Julian, but found little there to stimulate him. He would declare : 'Je suis élève de la rue !' – and drew his inspiration from Paris streets and markets, such as those in Clichy and Montparnasse. He watched and duly portrayed carters and rag-and-bone men, vagabonds and millhands, against a background of factory chimneys and crumbling walls. Such scenes may have reminded him of the more squalid areas of old Constantinople. But Chahine also excelled in portrayal of elegant ladies from the fashionable world. His evocations of mysterious beauties riding up and down the Bois de Boulogne or the Champs Elysées are unforgettable for their seductive suavity and social poise.

The year 1899 was crucial for the young Armenian : he exhibited two paintings, a drypoint and three etchings in the Salon of the

[1] Suzanne d'Arthez, *Mutafian* (Paris, 1978).

Société Nationale des Beaux-Arts. Leading bibliophiles and art dealers began to offer him commissions. At the 1900 World Exhibition in Paris, he received a gold medal for his engravings. Chahine participated in the 1901 Venice Biennale, and two years later Anatole France invited Chahine to illustrate his *Histoire Comique*. In 1906, Chahine produced his most successful illustrations : 110 soft-ground etchings for Gabriel Mourey's *Fêtes foraines de Paris*.

As in the case of Arshile Gorky, Edgar Chahine's life was dogged by tragedy and misfortune. His fiancée Mary Jacobson died of tuberculosis in 1906, and Chahine suffered a severe nervous breakdown. It took more than a decade for Chahine to regain his creative drive. In 1921, the artist married Simone Julia Gaumet, a Parisian art student, revisited Venice, and produced a number of engravings of that city – engravings which have been compared with those of Whistler. But his Paris studio was destroyed by fire in 1926, and two-thirds of his prints were burnt. A flood in 1942 caused extensive damage to his new studio at 11 Square Alboni, which also helps to explain the great rarity of Chahine's original engravings. In spite of his Western orientation, Chahine was a patriotic Armenian to the end. He supported Armenian cultural organizations in France, exhibited at Erevan in 1936, and was buried in 1947 in the Armenian cemetery in Paris.

Despite his incomparable perfection of style, Chahine has for too long been little known to the general public. An exhibition at the Lumley Cazalet Gallery in London in March 1977 made his work available in Great Britain. A friend has described Chahine's personality in glowing terms : 'An exceptional human being : a great judge of character, he was endowed with an intelligence full of sensitiveness and finesse. With all that he was modest and his heart was of pure gold.' All the signs point to a continued growth in Chahine's posthumous reputation. Since 1965, exhibitions of his prints have taken place in Paris, Moscow, Chicago, Venice, San Francisco and Stockholm.[1]

The qualities of artistic integrity, professional accomplishment, and instinctive sense of style are also exemplified in his younger compatriot, the world-famous photographer Yousuf Karsh, born in 1908 at Mardin, eastern Turkey. Karsh of Ottawa is a household word, so it is useless to exhaust oneself in superlatives. He has immortalized in his art such figures as Winston Churchill, Nikita Khrushchev, Albert Einstein,

[1] M. R. Tabanelli, *Edgar Chahine: Catalogue de l'Oeuvre gravée* (Milan, 1977).

20 Academician Henri Troyat of Paris, born 1911, biographer, historian and novelist. *(Courtesy Henri Troyat)*

21 William Saroyan at Haigazian College, Beirut. *(Armenian Missionary Association of America)*

22 Miss Gilda Buchakjian, student editor of *Haigazian College Herald* newspaper, in her Beirut office. *(Armenian Missionary Association of America)*

23 David of Sassoun, equestrian statue by Ervand Kochar. *(Armenian Society for Friendship and Cultural Relations)*

24 Arshile Gorky, study for painting, *Nude*, 1945. *(Arts Council of Great Britain)*

25 Ceramic by Vresh David Kanikanian, a London-based sculptor from Iraq. *(Iraqi Cultural Centre)*

Sibelius, Pablo Casals, Ernest Hemingway, Somerset Maugham and Pope John XXIII. Karsh has elevated the art of photography from the mechanical process of accurate reproduction of a subject or milieu to a fine art, in which the psychological qualities of his sitter come through to an uncanny degree, and bring a new element to our conception of the character portrayed. An uncanny feature of Karsh's work is to impart a three-dimensional quality to his portraits, so that we seem to be looking all round the subjects; thus, they gain the quality of being, one could say, photographic statues in the round.[1] During his long and fruitful career, Karsh has received many official honours and academic distinctions.

From photography we move naturally to the art of the cinema. Here, the great figure is Rouben Mamoulian, born in 1897. Mamoulian combines great technical originality with style and poetry. In 1932, he was already using synthetic sound, in *Dr Jekyll and Mr Hyde*. This treatment of Robert Louis Stevenson's spine-chilling story is important enough to warrant a whole chapter in a recent book about the film considered as a tale of terror.[2] It was also the first foreign film to be banned by the German censors after Hitler's accession to power in 1933. Mamoulian's *Becky Sharp* (1935) was the first film to make use of technicolour, though as yet he had only three colours with which to experiment. For Greta Garbo, Mamoulian created the scenic framework for what was perhaps her greatest role – as Queen Christina of Sweden (1933). Other outstanding Mamoulian films were *The Mark of Zorro* (1940) and *Blood and Sand* (1941). Among his important theatre productions was *Oklahoma* (1943). His musical productions, both on the stage and in the cinema are remarkable for the way in which the dance is used to further the action and to interpret character – as in one of his last triumphs, *Silk Stockings* (1957). In all, Mamoulian made sixteen films, many of them classics of cinema history.[3]

There is a flourishing film industry within Soviet Armenia, with a wealth of original talent to draw on. An absorbing film about life in early Soviet Armenia, *Nahapet* (1978), was shown successfully on BBC Television. It is all the more deplorable to have to record the unrelenting persecution by the Soviet establishment of the most talented con-

---

[1] *In Search of Greatness. Reflections of Yousuf Karsh* (New York, 1962); British *Who's Who*.

[2] S. S. Prawer, *Caligari's Children* (Oxford University Press, 1979).

[3] Tom Milne, *Rouben Mamoulian* (London, 1969); British *Who's Who*.

tempory Armenian film producer, Sarkis Paradjanov. After creating such exceptional films as *Shadows of our Forgotten Ancestors* and *The Colour of Pomegranates*, Paradjanov somehow fell foul of the Soviet regime in 1974, and was sentenced to five years in a strict-regime labour camp. He was accused of homosexuality, alleged to have raped a member of the Communist Party, and to have perverted an old lady of eighty with a pornographic pen! He was last heard of living in squalor in Tbilisi, forbidden to undertake any creative work, and reduced to begging in the streets.[1]

The harmonious synthesis of dramatic action, music and dance characteristic of Mamoulian's work has its roots in ancient Armenian tradition. A court theatre was already functioning in Armenia in the age of Julius Caesar, about 50 BC. Mummers and itinerant bards were busy performers in medieval times, both in royal palaces and at popular festivals. During the nineteenth century, original Armenian plays and operas were staged with success in Tbilisi and in Constantinople. At the Ottoman capital, the outstanding figure was Tigran Chukhajian (1837–98), unsurpassed as a melodist, and equally at home in grand opera and in light opera in the Offenbach mode. Armen Tigranian (1879–1950) composed the lyric drama *Anush*, which remains in the permanent repertory of the Erevan opera. In his opera *Almast*, Alexander Spendiarov or Spendiarian (1871–1928) treats Armenian and Persian themes with a sophistication which he had learnt at the feet of his teacher, Rimsky-Korsakov.[2] The dramatic element bulks large in the art of the late Aram Khatchaturian, whose *Spartacus* and *Gayané* ballets are favourites in the international repertoire.

Armenian opera singers excel in both the Armenian and in the standard Western repertoires. In the Soviet Union, Gohar Gasparian and Lucine Zakarian are admired sopranos. Lucine Amara appears regularly at the Metropolitan Opera in New York, and also made excellent recordings with Sir Thomas Beecham.

There are also younger Armenian sopranos established in Western Europe. German-speaking audiences respond warmly to the art of Luisa Bosabalian of the Hamburg Opera, and of Sona Ghazarian of Vienna. Luisa Bosabalian excels in the Puccini operas, and is much applauded when she sings the title roles in *Madame Butterfly* and *La Bohême*. Sona Ghazarian's rise to fame has been quite spectacular.

[1] H. Anassian, 'No future but beggary for a master of film', in *The Times*, London, 14 April 1980, p. 16.

[2] A. Shahverdyan, *A. A. Spendiaryan* (Erevan, 1971).

After her début as Violetta in *La Traviata* at Vienna in 1974, an Austrian newspaper commented : 'A star was born.' Sona Ghazarian was then twenty-seven years old; after her début as Rosina in *The Barber of Seville*, also in 1974, a Viennese critic commented : 'There seems to be no prospect of a halt in Miss Ghazarian's career.' Indeed, she still shows no sign of slowing down – during the past seven years, the Viennese public has heard her as Gilda in *Rigoletto* and as Julia in a rare opera by Bellini dealing with the story of Romeo and Juliet : *I Capuletti ed i Montecchi*. She broadcasts frequently and makes many recordings, so that British listeners have heard her in such varied works as *Fidelio*, Mozart's *Il Re Pastore*, *Arabella* by Richard Strauss, and Mendelssohn's Second Symphony, the so-called *Lobgesang*.

The operatic life of Austria has also been enriched by several Armenian male singers. The city of Linz owes much to the baritone Stefan Zadejan, born in Vienna in 1912. From 1945 onwards, Zadejan was a resident performer at the Linz opera house, later becoming its chief regisseur. Among his memorable roles were those of Hans Sachs in *Die Meistersinger*, and Boris Godunov in Mussorgsky's masterpiece. From 1950 until his retirement in 1972, Zadejan was director of the opera division of the Anton Bruckner Conservatory.

A promising lyric tenor is Albert Khadjesari (or Khadjesarian), born in Teheran in 1937, and a former pupil of the Vienna Music Academy. He has mastered the solo parts of the Armenian classical liturgy in the settings by Komitas and Yekmalian, and is much in demand at solemn church ceremonies. For the Viennese public, he appears regularly in the standard operetta repertory, including *The Gipsy Baron, Land of Smiles*, and *Madame Pompadour*.

Apart from Germany and Austria, Armenians are active as opera singers and producers in several other countries, including France and Greece. After singing with conductors of the calibre of Sir Thomas Beecham (in Grétry's exquisite *Zémire et Azor*), Arda Mandikian is now Administrator of the Greek National Opera in Athens. In 1980, the BBC broadcast a French performance of Auber's sparkling opera, *Le Cheval de Bronze* (1835), and two of the leading performers bore Armenian names.

A special word is called for regarding that well established favourite Cathy Berberian. In an interview with the London *Times* musical correspondent Alan Blyth in October 1972, Cathy Berberian admitted that she does not have perfect pitch, nor what is generally regarded as

a 'beautiful voice'. 'After all,' she said, 'I'm a bit of a "ham".' But
Cathy is also a tremendous character. Her range extends from Monte-
verdi to Berio and Stravinsky. She has an unlimited sense of humour,
and revels in parody and pastiche. She can sing in any style or idiom,
from Australian to Aztec. No wonder audiences applaud her wherever
she goes, and persistently clamour for more.

Among Armenian composers, the name of Aram Khatchaturian
naturally stands out. Although purists compare him unfavourably with
Shostakovich, the brash, breezy, inventive Khatchaturian is assured
of a place in the pantheon of Soviet and of world musicians. Arthur
Rubinstein, in his recent memoirs, strikes a discordant note, stating
that he took up Khatchaturian's Piano Concerto when it first appeared, during the Second World War, but soon gave it up, owing to
its 'inherent banality'. However, the Armenian composer's orchestral
works are in constant demand throughout the Soviet Union, and also
rate no less than twenty entries in a catalogue of records currently
available in the United States of America.[1] All the major British
orchestras play them from time to time, and British record catalogues
contain an impressive selection.

In the United States, there is one modern Armenian composer who
outstrips even Khatchaturian in the range of his recorded output. This
is Alan Hovhaness (born 1911), who boasts no less than thirty-four
entries in the current Armenian Record Guide published in New York.
He has composed twenty-five symphonies to date, of which the best
known is the Saint Vartan Symphony, composed in 1950 for the
1,500th anniversary of the Battle of Avarayr, fought by Armenian
Christians against invading Persian fire-worshippers in AD 451.
According to the *Penguin Stereo Record Guide*, the symphony (in
twenty-four movements) tends to sprawl. 'Some may be tempted on
hearing this work to feel that perhaps the Persians had a point.'
Although Hovhaness is criticized at times for putting more colour than
substance into his symphonic music, there is no denying his influence
on modern American and Armenian composers and executants.

An unusually discriminating orchestral conductor is Angelo Ephrikian, who specializes in concertos and choral works of the Baroque and
later-eighteenth-century periods. Working with chamber ensembles at
Bologna, Venice and elsewhere, Ephrikian has made masterly recordings of works by Vivaldi, Haydn and other composers of the age with

[1] John M. Sarian, *Record Guide, Armenian Musicians and Composers* (Ararat
Press, New York, 1979).

which he seems to have a special affinity.

Among organ virtuosi, pride of place belongs to Berj Zamkochian, resident organist of the Boston Symphony Orchestra, who has made several recordings of the Armenian Mass and of works by such composers as Liszt, Max Reger, and Mendelssohn. There are some enjoyable recent recordings of classical harp concertos made by the Armenian harpist Shushanik Miltonian, who has lived for some years in Belgium.

Many Armenian pianists have won distinction in concert halls all over the world. To give but one example, the London public was very favourably impressed by a recital in 1978 at the Queen Elizabeth Hall by Seta Tanyel, a prizewinner in the first Arthur Rubinstein International Piano Master competition. Her repertoire includes the sonatas of Haydn and Beethoven, and romantic masterpieces by Schumann and Liszt.

Armenians have a natural affinity with the violin, and extract the maximum of sweetness from the instrument. Within the Soviet Union, the Komitas Quartet has built up an enviable reputation over the years. In Great Britain, the father figure among Armenian violinists is Manoug Parikian, arguably the greatest virtuoso of the instrument resident in the country. Born at Mersin, Turkey, in 1920, Parikian was trained at the Trinity College of Music in London. At the age of twenty-seven he was appointed Leader of the Liverpool Philharmonia Orchestra; from 1949 to 1957, he was Leader of the Philharmonic Orchestra. Parikian has appeared in all European countries as solo violinist and given recitals at many important festivals. He introduced the Shostakovich Violin Concerto to Scandinavia at a Stockholm concert in 1956, and has consistently championed modern British composers. He toured the Soviet Union with success in 1961. In recent years, his career has taken on a new lease of life with the establishment of the Parikian/Fleming/Roberts trio, who currently give acclaimed performances of the piano trios of Mozart, Haydn, Beethoven, Schubert and Brahms.[1]

Parikian's work is worthily continued by another Armenian violinist, his nephew Levon Chilingirian. The Chilingirian Quartet is an ensemble of international standing. Its Schubert quartet cycle at the London Wigmore Hall was a musical sensation, and its Beethoven series there in June 1980 was sold out. The Chilingirian Quartet has made many recordings, including the three beautiful quartets of that ill-starred

[1] British *Who's Who*.

Spanish musical genius Arriaga. They are young players, with nimble fingers, fresh and spontaneous in approach, and possessing a rare sweetness of tone. Their musical sincerity and integrity are above praise.

Another young Armenian musician to win international acclaim is the London-based classical guitarist Julian Byzantine. An Associate of the Royal College of Music, Mr Byzantine has a special interest in the manuscripts of the early guitarists and lutenists, and he often performs on the baroque guitar. This early instrument is double strung, like the lute, and once had a strong tradition in many European countries; its sound is somewhere between that of the lute and that of the modern guitar, yet subtly different from either. Julian Byzantine has made many appearances at the Wigmore Hall and the Queen Elizabeth Hall, and also plays the concertos of Vivaldi, Giuliani, Castelnuovo-Tedesco, Villa Lobos and Rodrigo with the Royal Philharmonic and Birmingham Symphony Orchestras. In the modern music field, he has worked with Peter Maxwell Davies and Pierre Boulez, and has had works specially composed for him. Julian Byzantine has broadcast on BBC Radio 3, and makes records for the EMI company. He has toured the Middle and Far East, Australia and New Zealand, as well as appearing in Norway, Sweden, Yugoslavia and the United States of America.

Armenians possess a natural talent for dramatic presentation. They have mobile, expressive features, are excellent mimics, and have a real instinct for characterization. An important school of Armenian dramatists sprang up in the nineteenth century, producing heroic tragedies and genre comedies and dramas having their roots in ancient and modern Armenian life. The great names here are those of Gabriel Sundukian (1825–1912) and Alexander Shirvanzadé (1858–1935). Under the oppressive regime of Sultan 'Abdul Hamid, the Constantinople Armenian theatre operated under restrictions, and the most interesting developments took place in the Georgian capital of Tbilisi, and in some provincial towns of Russian Armenia. Several plays of Shakespeare were translated into Armenian during the nineteenth and early twentieth centuries, and many of his heroic roles were interpreted with distinction by the actor P. Adamian and many other talented exponents.

Armenians also excel in the technical side of stage production, and can achieve brilliant effects with modest resources. These factors contributed to the meteoric though tragically short career of Evgeny Vakhtangov (1883–1922), founder of the Moscow theatre which bears his name. Vakhtangov's revolutionary mode of directing, called 'fantastic realism', and his production techniques have influenced regisseurs working as far afield as Tel Aviv and New York.[1]

During recent years, the American Armenian community has built up an interesting, adventurous theatre of its own, using both English- and Armenian-language media. An outstanding figure here is William Saroyan, whose highly individual plays have built up a wide following.

Armenian literature has a continuous history going back to the fifth century AD, when its distinctive alphabet was invented.[2] Over the last decade, the important early chronicles of Agathangelos and Moses of Khorene have been translated into English by Professor R. W. Thomson of Harvard University. Mischa Kudian of London has given us a rendering of sections of the *Book of Lamentations* by the mystical poet Gregory of Narek (950–1010). The poet seeks to attain harmony with God by merging his sinful soul with the divine ethos. His moving work may be compared with the Psalms of David, and copies of it are endowed by simple Armenian folk with magical, talismanic properties.

An Armenian legend which ranks also as a national epic is the David of Sassoun cycle, associated with a mountain region in southwestern Armenia, now part of Turkey. It is difficult to classify the David of Sassoun stories as ancient, medieval or modern. The action takes place about a thousand years ago, during the Saracen domination over Armenia. However, the tales and poems were collected and put into shape by folklore specialists only towards the end of the nineteenth century. The mighty heroes of Sassoun are swashbuckling daredevils, Robin Hood style characters, equally successful in bed and on the battlefield. Their exploits make excellent reading, and are available in both English and French translation.[3]

Armenian romantic and epic poetry has flourished greatly from the second half of the nineteenth century onwards. Much of this material has become available to the English-speaking world through the efforts of the London Mashtotz Press, directed by Mischa Kudian, who is also the chief translator. Through this publishing house, we can ap-

[1] Nishan Parlakian, 'Evgenii Vakhtangov; Our Man in Moscow', in *Ararat*, New York, Spring 1969, pp. 34–7.

[2] D. M. Lang, *Armenia: Cradle of Civilization*, pp. 263–85; Charles Burney and D. M. Lang, *The Peoples of the Hills, Ancient Ararat and Caucasus* (London and New York, 1971), pp. 226–48.

[3] By Leon Surmelian, *Daredevils of Sassoun* (London, 1966); *David de Sassoun, épopée en vers*, trans. F. Feydit (Paris, 1964).

preciate the romantic narrative poems of Hovhannes Tumanian (1869–1923), known as the Bard of Lori. Two of his poems were turned into successful operas, by Armen Tigranian and Alexander Spendiarov respectively.

The same organization has published in English translation the selected poetic works of Avetik Issahakian (1875–1957), including his long philosophical poem *Abou Lala Mahari*, completed in 1909 and considered to be his masterpiece. The work deals symbolically with the life of a poet of old Baghdad who renounces the world and sets off into the desert with a caravan of camels, in search of eternal wisdom. In its general conception, the poem is in the tradition of Edward Fitzgerald's re-creation of Omar Khayyam, though the atmosphere of world-weariness and disillusionment is more pronounced in the poem by Issahakian.

The Mashtotz Press has also given us a translation of Hagop Baronian's lively satire, *Honourable Beggars*, which pillories the parasitical, half-baked Armenian intellectuals of Constantinople during the 1880s. Also strongly recommended is Mischa Kudian's selection of stories by Vahan Totovents, entitled *Tell Me, Bella*. Both these works give a vivid picture of life in Armenian communities in the Ottoman Empire before the 1915 holocaust.

During the period following the First World War, widely differing schools of writing sprang up in the Armenian diaspora. Given the traumatic experience of the genocide, it is understandable that there should have been an 'escapist' school of writing among the survivors in the emigration. The foremost exponent of this escapist trend was Michael Arlen, nom-de-plume of Dikran Kouyoumdjian (1895–1956), author of *The Green Hat*, a novel of scandalous high life of the 1920s.

Michael Arlen made a fortune from his witty and topical books, entirely divorced from Armenian life, and established himself as an international celebrity. He had a villa on the Riviera, and used to play tennis with Somerset Maugham at the Villa Mauresque – ingratiating himself with the touchy old master by letting him win most of the time. Many people found the snobbish boulevardier insufferable. In 1929, Sir Robert Bruce Lockhart attended a dinner party at Lord Beaverbrook's, and noted that Michael Arlen came in later, 'looking more opulent and conceited than ever'.[1] Arlen cultivated the friendship of the English composer Peter Warlock, and they frequented the salon of Lady Ottoline Morrell at Garsington. She took a dislike to the

---

[1] *Diaries*, ed. Kenneth Young (London, 1973), vol. 1, p. 108.

26 Composer Makar Yekmalian, 1855–1905, reviser and arranger of the liturgy of the Armenian Apostolic Church, as used all over the world today. (*Armenian Academy of Sciences*)

27 Manoug Parikian, born 1920, celebrated London and Oxford-based international violin virtuoso. (*Donald Southern*)

28 Seta Tanyel, prizewinner, First Arthur Rubinstein International Piano Master competition. (*Basil Douglas Ltd.*)

29 Julian Byzantine, London-based classical guitarist. *(Courtesy Julian Byzantine)*

30 Albert Khadjesari, lyric tenor, of Vienna. *(Victor Mory)*

pair of them, and confided to her diary that 'they seem to pollute the atmosphere and stifle me, and I have to escape from their presence – also I get very tired of the continual boasting of what they are going to do'.

Michael Arlen achieved very little after his initial successes of the 1920s. The family eventually emigrated to 75th Street, New York and the retired celebrity would hold court at lunch time in the fashionable St Regis Hotel. His son, Michael J. Arlen Jr, has become a staff writer on the *New Yorker* magazine, and written a moving account of his own rediscovery of his personal Armenian heritage.[1]

A complete antithesis to Michael Arlen is provided by the multi-faceted personality of William Saroyan, who was born at Fresno, California, in 1908. If Michael Arlen Sr. turned his back on his Armenian heritage, Saroyan has always revelled in it. By espousing the cause of the immigrant community generally – not only the Armenian one – Saroyan has been instrumental in building a bridge between old and new elements in American society, a feat which enhances the real merits of his whimsical, evocative prose. If one could make one criticism, it is that Saroyan's roseate view of human nature does not always match the hard realities of human life in the twentieth century, though it is soothing to feel that in the Great American Society all will turn out for the best in the long run.

At the time of writing, in 1981, the situation of Armenian literature all over the world is markedly healthy. In Soviet Armenia, a new generation of poets and novelists has grown up to replace those brutally liquidated during the Stalin-Beria purges. In Paris, the veteran French Armenian Academician Henri Troyat, now approaching his seventieth birthday, produces biographies and historical and popular novels with undiminished vigour. Some of his works of fiction appear in large paperback editions, and have been turned into films in France, with lyrics featuring Charles Aznavour. For the English-speaking public, there are several excellent anthologies of Armenian poetry in translation, as well as collections of colourful Armenian folk-tales.[2] A thriving school of young Armenian American writers now operates in North

---

[1] Michael J. Arlen, *Exiles* (London and New York, 1971); *Passage to Ararat* (London and New York, 1976).

[2] Among the best selections are: Diana Der Hovanessian and Marzbed Margossian, *Anthology of Armenian Poetry* (New York, Columbia University Press, 1978); Leon Surmelian, *Apples of Immortality, Folktales of Armenia* (London, 1968).

America, many of their stories, articles and poems appearing regularly in *Ararat*, the quarterly journal of the Armenian General Benevolent Union of New York.

Select Bibliography

NOTE: My earlier book, *Armenia: Cradle of Civilization*, contains an extensive bibliography, with special reference to works on Armenian archaeology, history and culture. There is now V. Nersessian's invaluable Index of articles on Armenian studies in Western Journals (Luzac & Company, London, 1976). As far as possible I have avoided duplication with entries in these two works.

1 Historical Introduction

ADONTZ, NICHOLAS, *Armenia in the period of Justinian*, translated by Nina G. Garsoïan (Lisbon, 1970).

AGATHANGELOS, *History of the Armenians*, translation and commentary by R. W. Thomson (Albany, 1976).

ARPEE, L. *Armenian Awakening. A history of the Armenian Church* (reprint, 1976).

BAUER, E., *Arménie. Son histoire et son présent* (Lausanne and Paris, 1977).

BEDOUKIAN, PAUL Z., *Coinage of the Artaxiads of Armenia* (London, Royal Numismatic Society, 1978).

BRENTJES, B., *Drei Jahrtausende Armenien*, 2nd edition (Vienna and Munich, 1976).

BURNEY, CHARLES, and LANG, D. M., *The Peoples of the Hills, Ancient Ararat and Caucasus* (London and New York, 1971).

DEDEYAN, GERARD, *Solidarité Franco-Arménienne à l'Epoque des Croisades* (Paris, 1970).

DER NERSESSIAN, SIRARPIE, *The Armenians* (London, New York, 1969).

GROUSSET, R., *Histoire de l'Arménie des origines à 1071*, reprint (Paris, 1973).

HEYER, F. (ed.), *Die Kirche Armeniens* (Stuttgart, 1978).

MACLEAN, SIR FITZROY, *To Caucasus, the End of all the Earth* (London, 1976).

MANANDIAN, H., *Tigrane II et Rome* (Lisbon, 1963).

MOSES KHORENATS'I., *History of the Armenians*, translation and commentary by R. W. Thomson (Harvard University Press, 1978).

MOVSES DASXURANCI (DASKHURANTSI), *The History of the Caucasian Albanians*, trans. C. J. F. Dowsett (Oxford University Press, 1961).

PIOTROVSKII, B. B., *Urartu: the Kingdom of Van and its Art*, trans. Peter S. Gelling (London, 1967).

2 Modern Armenian History and the Genocide

ADELSON, ROGER, *Mark Sykes, Portrait of an Amateur* (London, 1975).

ALAMUDDIN, IDA, *Papa Kuenzler and the Armenians* (London, 1970)

ALLEN, W. E. D. and MURATOFF, PAUL, *Caucasian Battlefields* (Cambridge, 1953).

ANDERSON, M. S., *The Eastern Question, 1774–1923* (London, 1966).

ARFA, General HASSAN, *Under Five Shahs* (London, 1964).

BEDOUKIAN, K., *The Urchin* (London, 1978).

BRYCE, JAMES, Viscount, *Transcaucasia and Ararat* (London, 1877).

BRYCE, JAMES, Viscount, *The Treatment of Armenians in the Ottoman Empire, 1915–16*, 2nd edition (Beirut, 1972).

CATCHPOOL, E. ST JOHN, *Candles in the Darkness* (London, 1966).

DUNSTERVILLE, Major-General L. C., *The Adventures of Dunsterforce* (London, 1920).

GIDNEY, JAMES B., *A Mandate for Armenia* (Ohio, 1967).

GÖKALP, ZIA, *The Principles of Turkism*, trans. Robert Devereux (Leiden, 1968).

HOSTLER, CHARLES W., *Turkism and the Soviets* (London, 1957).

HOUSEPIAN, MARJORIE, *Smyrna 1922: The Destruction of a City* (London, 1972).

HOVANNISIAN, RICHARD G., *Armenia on the Road to Independence, 1918* (University of California Press, 1967).

HOVANNISIAN, RICHARD G., *The Republic of Armenia, vol. 1: 1918–1919* (University of California Press, 1971).

KAYALOFF, JACQUES, *The Battle of Sardarabad* (The Hague and Paris, 1973).

KAZEMZADEH, F., *The Struggle for Transcaucasia (1917–1921)* (New York and Oxford, 1951).

KERR, STANLEY E., *The Lions of Marash* (Albany, N.Y., 1973).

KRIKORIAN, Very Reverend MESROP K., *Armenians in the Service of the Ottoman Empire, 1860–1908* (London, 1978).

LANG, D. M., and WALKER, CHRISTOPHER J., *The Armenians*, Minority Rights Group, Report No. 32 (revised edition, London, 1978).

LEPSIUS, JOHANNES, *Deutschland und Armenien, 1914–1918* (Potsdam, 1919).

LEWIS, BERNARD, *The Emergence of Modern Turkey* (2nd edition, London, 1968).

MATOSSIAN, MARY K., *The Impact of Soviet Policies in Armenia* (Leiden, 1962).

MEDLICOTT, W. N., *The Congress of Berlin and After* (2nd edition, London, 1963).

MORGENTHAU, HENRY, *Ambassador Morgenthau's Story* (New York, 1919).

NALBANDIAN, LOUISE, *The Armenian Revolutionary Movement* (California University Press, reprinted 1977).

NANSEN, F., *L'Arménie et le Proche Orient* (Paris, 1928).

NOGALES, RAFAEL DE, *Four Years beneath the Crescent* (London, 1926).

SARKISYANZ, M., *A Modern History of Transcaucasian Armenia* (Leiden, 1978).

SVAJIAN, S. G., *A Trip through Historic Armenia* (New York, 1977).

TORIGUIAN, SHAVARSH, *The Armenian Question and International Law* (Beirut, 1973).

TRUMPENER, ULRICH, *Germany and the Ottoman Empire, 1914–1918* (Princeton, 1968).

WALKER, CHRISTOPHER J., *Armenia*: *The Survival of a Nation* (London, 1980).

WERFEL, FRANZ, *The Forty Days* [*of Musa Dagh*], trans, G. Dunlop (London, 1934).

WINSTONE, H. V. F., *Gertrude Bell* (London, 1978).

ZURRER, W., *Kaukasien 1918–1921* (Düsseldorf, 1978).

ZURRER, W., *Die Nahostpolitik Frankreichs und Russlands, 1891–1898* (Wiesbaden, 1970).

3   *Diaspora*: *Armenian Communities Abroad*

ALGAR, HAMID, *Mirza Malkum Khan* (University of California Press, 1973).

ALTOUNYAN, TAQUI, *In Aleppo Once* (London, 1969).

ANTREASSIAN, A., *Jerusalem and the Armenians* (Jerusalem, 1968).

ARLEN, MICHAEL J., *Passage to Ararat* (London, 1976).

AVAKIAN, ARRA, *The Armenians in America* (Minneapolis, 1977).

BEDOUKIAN, PAUL Z., *Coinage of Cilician Armenia*, revised edition (Danbury, Connecticut, 1979).

BOASE, T. S. R. (ed.), *The Cilician Kingdom of Armenia* (Scottish Academic Press, 1978).

CHOPOURIAN, G. H., *The Armenian Evangelical Reformation*: *Causes and Effects* (New York, 1972).

COLLESS, B. C., 'The Traders of the Pearl', in *Abr Nahrain*, vols. 9–11 and 13–15, Leiden, 1970–5.

DACHKEVYTCH, YA, Articles on Armenian communities in Poland and the Ukraine, in *Revue des Études Arméniennes*, nouvelle série, vols. I–XIII, Paris, 1964–79.

DER NERSESSIAN, SIRARPIE, *Armenia and the Byzantine Empire* (Harvard, 1945).

GRIGOR OF AKANC', *History of the Nation of the Archers*, trans. Blake and Frye (Harvard, 1954).

GULBENKIAN, R., 'Jacome Abuna, an Armenian Bishop in Malabar (1503–1550)', in *Arquivos do Centro Cultural Português*, vol. IV, Paris, 1972.

LANG, D. M. *The Bulgarians* (London, 1976).

PANKHURST, R., 'The History of Ethiopian–Armenian relations', in *Revue des Études Arméniennes*, nouvelle série, vols XII–XIII, Paris, 1977–9.

PAPAZIAN, K. S., *Merchants from Ararat* (New York, 1979).

SANJIAN, A. K., *The Armenian communities in Syria under Ottoman dominion* (Harvard, 1965).

SETH, MESROVB J., *Armenians in India from the earliest times to the present day* (Calcutta, 1937).

ŞIMANSCHI, L., *Le Monastère de Zamca* (Bucharest, 1967).

TASHJIAN, JAMES H., *The Armenians of the United States and Canada* (Boston, 1947).

WAUGH, EVELYN, *When the Going was Good* (Penguin).

YAKOBSON, A. L., *Srednevekovy Krym* ('The medival Crimea': Russian), (Moscow and Leningrad, 1964).

4   *Armenian Cooking*

ANTREASSIAN, A., *Armenian Cooking Today* (New York, 1975).
DETROIT WOMEN'S CHAPTER OF THE ARMENIAN GENERAL BENEVOLENT UNION, *Treasured Armenian Recipes* (23rd printing, New York, 1976).
UVEZIAN, S., *The Cuisine of Armenia* (New York, 1974).

5   *Armenians and the Occult*

ANANIKIAN, M. H., *Armenian Mythology* (Boston, 1925).
BENNETT, JOHN G., *Gurdjieff : Making a New World* (London, 1976).
BUTKOVSKY-HEWITT, ANNA, *With Gurdjieff in St Petersburg and Paris* (London, 1978).
GURDJIEFF, G. I., *Beelzebub's Tales to his Grandson* (London, 1950).
GURDJIEFF, G. I., *Meetings with Remarkable Men* (London, 1963).
GURDJIEFF, G. I., *Views from the Real World* (London, 1976).
MARQUEZ, G. G., *A Hundred Years of Solitude* (London, 1970).
NOTT, C. S., *Teachings of Gurdjieff. The Journal of a Pupil* (London, 1961).
RUNCIMAN, Sir STEVEN, *The Medieval Manichee* (reprinted, Cambridge University Press, 1960).
WALKER, KENNETH, *Gurdjieff. A Study of his Teaching* (reprinted, London, 1979).
WEBB, JAMES, *The Harmonious Circle* (London, 1980).

6   *Architecture and the Arts*

AZARIAN, L., *Khatchkar . . . The Stone Crosses*, Italian and English texts (Milan, 1970) (Documents of Armenian Architecture, no. 2).
AZNAVOUR, CHARLES, *Yesterday when I was young* (London, 1979).
BACHMANN, W., *Kirchen und Moscheen in Armenien und Kurdistan* (Leipzig, 1913; reprinted 1978).
BERNARDOUT, R., *Caucasian Rugs* (London, 1978).
BERKIAN, ARA J., *Armenischer Wehrbau im Mittelalter* (Darmstadt, 1976).
CARSWELL, JOHN, *Kutahya tiles and pottery from the Armenian Cathedral of St James, Jerusalem,* (2 vols, Oxford, 1972).
CARSWELL, JOHN, *New Julfa. The Armenian churches and other buildings* (Oxford, 1968).
D'ARTHEZ, SUZANNE, *Mutafian* (Paris, 1978).
DER NERSESSIAN, SIRARPIE, *Armenian Art* (London, 1979).
DER NERSESSIAN, SIRARPIE, *Armenian Manuscripts in the Walters Art Gallery* (Baltimore, Maryland, 1973).
DER NERSESSIAN, SIRARPIE, *Études Byzantines et Arméniennes. Byzantine and Armenian Studies,* 2 vols. (Louvain, 1973).
DRAMPIAN, I. R., *Bazhbeuk-Melikyan* (Biography of the painter : Russian) (Moscow, 1970).

DRAMPIAN, I. R. and KORKHMAZIAN, E. M., *Khudozhestvennye sokrovischcha Matenadarana* ('Artistic treasures of the Erevan State Manuscript Museum called Matenadaran'), Russian text (Moscow, 1976).

GOMBOS, K., *Armenia: Landscape and Architecture* (Budapest, 1975).

KAMENSKY, A. A., *Sarian: Le Peintre du Bonheur* (Moscow, 1967).

KARSH, YOUSUF, *In Search of Greatness. Reflections* (New York, 1962).

KHATCHATRIAN, A., *L'architecture arménienne du 4e au 6e siècles* (Paris, 1971).

LEVY, JULIEN, *Gorky* (New York, 1962).

MANOUKIAN, AGOPIK and ARMEN (eds.), *Documents of Armenian Architecture*, Italian and English texts. vols 1–9, etc. (Milan, 1968). In progress. Comprises separate vols on leading Armenian architectural monuments, including Haghpat, Sanahin, S. Thadei Vank, Amberd, Goshavank and Aghtamar.

MARRISON, G. E. (ed.), *The Christian Orient* (The British Library, 1978).

MAZMANIAN, N., *The Art Gallery of Armenia* (Leningrad, 1975).

MILNE, TOM, *Rouben Mamoulian* (London, 1969).

NARKISS, B. and STONE, MICHAEL E., *Armenian Art Treasures of Jerusalem* (Massada Press, 1979).

NERSESSIAN, V. (ed.), *Essays on Armenian Music* (London, 1978).

NICKEL, HEINRICH L., *Kirchen, Burgen, Miniaturen. Armenien und Georgien während des Mittelalters* (Berlin, 1974).

NOVOUSPENSKY, N. N., *Aivazovsky* (Aurora Art Publishers, Leningrad, 1972), English, French, German and Russian texts.

ROSENBERG, HAROLD, *Arshile Gorky: the Man, the Time, the Idea* (New York, Horizon, 1962).

SARIAN, JOHN M., *Record Guide, Armenian Musicians and Composers* (New York, 1979).

SCHNEEDE, UWE M., *Surrealism. The Movement and the Masters* (New York, c. 1975).

SHAHVERDYAN, A., *A. A. Spendiaryan* (biography of the composer: English text) (Erevan, 1971).

STEPANIAN, N. and TCHAKMAKTCHIAN, A., *L'Art décoratif de l'Arménie médiévale* (Leningrad, 1971).

TABANELLI, M. R., *Edgar Chahine: Catalogue de l'Oeuvre gravée* (Milan, 1977).

TAHMIZIAN, N. K., *Teoriya muzyki v drevnei Armenii* ('The theory of music in ancient Armenia': Russian) (Erevan, 1977).

VAHRAMIAN, HERMAN, and others, *Aght'amar*, Italian and English texts (Milan, 1974) (Documents of Armenian Architecture, no. 8).

YETKIN, SERARE, *Early Caucasian carpets in Turkey*, 2 vols (London, 1978).

ZARIAN, RUBEN, *Ruben Adalian: Al'bom* (Armenian, Russian and English texts) (Erevan, 1978). An album of black-and-white reproductions of drawings and engravings by the contemporary Soviet Armenian artist.

7 *Literature*

ARLEN, MICHAEL J., *Exiles* (London and New York, 1971).

BARONIAN, HAGOP., *Honourable Beggars,* a satire, trans. and ed. by Mischa Kudian (London, 1978).

DER HOVANESSIAN, DIANA, and MARGOSSIAN, MARZBED (trans. and eds.), *Anthology of Armenian Poetry* (New York, 1978).

DOWNING, CHARLES (pseudonym), *Armenian Folk-tales and Fables* (Oxford University Press, 1972).

GREGORY OF NAREK (Grigor Narekatsi), *Lamentations: Mystic Soliloquies with God,* vol. 1, trans. M. Kudian (London, 1977).

ISSAHAKIAN, AVETIK, *Abu Lala Mahari. Poem in seven suras,* trans. Zabelle C. Boyajian (Erevan, 1975).

ISSAHAKIAN, AVETIK, *The Muse of Sheerak,* compiled and trans. by M. Kudian, (London, 1975).

KUDIAN, MISCHA, *Candy Floss. Satirical Poems* (London, 1980).

KUDIAN, MISCHA, *The Saga of Sassoun* (London, 1970).

KUDIAN, MISCHA, *Soviet Armenian Poetry* (compiler and translator) (London, 1974).

KUDIAN, MISCHA, *Three Apples fell from Heaven* (London, 1969).

NERSESSIAN, V., *Catalogue of Early Armenian books* (London, British Library, 1980).

SANJIAN, A. K., *A Catalogue of Medieval Armenian Manuscripts in the United States* (University of California Press, 1976).

SHAHNOUR, SHAHAN, *Retreat without Song* (London, 1981).

TOTOVENTS, VAHAN, *Scenes from an Armenian Childhood,* trans. M. Kudian (2nd edition, London, 1980).

TOTOVENTS, VAHAN, *Tell me, Bella,* Stories, trans. M. Kudian (London, 1972).

TOUMANIAN, HOVANNES, *The Bard of Loree,* selected works, trans. by M. Kudian (London, 1970).

Index

Note: Due to the large number of personal and geographical names mentioned in the text, this Index has of necessity been compiled on a selective basis.

7294